FINANCIAL INSTITUTIONS AND SERVICES

MULTILATERAL DEVELOPMENT BANKS AND INTERNATIONAL FINANCE

FINANCIAL INSTITUTIONS AND SERVICES

Additional books in this series can be found on Nova's website under the Series tab.

Additional E-books in this series can be found on Nova's website under the E-books tab.

FINANCIAL INSTITUTIONS AND SERVICES

MULTILATERAL DEVELOPMENT BANKS AND INTERNATIONAL FINANCE

LEAH M. GROFFE
EDITOR

Nova Science Publishers, Inc.
New York

Copyright © 2010 by Nova Science Publishers, Inc.

All rights reserved. No part of this book may be reproduced, stored in a retrieval system or transmitted in any form or by any means: electronic, electrostatic, magnetic, tape, mechanical photocopying, recording or otherwise without the written permission of the Publisher.

For permission to use material from this book please contact us:
Telephone 631-231-7269; Fax 631-231-8175
Web Site: http://www.novapublishers.com

NOTICE TO THE READER

The Publisher has taken reasonable care in the preparation of this book, but makes no expressed or implied warranty of any kind and assumes no responsibility for any errors or omissions. No liability is assumed for incidental or consequential damages in connection with or arising out of information contained in this book. The Publisher shall not be liable for any special, consequential, or exemplary damages resulting, in whole or in part, from the readers' use of, or reliance upon, this material. Any parts of this book based on government reports are so indicated and copyright is claimed for those parts to the extent applicable to compilations of such works.

Independent verification should be sought for any data, advice or recommendations contained in this book. In addition, no responsibility is assumed by the publisher for any injury and/or damage to persons or property arising from any methods, products, instructions, ideas or otherwise contained in this publication.

This publication is designed to provide accurate and authoritative information with regard to the subject matter covered herein. It is sold with the clear understanding that the Publisher is not engaged in rendering legal or any other professional services. If legal or any other expert assistance is required, the services of a competent person should be sought. FROM A DECLARATION OF PARTICIPANTS JOINTLY ADOPTED BY A COMMITTEE OF THE AMERICAN BAR ASSOCIATION AND A COMMITTEE OF PUBLISHERS.

Additional color graphics may be available in the e-book version of this book.

LIBRARY OF CONGRESS CATALOGING-IN-PUBLICATION DATA
Multilateral development banks and international finance / editor, Leah M.
Groffe.
p. cm.
Includes index.
ISBN 978-1-61728-883-8 (hardcover)
1. Development banks. 2. International finance. 3. Debt
relief--Developing countries. 4. Economic assistance. 5. Economic
assistance, American. I. Groffe, Leah M.
HG1975.M849 2010
332.1'53--dc22
2010026981

Published by Nova Science Publishers, Inc. ✦New York

CONTENTS

Preface		**vii**
Chapter 1	Multilateral Development Banks: Overview and Issues for Congress *Rebecca M. Nelson*	**1**
Chapter 2	The African Development Bank Group *Martin A. Weiss*	**29**
Chapter 3	Multilateral Development Banks: U.S. Contributions FY1998-FY2009 *Jonathan E. Sanford*	**35**
Chapter 4	The International Financial Institutions: A Call for Change *A Report to the Committee on Foreign Relations*	**45**
Chapter 5	The World Bank's International Development Association (IDA) *Martin A. Weiss*	**107**
Chapter 6	The Multilateral Debt Relief Initiative *Martin A. Weiss*	**123**
Chapter 7	Developing Countries: The United States has not Fully Funded its Share of Debt Relief, and the Impact of Debt Relief on Countries' Poverty-Reducing Spending is Unknown *United States Government Accountability Office*	**129**
Index		**183**

PREFACE

Multilateral Development Banks (MDBs) are institutions that provide loans and grants to developing countries in order to promote economic and social development. Congressional interest in the MDBs has increased since the outbreak of the current global financial crisis. Following the crisis, the MDBs ramped up financial assistance to developing countries, and each of the MDBs has requested increased funding from their member states to increase lending to middle-income countries. This book explores the history of the MDBs, their operations, major donor contributions, their organization, and debates the effectiveness of MDB financial assistance.

Chapter 1 - Overview: The multilateral development banks (MDBs) include the World Bank and four smaller regional development banks: the African Development Bank (AfDB), the Asian Development Bank (AsDB), the European Bank for Reconstruction and Development (EBRD), and the Inter- American Development Bank (IDB). The United States is a member of each of the MDBs. The MDBs provide financial assistance to developing countries to promote economic and social development. They primarily fund large infrastructure and other development projects and, increasingly, provide loans tied to policy reforms by the government. Most of the MDBs have two facilities from which they make loans (loan windows): a non-concessional lending window that provides loans to middle-income countries at market-based interest rates, and a concessional lending window that provides loans at below-market interest rates and grants to low-income countries.

Debate over the effectiveness of MDB financial assistance is contentious. Critics argue that the MDBs focus on "getting money out the door" (rather than delivering results in developing countries), are not transparent, and lack a clear division of labor. They also argue that providing aid multilaterally relinquishes U.S. control over where and how the money is spent. Proponents argue that providing aid to poor countries is the "right" thing to do and has been successful in helping developing countries make strides in health and education over the past four decades. They also argue that providing foreign aid to the MDBs is important for leveraging funds from other donors, tying policy reforms to financial assistance, and enhancing U.S. leadership. Most U.S. aid for economic and social development is provided directly to projects and programs in developing countries (bilateral aid) rather than to multilateral organizations, like the MDBs (multilateral aid).

Issues for Congress: Congressional legislation is required for U.S. financial contributions to the MDBs. Replenishments of the concessional windows occur regularly; capital increases for the non-concessional windows happen more infrequently. Unusually, all the MDBs have currently requested capital increases, generally because MDB lending has increased following the global financial crisis.

In addition to congressional hearings on the MDBs, Congress exercises oversight over U.S. participation in the MDBs through legislative mandates. These mandates direct the U.S. Executive Directors to the MDBs to advocate certain policies and how they should vote at the MDBs on various issues. Congress also issues reporting requirements for the Treasury Department on issues related to MDB activities. Finally, Congress can withhold funding for the MDBs unless certain institutional reforms are met ("power of the purse").

More than $30 billion in contracts are awarded each year to complete projects financed by the MDBs. Some of these contracts are awarded to U.S. companies. Major changes are underway at the World Bank, the biggest MDB, that would alter how companies bid on World Bank projects. The World Bank argues that these changes will strengthen national institutions, while opponents argue that they will weaken existing procurement standards. Finally, the G-20 has proposed voting reform at the World Bank to reflect the increased role of emerging-markets in the world economy. While the voting power of the United States is unlikely to be affected, these proposals are likely to be a focus of discussion about the World Bank moving forward.

Chapter 2 - The African Development Bank (AfDB) Group is a regional development bank currently based in Tunis, Tunisia. It comprises three lending facilities: the market rate facility, the AfDB; a concessional lending facility, the African Development Fund; and a trust fund established by Nigeria to lend to low-income African countries. The Bank has 53 African members, as well as 24 non-regional members, including the United States.

Chapter 3 - This chapter shows in tabular form how much the Administration requested and how much Congress appropriated during the past 11 years for U.S. payments to the multilateral development banks (MDBs). It also provides a brief description of the MDBs and the ways they fund their operations.

Chapter 4 - The International Monetary Fund, World Bank, African Development Bank, Asian Development Bank, European Bank for Reconstruction and Development, and Inter-American Development Bank are foreign policy tools that allow the United States to leverage the contributions of other countries to promote our national security and humanitarian interests in alleviating poverty and promoting progress around the world. For this reason, the U.S. Congress regularly supports appropriations for subsidized loan and grant programs through the multilateral development banks and recently provided a loan to the IMF. As one of the largest shareholders in these institutions, the United States enjoys an opportunity to influence their policies and programs. We must be cautious about forfeiting our leadership positions at these institutions.

Chapter 5 - The World Bank is a Multilateral Development Bank (MDB) that makes loans and grants to low and middle-income countries to reduce poverty and promote economic development. Both the World Bank and the International Monetary Fund (IMF) were founded at the Bretton Woods Conference in 1944. Two of the World Bank facilities, the International Bank for Reconstruction and Development (IBRD) and International Development Association (IDA) lend directly to governments to finance projects and programs.

IDA was established in 1960, 16 years after the creation of the World Bank to address concern that the poorest countries could not afford to borrow at the near- market rate terms offered by the IBRD. Consequently, IDA was established as a revolving fund, providing concessional loans to the poorest countries subsidized by donor contributions and transfers from the IBRD. IDA assistance is highly discounted, it is increasingly provided as grants, and only available to low-income member countries. Since IDA provides loans and grants to the poorest countries at subsidized rates, its resources must be periodically replenished. Donor nations have replenished IDA 14 times since its founding.

On March 5, 2007, donor nations began to discuss a possible fifteenth replenishment of funds for IDA. This is the first replenishment since the G8 summit at the Gleneagles Resort in Scotland in 2005 where world leaders proposed the creation of the Multilateral Debt Relief Initiative (MDRI). The MDRI cancels the remaining debt of the world's poorest countries and pledges to double the amount of aid to Sub-Saharan Africa between 2004 and 2010, primarily in the form of grant- based assistance.

Donor governments selected three themes for IDA-15: (1) IDA's role in the international foreign aid system, (2) the role of the World Bank in post-conflict reconstruction and fragile states, and (3) the need to improve the effectiveness of IDA assistance. This chapter provides brief background material on the World Bank's IDA, the U.S. role at the institution, and information on the status of the current IDA-14 replenishment. It then examines the negotiations for IDA-15, and analyzes the three core themes identified for IDA-15.

Chapter 6 - In June 2005, G8 finance ministers proposed the new Multilateral Debt Relief Initiative (MDRI). The MDRI proposes to cancel debts of some of the world's poorest countries owed to the International Monetary Fund, World Bank, and African Development Bank. This chapter discusses MDRI's implementation and raises some issues regarding debt relief's effectiveness as a form of foreign assistance for possible congressional consideration.

The Multilateral Debt Relief Initiative (MDRI) is the most recent effort by the International Monetary Fund (IMF), World Bank, and African Development Bank (AfDB) to provide poor country debt relief. Proposed by G8 finance ministers in June 2005, the MDRI provides 100% debt relief to select countries that are already participating in the joint-IMF/World Bank Heavily Indebted Poor Countries (HIPC) program.[1] The goal of the MDRI program is to free up additional resources for the poorest countries in order to help them reach the United Nations' Millennium Development Goals (MDGs), which are focused, among other things, on reducing world poverty by half by 2015.[2]

Chapter 7 - In 1996, the Heavily Indebted Poor Countries (HIPC) Initiative was created to provide debt relief to poor countries that had reached unsustainable levels of debt. In 2005, the Multilateral Debt Relief Initiative (MDRI) expanded upon the HIPC Initiative by eliminating additional debt owed to four international financial institutions (IFI): the International Monetary Fund (IMF), World Bank's International Development Association (IDA), African Development Fund (ADF), and Inter-American Development Bank (IaDB). These four IFIs are projected to provide $58 billion in total debt relief to 41 countries. GAO (1) analyzed the U.S. financing approach for debt relief efforts; (2) reviewed the extent to which MDRI might affect resources available to countries for poverty-reducing activities; and (3) assessed revisions to the analyses conducted by the World Bank and IMF to review and promote future debt sustainability. GAO analyzed Treasury, IFI, and country documents and data, and interviewed officials at Treasury and the four IFIs.

In: Multilateral Development Banks and International Finance   ISBN: 978-1-61728-883-8
Editor: Leah M. Groffe   © 2010 Nova Science Publishers, Inc.

Chapter 1

MULTILATERAL DEVELOPMENT BANKS: OVERVIEW AND ISSUES FOR CONGRESS[*]

Rebecca M. Nelson

SUMMARY

Overview: The multilateral development banks (MDBs) include the World Bank and four smaller regional development banks: the African Development Bank (AfDB), the Asian Development Bank (AsDB), the European Bank for Reconstruction and Development (EBRD), and the Inter- American Development Bank (IDB). The United States is a member of each of the MDBs. The MDBs provide financial assistance to developing countries to promote economic and social development. They primarily fund large infrastructure and other development projects and, increasingly, provide loans tied to policy reforms by the government. Most of the MDBs havetwo facilities from which they make loans (loan windows): a non-concessional lending window that provides loans to middle-income countries at market-based interest rates, and a concessional lending window that provides loans at below-market interest rates and grants to low-income countries.

Debate over the effectiveness of MDB financial assistance is contentious. Critics argue that the MDBs focus on "getting money out the door" (rather than delivering results in developing countries), are not transparent, and lack a clear division of labor. They also argue that providing aid multilaterally relinquishes U.S. control over where and how the money is spent. Proponents argue that providing aid to poor countries is the "right" thing to do and has been successful in helping developing countries make strides in health and education over the past four decades. They also argue that providing foreign aid to the MDBs is important for leveraging funds from other donors, tying policy reforms to financial assistance, and enhancing U.S. leadership. Most U.S. aid for economic and social development is provided

---

[*] This is an edited, reformatted and augmented version of a CRS Report for Congress publication, Report #R41170, dated April 9, 2010.

directly to projects and programs in developing countries (bilateral aid) rather than to multilateral organizations, like the MDBs (multilateral aid).

Issues for Congress: Congressional legislation is required for U.S. financial contributions to the MDBs. Replenishments of the concessional windows occur regularly; capital increases for the non-concessional windows happen more infrequently. Unusually, all the MDBs have currently requested capital increases, generally because MDB lending has increased following the global financial crisis.

In addition to congressional hearings on the MDBs, Congress exercises oversight over U.S. participation in the MDBs through legislative mandates. These mandates direct the U.S. Executive Directors to the MDBs to advocate certain policies and how they should vote at the MDBs on various issues. Congress also issues reporting requirements for the Treasury Department on issues related to MDB activities. Finally, Congress can withhold funding for the MDBs unless certain institutional reforms are met ("power of the purse").

More than $30 billion in contracts are awarded each year to complete projects financed by the MDBs. Some of these contracts are awarded to U.S. companies. Major changes are underway at the World Bank, the biggest MDB, that would alter how companies bid on World Bank projects. The World Bank argues that these changes will strengthen national institutions, while opponents argue that they will weaken existing procurement standards. Finally, the G-20 has proposed voting reform at the World Bank to reflect the increased role of emerging-markets in the world economy. While the voting power of the United States is unlikely to be affected, these proposals are likely to be a focus of discussion about the World Bank moving forward.

INTRODUCTION

Multilateral Development Banks (MDBs) are international institutions that provide loans and grants to developing countries in order to promote economic and social development. The term MDBs typically refers to the World Bank and four smaller regional development banks:

- the African Development Bank (AfDB);
- the Asian Development Bank (AsDB);
- the European Bank for Reconstruction and Development (EBRD); and
- the Inter-American Development Bank (IDB).[1]

The United States is a member of each of these institutions.[2]

Congressional interest in the MDBs has increased since the outbreak of the current global financial crisis. Following the onset of the crisis in fall 2008, the MDBs ramped up financial assistance to developing countries, and each of the MDBs has requested increased funding from their member states to increase lending to middle-income countries. A capital increase for an MDB is unusual and simultaneous requests for capital increases by all the MDBs has not happened since the 1970s. Any U.S. financial contribution to the MDBs requires congressional authorization and appropriation legislation. Negotiations for increasing MDB resources are currently underway, and it is expected that any increases would be included in the FY2011 budget (for the AsDB) or FY2012 budget (for the other MDBs). Hearings may be held in 2010.

This chapter provides an overview of the MDBs and highlights major current issues for Congress. The first section discusses the history of the MDBs, their operations, major donor contributions, their organization, and debates about the effectiveness of MDB financial assistance. The second section discusses issues of particular interest to Congress, including congressional legislation authorizing and appropriating U.S. contributions to the MDBs, congressional oversight of the MDBs, and U.S. commercial interests in the MDBs. It also discusses recent proposals for increasing the voting power of emerging-markets at the World Bank.

OVERVIEW OF THE MULTILATERAL DEVELOPMENT BANKS

The MDBs provide financial assistance to developing countries, typically in the form of loans and grants, for investment projects and policy-based loans. Project loans include large infrastructure projects, such as highways, power plants, port facilities, and dams, as well as social projects, including health and education initiatives. Policy-based loans provide governments with financing simultaneous with agreement by the borrower country government that it will undertake particular policy reforms, such as the privatization of state-owned industries or reform in agriculture or electricity sector policies. Policy-based loans can also provide budgetary support to developing country governments. In order for the disbursement of a policy-based loan tocontinue, the borrower must implement the specified economic or financial policies. Some have expressed concern over the increasing budgetary support provided to developing countries by the MDBs. Traditionally, this has been the province of the International Monetary Fund (IMF).

Most of the MDBs have two funds, often called lending windows or lending facilities. One type of lending window is used to make loans at market-based interest rates.[3] Such non-concessional loans are, depending on the MDB, extended to governments and private sector firms in middle- income and some creditworthy low-income countries. The other type of lending window is used to make loans at below-market interest rates (concessional loans) and grants to the governments of low-income countries.

Historical Background

World Bank

The World Bank is the oldest and largest of the MDBs. The World Bank Group comprises three sub-institutions that make loans and grants to developing countries: the International Bank for Reconstruction and Development (IBRD), the International Development Association (IDA), and the International Finance Corporation (IFC).[4]

The famous 1944 Bretton Woods Conference led to the establishment of the World Bank, the IMF, and the institution that would eventually become the World Trade Organization (WTO). The IBRD was the first World Bank affiliate created, when its Articles of Agreement became effective in 1945 with the signatures of 28 member governments. Today, the IBRD has near universal membership with 186 member nations. Only Cuba and North Korea, and a few micro-states suchas the Vatican, Monaco, and Andorra, are non-members. The IBRD lends mainly to the governments of middle-income countries at market-based interest rates.

In 1960, at the suggestion of the United States, IDA was created to make concessional loans (with low interest rates and long repayment periods) to the poorest countries. IDA also now provides grants to these countries. The IFC was created in 1955 to extend loans and equity investments to private firms in developing countries. The World Bank initially focused on providing financing for large infrastructure projects. Over time, this has broadened to also include social projects and policy-based loans.

Regional Development Banks

Inter-American Development Bank

The IDB was created in 1959 in response to a strong desire by Latin American countries for a bank that would be attentive to their needs, as well as U.S. concerns about the spread of communism in Latin America.[5] Consequently, the IDB has tended to focus more on social projects than large infrastructure projects, although the IDB began lending for infrastructure projects as well in the 1970s. From its founding, the IDB has had both non-concessional and concessional lending windows. The IDB's concessional lending window is called the Fund for Special Operations (F SO). The IDB Group also includes the Inter-American Investment Corporation (IIC) and the Multilateral Investment Fund (MIF), which extend loans to private sector firms in developing countries, much like the World Bank's IFC.

African Development Bank

The AfDB was created in 1964 and was for nearly two decades an African-only institution, reflecting the desire of African governments to promote stronger unity and cooperation among the countries of their region. In 1973, the AfDB created a concessional lending window, the African Development Fund (AfDF), to which non-regional countries could become members and contribute. The U.S. joined the AfDF in 1976. In 1982, membership in the AfDB nonconcessional lending window was officially opened to non-regional members. The AfDB makes loans to private sector firms through its non-concessional window and does not have a separate fund specifically for financing private sector projects with a development focus in the region.

Asian Development Bank

The AsDB was created in 1965 to promote regional cooperation. Similar to the World Bank, and unlike the IDB, the AsDB's original mandate focused on large infrastructure projects, rather than social projects or direct poverty alleviation. The AsDB's concessional lending facility, the Asian Development Fund (AsDF), was created in 1973. Like the AfDF, the AsDB does not have a separate fund specifically for financing private sector projects, and makes loans to private sector firms in the region through its non-concessional window.

Table 1. Overview of MDB Lending Windows

MDB	Type of Financing	Type of Borrower	Year Founded	Commitments, 2008 or FY2009 (Billion US$)
World Bank Group				
International Bank for Reconstruction and Development (IBRD)	Non-concessional loans	Primarily middle-income governments, also some creditworthy low-income countries	1944	32.9
International Development Association (IDA)	Concessional loans and grants	Low-income governments	1960	14.0
International Finance Corporation (IFC)	Non-concessional loans and equity investments	Private sector firms in developing countries	1955	10.5
African Development Bank (AfDB)	Non-concessional loans	Middle-income governments, some creditworthy low- income governments, and private sector firms in the region	1964	2.8
African Development Fund (AfDF)	Concessional loans and grants	Low-income governments in the region	1973	2.6
Asian Development Bank (AsDB)	Non-concessional loans	Middle-income governments, some creditworthy low- income governments, and private sector firms in the region	1965	8.7
Asian Development Fund (AsDF)	Concessional loans and grants	Low-income governments in the region	1973	1.8
European Bank for Reconstruction and Development (EBRD)	Non-concessional loansand equity investments	Primarily private sector firmsin developing countries in the region, also developing- country governments in the region	1990	7.4
Inter-American Development Bank (IDB)	Non-concessional loans	Middle-income governments, some creditworthy low-income governments, and private sector firms in the region	1959	11.1
Fund for Special Operations (FSO)	Concessional loans and grants	Low-income governments in the region	1959	0.1

Source:MDB Annual Reports. World Bank data is for FY2009 (July 2008 – June 2009). Regional development bank data is for 2008 (calendar year). Most of the MDBs also have additional funds that they administer, typically funded by a specific donor and/or targeted towards narrowly defined projects. These special funds tend to be very small in value and are not included in this chapter.

European Bank for Reconstruction and Development

The EBRD is the youngest MDB, founded in 1990. The motivation for creating the EBRD was to ease the transition of the former communist countries of Central and Eastern Europe (CEE) and the former Soviet Union from planned economies to free-market economies. The EBRD differs from the other regional banks in two fundamental ways. First, the EBRD has an explicitly political mandate: to support democracy-building activities. Second, the EBRD does not have a concessional loan window. The EBRD's financial assistance is heavily targeted on the private sector, although the EBRD does also extend some loans to governments in CEE and the former Soviet Union.

Table 1 summarizes the different lending windows for the MDBs, noting what types of financial assistance they provide, who they lend to, when they were founded, and how much financial assistance they committed to developing countries in 2008 or FY2009.[6] The World Bank accounted for more than 60% of total MDB financial assistance commitments to developing countries in 2008 or FY2009.[7] Also, more than 60% of the financial assistance provided by the MDBs to developing countries in 2008 or FY2009 was on non-concessional terms.

Operations: Financial Assistance to Developing Countries

Financial Assistance over Time

Figure 1 shows MDB financial commitments to developing countries since 2000. As a whole, non-concessional MDB financial assistance was relatively flat until the current global financial crisis prompted major member countries to press for increased financial assistance. In response to the financial crisis and at the urging of its major member countries, the IBRD dramatically increased lending between FY2008 and FY2009. When the 2009 lending data for the regional development banks is released later this year (2010), they are also expected to show substantial upticks in lending.

Figure 2 shows concessional financial assistance provided by the MDBs to developing countries from 2000 to 2008-2009. The World Bank's concessional lending arm, IDA, has grown steadily over the decade in nominal terms, while the regional development bank concessional lending facilities, by contrast, have remained relatively stable in nominal terms over the past several years. When the 2009 data for the regional development banks becomes available, however, it is expected that these figures will show an increase in concessional assistance as the regional banks responded to the financial crisis.

Recipients of MDB Financial Assistance

Figures 3-7 show which countries received commitments for financial assistance from the MDBs in the most recent year available (FY2009 for the World Bank and 2008 for the regional development banks). Additionally, Figure 3 shows how much, on a per capita basis, each country received. Darker regions in the graphs indicate higher levels of MDB financial assistance per capita. The data used is a sum of total financial assistance – concessional and non-concessional – for each MDB.

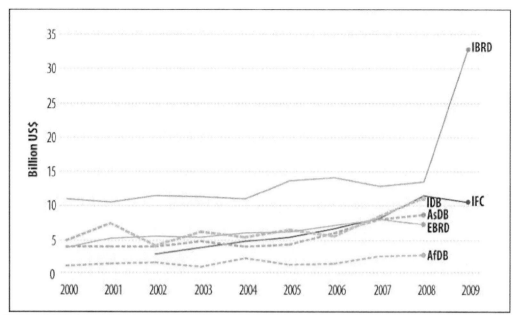

Source: MDB Annual Reports.
Notes: World Bank data is for FY2009 (July 2008 – June 2009). Regional development bank data is for 2008 (calendar year).

Figure 1. MDB Non-Concessional Financial Assistance, 2000-2009

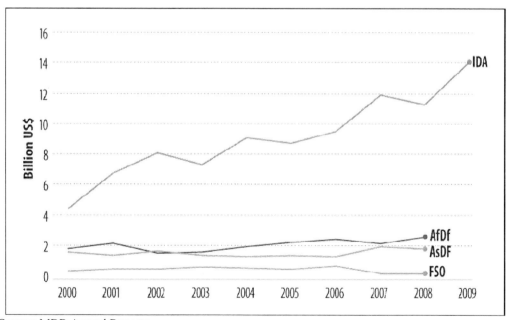

Source: MDB Annual Reports.
Notes: World Bank data is for FY2009 (July 2008 – June 2009). Regional development bank data is for 2008 (calendar year).

Figure 2. MDB Concessional Financial Assistance, 2000-2009

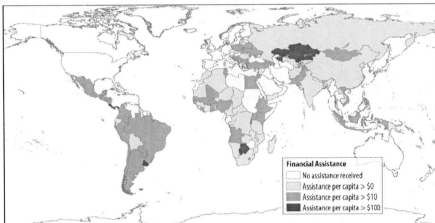

Source: World Bank Projects & Operations Database, http://go.worldbank.org/0FRO32VEI0. IFC FY09 Project & Portfolio Information, http://www.ifc.org/ifcext/annualreport.nsf/Content/AR2009_Projects_Portfolio.

Notes: Includes concessional and non-concessional financial assistance from lending windows listed in Table 1 (IBRD, IDA, and IFC). Excludes regional assistance, which is typically a small portion of the banks' lending portfolios.

Figure 3. World Bank: Commitments of Financial Assistance, FY2009.

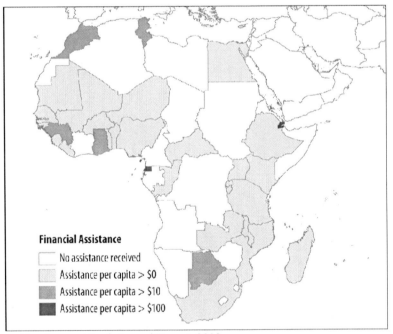

Source: African Development Bank Annual Report, 2008.

Notes: Includes concessional and non-concessional financial assistance from lending windows listed in Table 1. Excludes regional assistance, which is typically a small portion of the banks' lending portfolios.

Figure 4. African Development Bank: Commitments of Financial Assistance, 2008.

Multilateral Development Banks: Overview and Issues for Congress 9

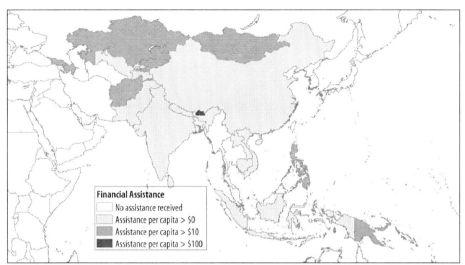

Source: Asian Development Bank Annual Report, 2008.
Notes: Includes concessional and non-concessional financial assistance from lending windows listed in Table 1. Excludes regional assistance, which is typically a small portion of the banks' lending portfolios.

Figure 5. Asian Development Bank: Commitments of Financial Assistance, 2008

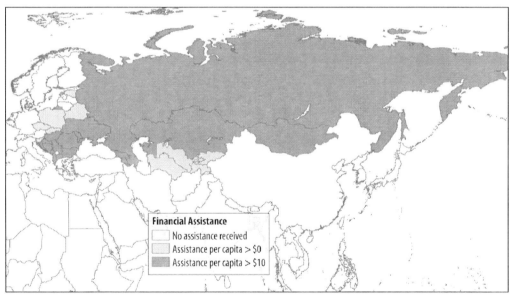

Source: European Bank for Reconstruction and Development Annual Report, 2008.
Notes: EBRD only provides non-concessional loans. Excludes regional assistance. Excludes regional assistance, which is typically a small portion of the banks' lending portfolios.

Figure 6. European Bank for Reconstruction and Development: Commitments of Financial Assistance, 2008

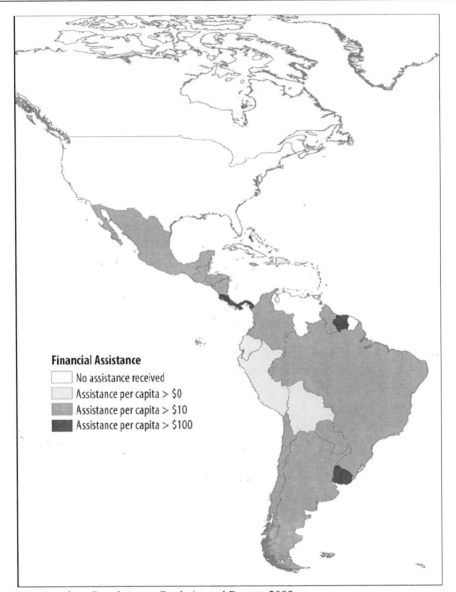

Source: Inter-American Development Bank Annual Report, 2008.
Notes: Includes concessional and non-concessional financial assistance from lending windows listed in Table 1. Excludes regional assistance, which is typically a small portion of the banks' lending portfolio.
Figure 7. Inter-American Development Bank: Commitments of Financial Assistance, 2008

Generally, Latin America and Eastern and Central Europe (CEE) received the highest levels of financial assistance per capita from the World Bank in FY2009, although there are notable instances in Asia and Africa, such as Kazakhstan and Botswana. For the AfDB, financial assistance per capita in 2008 was concentrated in Western and Eastern Africa, with some lending in Northern African (particularly Morocco and Egypt) and Southern Africa (particularly Botswana and South Africa). For the AsDB, Mongolia, Kazakhstan, Georgia, Papua New Guinea, and the Cook Islands were among the top recipients of financial assistance per capita in 2008. Regional economic powers China and India were also among the recipients of lower levels of financial assistance per capita from the AsDB in 2008. For the EBRD and the IDB, financial assistance per capita was spread fairly evenly throughout the region in 2008. For the EBRD, Bosnia and Herzegovina, Georgia, Moldova, and Albania received the highest levels of financial assistance per capita in 2008. Russia also received substantial assistance from the EBRD in 2008. For the IDB, the Bahamas, Costa Rica, Panama, and Barbados received high levels of financial assistance per capita. Mexico and Brazil also received lower levels of financial assistance from the IDB in 2008, among others.

The above Figures show that several large, emerging-market countries, such as the "BRICs" (Brazil, Russia, India, and China), receive a steady flow of financial assistance from the MDBs. This trend is somewhat controversial. Some argue that, instead of using MDB resources, these countries should rely on their own resources, particularly countries like China which has substantial foreign reserves holdings and can easily get loans from private capitalmarkets to fund development projects. MDB assistance, it is argued, would be better suited to focusing on the needs of the world's poorest countries, which do not have the resources to fund development projects and cannot borrow these resources from international capital markets.

Others argue that MDB financial assistance provided to large, emerging-market countries is important, because these countries have substantial numbers of people living in poverty and MDBs provide financial assistance for projects for which the government might be reluctant to borrow. Additionally, MDB assistance helps address environmental issues, promotes better governance, and provides important technical assistance to which emerging-market countries might not otherwise have access. Finally, supporters point out that because MDB assistance to emerging-market countries takes the form of loans with market-based interest rates, rather than concessional loans or grants, this assistance is relatively inexpensive to provide.

Funding: Donor Commitments and Contributions

MDBs are able to make loans and grants to developing countries due to the financial commitments of their more prosperous member countries. This support takes several forms, depending on the type of assistance (non-concessional or concessional) provided to developing countries. The MDBs use money contributed or subscribed by their member countries to support their assistance programs. They fund their operating costs from money earned on nonconcessional loans to borrower countries. Some of the MDBs transfer a portion of their surplus net income annually to help fund their concessional aid programs.

Non-Concessional Lending Windows

To offer non-concessional loans, the MDBs borrow money from international capital markets and then re-lend the money to developing countries. MDBs are able to borrow from international capital markets because they are backed by the guarantees of their member governments. This backing is provided through the ownership shares that countries subscribe as a consequence of their membership in each bank.[8] Only a small portion (typically less than 5-10%) of the value of these capital shares is actually paid to the MDB ("paid-in capital"). The bulk of these shares is a guarantee that the donor stands ready to provide to the bank if needed. This is called "callable capital," because the money is not actually transferred from the donor to the MDB unless the bank needs to call on its members' callable subscriptions. Banks may call upon their members' callable subscriptions only if their resources are exhausted and they still need funds to repay bondholders. To date, no MDB has ever had to draw on its callable capital. In recent decades, theMDBs have not used their paid-in capital to fund loans. Rather it has been put in financial reserves to strengthen the institutions' financial base.

Due to the financial backing of their member country governments, the MDBs are able to borrow money in world capital markets at the lowest available market rates, generally the same rates at which developed country governments borrow funds inside their own borders. The banks are able to relend this money to their borrowers at much lower interest rates than the borrowers would generally have to pay for commercial loans, if, indeed, such loans were available to them. As such, the MDBs' non-concessional lending windows are self-financing and even generate net income.

Periodically, when donors agree that future demand for loans from an MDB is likely to expand, they increase their capital subscriptions to an MDB's non-concessional lending window in order to allow the MDB to increase its level of lending. This usually occurs because the economy of the world or the region has grown in size and the needs of their borrowing countries have grown accordingly, or to respond to a financial crisis. An across the board increase in all members' shares is called a "general capital increase" (GCI). This is in contrast to a "selective capital increase" (SCI), which is typically small and used to alter the voting shares of member countries. The voting power of member countries in the MDB is determined largely by the amount of capital contributed and through selective capital increases; some countries subscribe a larger share of the new capital stock than others to increase their voting power in the institutions. GCIs happen infrequently. For example, the World Bank's main non-concessional lending window, the IBRD, has had only three GCIs since it was created in 1945. Since the onset the current international financial crisis in fall 2008, all the MDBs have been planning to seek new GCIs. Simultaneous requests for capital increases from all the MDBs is quite unusual and has not occurred since the mid-1970s.

Table 2. MDB Non-Concessional Lending Windows: U.S. Share of CapitalSubscriptionsCurrent subscriptions, including paid-in capital and callable capital, as of 2008 or FY2009

MDB	U.S. Subscription Billion US$	Total Subscription Billion US$	U.S. Share %
IBRD	32.0	189.9	17
IFC	0.6	2.4	24
AfDB	2.2	33.5	6
AsDB	8.5	54.9	16
EBRD	2.9	28.7	10
IDB	30.3	100.9	30
Total	**76.5**	**410.3**	**19**

Source: MDB Annual Reports.

Notes: World Bank data is for FY2009 (July 2008 – June 2009). Regional development bank data is for 2008 (calendar year).

Table 2 summarizes current U.S. capital subscriptions to the MDB non-concessional lending windows. The largest U.S. share of subscribed MDB capital is with the IDB at 30% while its smallest share among the MDBs is with the AfDB at 6%.

Table 3 shows the top donor countries to the MDB non-concessional facilities. Cumulatively, the United States has the largest financial commitments to the non-concessional lending windows at the IBRD, the IFC, the IDB, and the EBRD. At the AfDB, the United States has the second largest financial commitment after Nigeria. At the AsDB, the United States is tied with Japan for the largest financial commitment.

Table 3. MDB Non-Concessional Lending Windows: Top Donors
Current subscriptions to capital, including paid-in capital and callable capital, as of 2008 or FY2009

World Bank			
IBRD	%	IFC	%
United States	16.83	United States	24.03
Japan	8.07	Japan	5.96
Germany	4.60	Germany	5.44
United Kingdom	4.41	United Kingdom	5.11
France	4.41	France	5.11
Canada	2.85	Canada	3.43
China	2.85	India	3.43
India	2.85	Italy	3.43
Russia	2.85	Russia	3.43
Saudi Arabia	2.85	Netherlands	2.37

Regional Development Banks							
AfDB	**%**	**AsDB**	**%**	**EBRD**	**%**	**IDB**	**%**
Nigeria	8.88	Japan	15.57	United States	10.10	United States	30.03
United States	6.44	United States	15.57	France	8.61	Argentina	10.76
Japan	5.49	China	6.43	Germany	8.61	Brazil	10.76
Egypt	5.14	India	6.32	Italy	8.61	Mexico	6.92
South Africa	4.56	Australia	5.77	Japan	8.61	Venezuela	5.76
Germany	4.12	Indonesia	5.43	United Kingdom	8.61	Japan	5.00
Algeria	3.97	Canada	5.22	Russia	4.04	Canada	4.00
Libya	3.84	S. Korea	5.03	Canada	3.44	Chile	2.95
Canada	3.75	France	4.32	Spain	3.44	Colombia	2.95
France	3.75	Malaysia	2.72	EC[a]	3.03	France	1.90
				EIB[b]	3.03	Germany	1.90
						Spain	1.90

Source: MDB Annual Reports.

Notes: World Bank data is for FY2009 (July 2008 – June 2009). Regional development bank data is for 2008 (calendar year). a. European Community. b. European Investment Bank.

Table 4. MDB Concessional Lending Windows: U.S. Share of Cumulative Contributions Cumulative contributions as of 2008 or FY2009

MDB	U.S. Contribution Billion US$	Total Contribution Billion US$	U.S. Share %
IDA	42.7	199.4	21
AfDF	3.0	28.3	11
AsDF	3.8	23.3	16
EBRD	---	---	---
IDB: FSO	4.8	9.6	50
Total	**54.3**	**260.6**	**21**

Source: MDB Annual Reports.

Notes: EBRD does not have a concessional lending window. World Bank data is for FY2009 (July 2008 – June 2009). Regional development bank data is for 2008 (calendar year).

Other top donor states include Western European countries, Japan, and Canada. Additionally, several regional members have large financial stakes in the regional banks. For example, among the regional members, China and India are large contributors to the AsDB; Egypt and South Africa are large contributors to the AfDB; Argentina, Brazil, and Venezuela are large contributors to the IDB; and Russia is a large contributor to the EBRD.

Concessional Lending Windows

Concessional lending windows do not issue bonds; their funds are contributed directly from the financial contributions of their member countries. Most of the money comes from the more prosperous countries, while the contributions from borrowing countries are generally more symbolic than substantive. The MDBs have also transferred some of the net income from theirnon-concessional windows to their concessional lending window in order to help fund concessional loans and grants.

As the MDB extends concessional loans and grants to low-income countries, the window's resources become depleted. The donor countries meet together periodically to replenish those resources. Thus, these increases in resources are called replenishments, and most occur on a planned schedule ranging from three to five years. If these facilities are not replenished on time, they will run out of lendable resources and have to substantially reduce their levels of aid to poor countries.

Table 4 summarizes cumulative U.S. contributions to the MDB concessional lending windows. The U.S. share of total contributions is highest to the IDB's concessional lending window (5 0%) and lowest to the AfDB's concessional lending window (11%).

Table 5 shows the top donor countries to the MDB concessional facilities. The United States has made the highest cumulative contributions to IDA and the IDB's FSO, and the second highest cumulative contributions to the AfDF and the AsDF, after Japan. Other top donor states includethe more prosperous member countries: Japan, Canada, and those in Western Europe. Within the FSO, Brazil, Argentina, and Mexico have also made substantial contributions. In recent years, theU.S. contributions to IDA have been well below its historical share on some occasions and other countries (notably the United Kingdom) have played a predominant role.

Table 5. MDB Concessional Lending Windows: Top Donors
Cumulative contributions as of 2008 or FY2009

IDA	%	AfDF	%	AsDF	%	IDB: FSO	%
United States	21.40	Japan	11.96	Japan	36.94	United States	50.22
Japan	19.44	United States	10.54	United States	16.18	Japan	6.14
Germany	11.04	France	10.47	Canada	6.79	Brazil	5.65
United Kingdom	10.16	Germany	10.29	Australia	6.57	Argentina	5.24
France	7.29	United Kingdom	7.81	Germany	6.35	Mexico	3.41
Italy	4.41	Canada	7.63	France	4.71	Canada	3.21
Canada	4.37	Italy	5.91	United Kingdom	4.51	Germany	2.39
Netherlands	3.70	Sweden	5.21	Italy	3.93	France	2.29
Sweden	2.99	Norway	4.50	Netherlands	2.52	Spain	2.24
Switzerland	1.61	Netherlands	4.04	Spain	1.27	Italy	2.24

Source: MDB Annual Reports.

Note: FSO is the Fund for Special Operations, the IDB's concessional lending window. World Bank data is for FY2009. Regional development bank data is for 2008 (calendar year).

Structure and Organization

Relation to Other International Institutions

The World Bank is a specialized agency of the United Nations. However, it is autonomous in its decision-making procedures and its sources of funds. It also has autonomous control over its administration and budget. The regional development banks are independent international agencies and are not affiliated with the United Nations system. All the MDBs must comply with directives (for example, economic sanctions) agreed to (by vote) by the U.N. Security Council. However, they are not subject to decisions by the U.N. General Assembly or other U.N. agencies.

Internal Organization

The MDBs have similar internal organizational structures. Run by their own management and staffed by international civil servants, each MDB is supervised by a Board of Governors and a Board of Executive Directors. The Board of Governors is the highest decision-making authority, and each member country has its own governor. Countries are usually represented by their Secretary of the Treasury, Minister of Finance, or Central Bank Governor. The United States is currently represented by Treasury Secretary Timothy Geithner. The Board of Governors meets annually, though may act more frequently through mail-in votes on key decisions.

Table 6. U.S. Executive Directors

MDB	U.S. Executive Director
World Bank	Ian Solomon
AfDB	Walter Crawford Jones
AsDB	Curtis S. Chin[a]
EBRD	James Hudson
IDB	Gustavo Arnavat

Source: MDB websites.

Notes: a. Robert M. Orr has been nominated by the Obama Administration to be the U.S. Executive Director to AsDB, pending approval by the Senate (see p. 28).

Table 7. U.S. Voting Power in the MDBs

MDB	U.S. Voting Share (%)
IBRD	16.36
IDA	12.16
IFC	23.59
AfDB	6.34
AsDB	12.76
IDB	30.00
EBRD	10.15

Source: MDB Annual Reports.

While the Boards of Governors in each of the Banks retain power over major policy decisions, such as amending the founding documents of the organization, they have delegated day-to-day authority over operational policy, lending, and other matters to their institutions' Board of Executive Directors. The Board of Executive Directors in each institution is smaller than the Board of Governors. There are 24 members on the World Bank's Board of Executive Directors, and fewer for some of the regional development banks. Each MDB Executive Board has its ownschedule, but they generally meet at least weekly to consider MDB loan and policy proposals and oversee bank activities. The current U.S. Executive Directors to the MDBs are listed in Table 6.

Decisions are reached in the MDBs through voting. Each member country's voting share is weighted on the basis of its cumulative financial contributions and commitments to theorganization.[9] Table 7 shows the U.S. voting power in each institution. The voting power of the United States is large enough to veto major policy decisions at the World Bank and the IDB, suchas amending the World Bank's Articles of Agreement. However, the United States cannot unilaterally veto more day-to-day decisions, such as individual loans.

Debates about Effectiveness of the MDBs

Effectiveness of Foreign Aid

The effectiveness of foreign aid, including the aid provided by MDBs, in spurring economic development and reform in developing countries is hotly debated. The most prominent academic, peer-reviewed studies of foreign aid effectiveness typically attempt to examine the effect of total foreign aid provided to developing countries, including both bilateral aid and multilateral aid. With bilateral aid, most U.S. resources go directly to programs and projects in developing countries. With multilateral aid, multilateral organizations, like the MDBs, pool money from different donors and then provide money to fund programs and projects in developing countries. The results of these studies that examine the effectiveness of bilateral and multilateral aid are mixed, with conclusions ranging from (a) aid is ineffective at promoting economic growth[10] to (b) aid is effective at promoting economic growth[11] to (c) aid is effective at promoting growth in some countries under specific circumstances (such as when developing-country policies are strong).[12] The divergent results of these academic studies make it difficult to reach firm conclusions about the overall effectiveness of aid.

Beyond the debates about the overall effectiveness of foreign aid, there are also criticisms of the providers of foreign aid. Many of these criticisms are made broadly about multilateral aid organizations and government aid agencies, and are not targeted at the MDBs specifically. For example, it is argued that the national and international bureaucracies that dispense foreign aid focus on "getting money out the door" to developing countries, rather than on delivering services to developing countries; emphasize short-term outputs like reports and frameworks but do not engage in long-term activities like the evaluation of projects after they are completed; and put enormous administrative demands on developing-country governments.[13] Bilateral and multilateral foreign aid agencies have also been criticized for their lack of transparency about their operating costs and how they spend their aid money; the fragmentation of foreign aid across many small aid bureaucracies that are not well coordinated; and the proportion of foreign aid that goes to corrupt leaders or is spent ineffectively. [14] (However, some analysts contend that among government and international foreign agencies, MDBs ranked among the best for adhering to foreign aid "best practices."[15]) Many of these criticisms and proposals for change are discussed ina March 2010 report by the Senate Foreign Relations Committee on the international financial institutions (IFIs).[16]

Proponents of foreign aid argue that, despite some flaws, such aid at its core serves vital economic and political functions. With 1.4 billion people in the developing world (one in four people in the developing world) living on less than $1.25 a day in 2005,[17] some argue that not providing assistance is simply not an option; providing aid to the world's poorest countries is the "right" thing to do and part of "the world's shared commitments to human dignity and survival."[18] These proponents typically point to the use of foreign aid to provide basic necessities, such as food supplements, vaccines, nurses, and access to education, to the world's poorest countries. Additionally, proponents of foreign aid argue that, even if foreign aid has not been effective at raising overall levels of economic growth, foreign aid has been successful in dramatically improving health and education in developing countries over the past four decades. For example, it is argued that foreign aid contributed to rising life expectancy in developing countries from 48 years to 68 years over the past four decades, and lowering infant mortality from 131 out of every 1,000 babies born in developing countries to 36 out of every 1,000 babies.[19] It is also argued that providing foreign aid is an important component of U.S. national security policy and U.S. leadership in the world.

Bilateral vs. Multilateral Aid

There are also policy debates about the merits of bilateral versus multilateral aid.[20] There are different advantages to each approach. Bilateral aid gives donors more control over where the money goes and how the money is spent. For example, donor countries may have more flexibility to allocate funds to countries that are of geopolitical strategic importance, but not facing the greatest development needs, than might be possible by providing aid through a multilateral organization. By building a clear link between the donor country and the recipient country, bilateral aid may also garner the donor country more goodwill from the recipient country than if the funds had been provided through a multilateral organization.

Providing aid through multilateral organizations offers different benefits for donor countries. Multilateral organizations pool the resources of several donors, allowing donors to share the cost of development projects (often called burden-sharing). Additionally, donor countries may find it politically sensitive to attach policy reforms to loans or to enforce these policy reforms. Multilateral organizations can usefully serve as a scapegoat for imposing and enforcingconditionality. Finally, many believe that providing funds to multilateral organizations is important for enhancing and symbolizing U.S. leadership in the world economy.

The United States provides most of its foreign aid for promoting economic and social development bilaterally rather than multilaterally. Data from the Organization for Economic Cooperation and Development (OECD) Development Assistance Committee (DAC) reports that in 2008, 11% of U.S. foreign aid disbursed to developing countries with the purpose of promoting economic and social development was provided through multilateral institutions, while 89% was provided bilaterally.[21] Figure 8 shows that the level of multilateral aid disbursed by the United States has remained fairly constant between 2001 and 2008, although U.S. bilateral aid for development has increased.

OECD-DAC data allows comparison of the United States with other developed countries. Generally, other developed countries disbursed a higher proportion of their foreign aid through multilateral institutions than the United States did in 2008. For example, 29% of Japan's, 33% of Germany's, and 36% of the United Kingdom's foreign aid for economic and social development in 2008 was disbursed to multilateral organizations. One exception is Australia, who disbursed only 10% of foreign aid through multilateral organizations in 2008.

An alternative data source for U.S. multilateral and bilateral economic assistance to developing countries is *U.S. Overseas Loans and Grants: Obligations and Loan Authorization*, published by U.S. Agency for International Development (USAID).[22] This publication is commonly referred toas the Greenbook. According to this publication, 6.7% of U.S. economic assistance in 2008 was provided to multilateral organizations. The data is drawn from the same source as the dataprovided by the United States to the OECD-DAC, but the totals are different due to differences between the definitions of economic assistance used by the OECD-DAC and by the Greenbook.

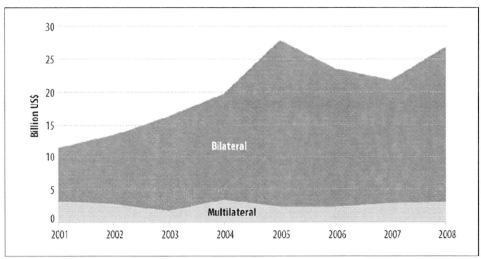

Source: OECD Development Assistance Committee (DAC) (www.oecd.org/dac/stats).
Notes: DAC reports data on disbursements of official development assistance (ODA), which is defined as flows to developing countries and multilateral institutions which are administered with the promotion of economic development and is concessional in character and conveys a grant element of at least 25%. DAC data does not include, for instance, other official flows including military assistance. DAC data also focuses on the disbursements of ODA, and would not include, for example, the callable capital committed by the United States to the MDBs, because this money has never actually been disbursed from the United States to the MDBs. Also, multilateral organizations not only include the MDBs but also U.N. agencies.

Figure 8. U.S. Bilateral and Multilateral Official Development Assistance, 2001-2008 Billion US$ (Current)

ISSUES FOR CONGRESS

This section discusses current issues of particular interest to Congress, including authorizing and appropriating legislation for U.S. contributions to the MDBs, congressional oversight of the MDBs, U.S. commercial interests in the MDBs, and proposed voting reforms at the World Bank.

Authorizing and Appropriating U.S. Contributions to the MDBs

Frequency and Process
Replenishments of the MDB concessional windows happen regularly, while capital increases for the MDB non-concessional windows occur much more infrequently. Quite unusually, all the MDBs are currently requesting capital increases, primarily to address the increase in demand for loans that resulted from the financial crisis, prepare for future crises, and, in the case of the IDB, recover from financial losses resulting from the financial crisis. Simultaneous capital increases for all the MDBs has not happened since the 1970s. Negotiations over the capital increases are ongoing, and hearings may be held as early as

Spring 2010. Any U.S. participation in the capital increases would require legislation. The Administration has requested that U.S. contributions to the Asian Development Bank (AsDB) capital increase be included in the FY2011 budget. Capital increases for the other MDBs, if agreed to, would likely be included in the FY2012 budget.

Authorizing and appropriations legislation is required for U.S. contributions to the MDBs. The Senate Committee on Foreign Relations and the House Committee on Financial Services are responsible for managing MDB authorization legislation. During the past several decades, authorization legislation for the MDBs has not passed as freestanding legislation. Instead, it has been included through other legislative vehicles, such as the annual foreign operations appropriations act, a larger omnibus appropriations act, or a budget reconciliation bill.

The Foreign Operations Subcommittees of the House and Senate Committees on Appropriations manage the relevant appropriations legislation. MDB appropriations is included in the annual foreign operations appropriations act or a larger omnibus appropriations act. For FY2010appropriations legislation for the MDBs, see CRS Report R40693, *State, Foreign Operations, and Related Programs: FY2010 Budget and Appropriations*, by Susan B. Epstein, Kennon H. Nakamura, and Marian Leonardo Lawson.

Administration's Request for FY2011

The Administration has requested authorizations and appropriations for U.S. contributions to the MDBs for FY2011.[23]

Authorizations

The Administration's request for authorization of appropriations for FY20 11 has three major components: authorization for U.S. contributions to the AsDB general capital increase, authorization for U.S. contributions to the replenishments of the AsDF, and authorization for U.S. contributions to a variety of smaller funds associated with the World Bank.

First, the Administration has requested authorization for U.S. contributions to AsDB's capital increase. This includes a request to authorize $532 million paid-in capital and $12.79 billion callable capital. The Administration has requested that these funds be appropriated over a five- year period. Second, the Administration is seeking authorization of $461 million for the most recent replenishment of the ADF, to be appropriated over a four year period. Third, the Administration has requested authorization for U.S. contributions to a new Multilateral Food Security Fund (to be established at the World Bank); authorization of $1,625 million for the Climate Investment Funds (of which the World Bank serves as the trustee); and an extension of authorization for U.S. contributions to the Heavily Indebted Poor Country (HIPC) Initiative and HIPC Trust Fund (administered by the World Bank).

Appropriations

The Administration's request for appropriations to the MDBs for FY20 1 1is listed in Table 8.[24] There are three major components to the Administration's appropriations request: appropriations for U.S. contributions to a capital increase at the AsDB, appropriations for U.S. contributions to the replenishments of IDA, the AfDF, and the AsDB, and appropriations for U.S. contributions to a variety of smaller funds associated with the MDBs.

First, for FY2011, the Administration has requested appropriations for the capital increase of the AsDB's non-concessional lending window. General capital increases entail paid-in and callable capital. Since 1981, only paid-in capital has been appropriated. For callable capital, Congress has annual program ceilings in the annual Foreign Operations Appropriations legislation specifyingthe amount of callable capital the United States may be subscribed to in each MDB during the current fiscal year. The Administration has requested $106.6 million paid-in capital and roughly $5 billion callable capital for FY2011 as the first of five annual U.S. contributions to the AsDB general capital increase.[25]

Table 8. Administration Request for Appropriations to the MDBs, FY2011Million US$

	Amount
Capital increases for non-concessional lending windows	
Asian Development Bank (AsDB), paid-in capital	106.6
Asian Development Bank (AsDB), callable capital	5,000.0[a]
Replenishments for concessional lending windows	
International Development Association (IDA)	1,285.0
African Development Fund (AfDF)	155.9
Asian Development Fund (AsDF)	115.3
Contributions to funds administered by or affiliated with an MDB, or where an MDB serves as the trustee	
Multilateral Investment Fund (MIF)[b]	25.0
Inter-American Investment Corporation (IIC)[b]	21.0
Multilateral Food Security Fund[c]	408.4
Clean Technology Fund (CTF)[d]	400.0
Strategic Climate Fund (SCF)[d]	235.0
Global Environment Facility (GEF)[d]	175.0
Heavily Indebted Poor Countries (HIPC) Initiative[e]	75.0

Source: U.S. Department of Treasury, *International Programs: Justification for Appropriations, FY2011 BudgetRequest,* http://www.treas.gov/offices/international-affairs/intl/fy2011/FY%202011%20CPD%20for%20web.pdf.

Notes: Does not include the $30 million request for the International Fund for Agricultural Development (IFAD). IFAD is a multilateral organization focused on reducing rural poverty and hunger. The IFAD is not covered in this chapter.

a. Since 1981, the United States no longer appropriates money to back its callable capital subscriptions to the MDBs. Rather Congress sets annual program ceilings in the annual Foreign Operations Appropriations Act specifying the amount of callable capital the United States may subscribe in each MDB during the current fiscal year.

b. Affiliate of the Inter-American Development Bank (IDB).

c. Administered by the World Bank.

d. The World Bank serves as the trustee for this fund.

e. The Administration has proposed using the requested funds for the Heavily Indebted Poor Countries (HIPC) Trust Fund, which is administered by the World Bank.

Second, the United States has previously committed to replenishments of IDA, the AfDF, and the AsDF, and these payments were scheduled in the replenishment agreements to occur over a period of three to four years. To meet these previous commitments, the Administration has requested appropriations for $1,285 million for the second of three payments for the 15th replenishment of IDA (IDA-15), $155 million for the third and final payment for the 11th replenishment of the AfDF (AfDF- 11), and $115.3 million for the second of four payments to the 10th replenishment of the AsDF (AsDF- 10).

Third, the Administration has also requested appropriations for U.S. contributions to several smaller funds. These include funds that are administered by or affiliated with an MDB, or funds where an MDB servers as the trustee. These appropriations requests include:

- $25 million for the Multilateral Investment Fund (MIF), an affiliate of the IDB that promotes small-and medium-size enterprise growth in the Western Hemisphere. This funding would be for the fifth of six installments of the first replenishment of the MIF.
- $21 million for the Inter-American Investment Corporation (ICC), an affiliate of the IDB that supports small- and medium-sized enterprises in Latin America and the Caribbean. This funding would be used to clear arrears for the U.S. payment of subscribed shares from the 1999 capital increase.
- $408.4 million for a new Multilateral Food Security Fund to be administered by the World Bank. The Fund will finance developing country efforts to create and sustain improvements in their food security by strengthening agricultural productivity, nutrition, and access to food.
- $400 million for the Clean Technology Fund (CTF), for which the World Bank serves as the trustee. The CTF seeks to reduce the growth of greenhouse gas emissions in developing countries by financing the additional costs of cleaner technologies.
- $235 million for the Strategic Climate Fund (SCF), for which the World Bank servers as the trustee. It seeks to pilot new approaches to address climate change challenges in developing countries, such as scaling-up renewable energy in low-income countries. The Administration proposes using the funds for three programs within the SCF: the Pilot Program for Climate Resilience ($90 million), the Forest Investment Program ($95 million), and the Program for Scaling-Up Renewable Energy in Low Income Countries ($50 million).
- $175 million for the Global Environment Facility (GEF), for which the World Bank serves as the trustee.[26] The GEF finances projects that aim to improve the environment. The Administration proposes $170 million for the first payment of the GEF replenishment and $5 million to pay off a portion of U.S. arrears to the GEF.
- $50 million for the Enhanced HIPC Initiative. The Administration proposes using the funds to meet the $75.4 million in U.S. pledges to the HIPC Trust Fund, administered by the World Bank. For qualifying countries, the HIPC Trust Fund will either prepay or purchase a portion of the debt owed to a multilateral creditor and cancel such debt or pay debt service as it comes due.[27]

Congressional Oversight

As international organizations, the MDBs are generally exempt from U.S. law. The President has delegated the authority to manage and instruct U.S. participation in the MDBs to the Secretary of Treasury. Within the Treasury Department, the Office of International Affairs has the lead role in managing day-to-day U.S. participation in the MDBs. The President appoints the U.S. Executive Directors, and their alternates, with the advice and consent of the Senate. Thus, the Senate canexercise oversight through the confirmation process.

Over the years, Congress has played a major role in U.S. policy towards the MDBs. In addition to congressional hearings on the MDBs, Congress has enacted a substantial number of legislative mandates that oversee and regulate U.S. participation in the MDBs. These mandates generally fall into one of four major types. More than one type of mandate may be used on a given issue area.

First, numerous legislative mandates direct how the U.S. representatives at the MDBs can vote on various policies. Examples include mandates that require the U.S. Executive Directors to oppose: (a) financial assistance to specific countries, such as Burma, until sufficient progress is made on human rights and implementing a democratic government;[28] (b) financial assistance to broad categories of countries, such as major producers of illicit drugs;[29] and (c) financial assistance for specific projects, such as the production of palm oil, sugar, or citrus crops for export if the financial assistance would cause injury to United States producers.[30] Some legislative mandates require the U.S. Executive Directors to support, rather than oppose, financial assistance. For example, a current mandate allows the Treasury Secretary to instruct the U.S. Executive Directors to vote in favor of financial assistance to countries that have contributed to U.S. efforts to deter and prevent international terrorism.[31]

Second, legislative mandates direct the U.S. representatives at the MDBs to advocate for policies within the MDBs. One example is a mandate that instructs the U.S. Executive Director of the IBRD to urge the IBRD to support an increase in loans that support population, health, and nutrition programs.[32] Another example is a mandate that requires the U.S. Executive Directors to take all possible steps to communicate potential procurement opportunities for U.S. firms to the Secretary of Treasury, the Secretary of State, the Secretary of Commerce, and the business community.[33] Mandates that call for the U.S. Executive Director to both vote and advocate for a particular policy are often called "voice and vote" mandates.

Third, Congress has also passed legislation requiring the Treasury Secretary to submit reports on various MDB issues (reporting requirements). Some legislative mandates call for one-off reports; other mandates call for reports on a regular basis, typically annually. For example, current legislation requires the Treasury Secretary to submit an annual report to the appropriate congressional committees on the actions taken by countries that have borrowed from the MDBs to strengthen governance and reduce the opportunity for bribery and corruption.[34]

Fourth, Congress has also attempted to influence policies at the MDBs through "power of the purse" – that is, withholding funding from the MDBs or attaching stipulations on the MDBs 's use of funds. For example, the FY20 10 Consolidated Appropriations Act stipulates that 10% of the funds appropriated to the AsDF will be withheld until the Treasury Secretary

U.S. Commercial Interests and "Country Systems"

Billions of dollars of contracts are awarded to private firms each year in order to acquire the goods and services necessary to implement projects financed by the MDBs. **Table 9** shows that this figure was above $30 billion in 2008. MDB contracts are awarded through international competitive bidding processes, although most MDBs allow the borrowing country to give some preference to domestic firms in awarding contracts for MDB-financed projects in order to help spur development.

Among the regional development banks, only a very small fraction (less than 1.5%) of these contracts are known to have been awarded to U.S. companies. Data on contracts awarded by the World Bank by firm nationality is not available,[36] nor is data on the nationality of subcontractors that participate in carrying out projects financed by the MDBs.

As the largest MDB, the World Bank awards the biggest number and the highest volume of contracts each year. Major policy changes are currently underway at the World Bank that wouldalter how companies bid on World Bank projects. Currently, the World Bank has one centralizedprocurement system for awarding World Bank contracts, regardless of which country the projectis being implemented in. The new system being proposed would award contracts using systemsdevised by the borrowing governments, provided that the system meet certain standards and criteria. The emphasis on the borrowing country's design and implementation of procurement,unique to each country, has led this system of procurement to be termed "country systems."

The World Bank has not implemented country systems yet, but it has been in the process of moving towards country systems over the past several years. In 2005, Congress stipulated that20% ($31 million) of the funds appropriated to IDA would be withheld unless the Treasury Secretary could verify that the Bank had, among other things, withdrawn its proposal on increasing the use of country systems in procurement.[37] The World Bank did not withdraw the country systems proposal, and Congress withheld the funds. Currently, the World Bank has plans to launch pilot programs of country systems in eight developing countries, possibly as soon 2010.[38] The Bank has completed assessments of the country procurement systems in 18 countries,although getting beyond the benchmarking exercise has been slower than initially hoped by the Bank.[39]

Scholars have argued that "although little discussed... the World Bank's planned use of country systems for public procurement has the potential to be one of its most significant policy changes in the next ten years."[40] The World Bank argues that country systems will strengthen national institutions in developing countries for public expenditures, whether they come from World Bank funds, taxes, or other donors.[41] It is also argued that country systems would help harmonize aid flows, streamline the disbursement of funds, reduce donor overhead costs, and return control over aid flows to borrowing countries.[42]

Table 9. MDB Contracts Identifiably Awarded to U.S. Companies
Calendar Year 2008, Million US$

MDB	Contracts Awarded to U.S. Companies	Total Contracts Awarded	Percent of Contracts Awarded to U.S. Firms
World Bank	n.a.[a]	20,000.0[b]	n.a.
AsDB[c]	40.5	4,487.0	0.9%
AfDB[c]	36.0	2,866.3	1.3%
EBRD[d]	0.7	1,730.0	0.0%
IDB[d]	12.6	2,529.8	0.5%

Source: World Bank Contracts Award website (http://go.worldbank.org/GM7GBOVGS0); ADB Annual Report; AfDB Annual Report; IDB Procurement Portal website http://www5.iadb.org/i dbppi/aspx/ppProcurement.aspx; EBRD Procurement Department, *Annual Procurement Review*, 2008.

Notes: In some cases, contracts have been awarded to firms in one country that intend to subcontract major elements of the work to firms in other countries. It is not clear to what extent the data capture subcontracting.

a. n.a. denotes not available. World Bank Contracts Award website (http://go.worldbank. org/GM7GBOVGS0) reports firm nationality for only a fraction of total contracts awarded.

b. Estimate of annual contracts awarded by the World Bank from World Bank Contracts Award website (http://go.worldbank.org/GM7GBOVGS0).

c. Contracts awarded by country of origin (where the goods are mined, produced, grown, assembled and/or manufactured).

d. Contracts awarded by nationality of firm (where the primary contractor is located).

Others, particularly among the business community that bids on World Bank contracts, have been skeptical of the World Bank's use of country systems. Critics note that harmonization of procedures within countries would likely come at the expense of harmonization of uniformity in the overall activities funded by the MDBs. Additionally, there is concern that standards used by the World Bank to evaluate a country's procurement policies and overall eligibility for country systems have been watered down over time, especially since the country systems idea was first seriously floated by the Bank in 2005. Lowering standards, it is argued, increases the scope for corruption in the procurement process. Also, since the use of country systems allows each country to have a unique procurement process as long as that process meets certain standards and criteria, there is concern that country systems would disadvantage small- and medium-sized businesses in bidding on World Bank contracts, since smaller businesses are less likely to have the resources to invest in learning dozens of different procurement processes. Finally, there is concern that weak bureaucracies in developing countries simply lack the capacity to administer the procurement process and would be better suited to remain in the purview of the World Bank, even if transitioning to country systems would reduce the overhead costs of the Bank.[43]

Proposals for Voting Reform at the World Bank

At the September 2009 G-20 meeting in Pittsburgh, leaders of the G-20 nations pledged to reform the voting shares of member states at the World Bank.[44] In particular, the G-20 leaders called for "adopting a dynamic formula at the World Bank which primarily reflects countries' evolving economic weight and the World Bank's development mission, and that generates an increase of at least 3% of voting power for developing and transition countries, to the benefit of underrepresented countries."[45] The G-20 leaders pledged to reach an agreement by the IMF and World Bank's 2010 Spring Meetings, which are to be held April 24-25, 2010. No agreement has yet been announced.

Negotiations are expected to be contentious, particularly among European countries which are largely expected to lose voting power if any voting reform is enacted. **Figure 9** shows that Belgium, the Netherlands, and Switzerland, for example, have voting power at the IBRD that is larger than their economic weight in the world economy, suggesting that these countries are overrepresented at the World Bank. By contrast, voting at the World Bank has not been reformed to reflect the increased weight in the world economy of large-emerging market countries. Voting power at the World Bank is tied closely to the financial commitments of countries, so presumably any increase of voting power for large emerging-market countries would also come with increased financial commitments.

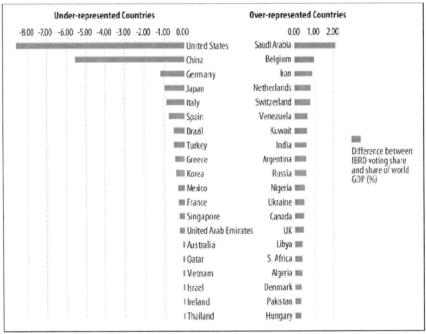

Source: IMF World Economic Outlook; World Bank Annual Report.
Notes: The 20 IBRD members with the smallest and largest differences between share of world GDP (2009 data at current prices) and voting share in the IBRD. These calculations are for illustrative purposes only. Alternative calculations could be made, for example, using voting power at IDA or GDP adjusted for differences in price levels among countries. These alternative calculations would likely produce different results.

Figure 9. Comparison of IBRD Voting Share and Share of World GDP

The United States is considered to be an under-represented country at the World Bank, as its current voting share at the IBRD, for example, is smaller than its weight in the internationaleconomy (Figure 9). The United States has lowered its share over time to allow new countries tojoin and reduce its financial commitment to the institution. It is unlikely the United States would lose or gain voting power if the G-20 proposals to shift voting power to under-representedcountries are implemented. However, the G-20's calls for voting reform at the World Bank are likely to be a central focus of debates about the World Bank moving forward.

End Notes

[1] There are also several sub-regional development banks, such as, the Caribbean Development Bank and the Andean Development Corporation. However, the United States is not a member of these sub-regional development institutions. This chapter does not discuss the North American Development Bank (NADBank), a binational financial institution capitalized and governed equally by the United States and Mexico.

[2] The International Monetary Fund (IMF), whose mandate is to ensure international financial stability, is not an MDB. The IMF does lend to developing countries on concessional terms (defined on p. 2), but this lending is primarily used to address balance of payments problems. However, the IMF provides some financial assistance to low-income countries, and the MDBs provide some balance of payments support through policy-based loans. This has led to some criticism in recent years about duplication of IMF and MDB efforts. Broadly speaking, though, the IMF focuses on providing financial support to countries facing balance of payments difficulties, and the MDBs provide financial support for economic and social development.

[3] These carry repayment terms that are lower than those normally required for commercial loans, but they are not subsidized. See the discussion of financing below.

[4] In addition to the IBRD, IDA, and the IFC, the World Bank Group also includes the Multilateral Investment Guarantee Agency (MIGA) and the International Centre for Settlement of Investment Disputes (ICSID). The term "World Bank" typically refers to IBRD and IDA specifically. MIGA and ICSID are not covered in this chapter, even though they arguably play an important role in fostering economic development, because they do not make loans and grants to developing countries. MIGA provides political risk insurance to foreign investors, in order to promote foreign direct investment (FDI) into developing countries. The ICSID provides facilities for conciliation and arbitration of disputes between governments and private foreign investors.

[5] Sarah Babb, *Behind the Development Banks: Washington Politics, World Poverty, and the Wealth of Nations* (Chicago: University of Chicago Press, 2009).

[6] World Bank commitments are for FY 2009 (July 2008 – June 2009). Regional bank commitments are for 2008 (calendar year).

[7] Including IBRD, IFC, and IDA.

[8] In most cases, the banks do not use the capital subscribed by their developing country members as backing for the bonds and notes they sell to fund their market-rate loans to developing countries, but instead just use the capital subscribed by their developed country members.

[9] This is not necessarily the case with the MDBs' concessional windows, though. In order to insure that borrower countries have at least some say in these organizations, the contributions of donor countries in some recent replenishments have not given the donor countries additional votes. In all cases, though, the donor countries together have a comfortable majority of the total vote.

[10] E.g., see William Easterly, "Can Foreign Aid Buy Growth?," *Journal of Economic Perspectives*, vol. 17, no. 3 (Summer 2003), p. 23–48.

[11] E.g., see Carl-Johan Dalgaard and Henrik Hansen, "On Aid, Growth, and Good Policies," *Journal of Development Studies*, vol. 37, no. 6 (August 2001), pp. 17-41.

[12] E.g., see Craig Burnside and David Dollar, "Aid, Policies, and Growth," *American Economic Review*, vol. 90, no. 4 (September 2000), p. 847–868.

[13] William Easterly, "The Cartel of Good Intentions," *Foreign Policy*, vol. 131 (July-August 2002), pp. 40-49.

[14] William Easterly and Tobias Pfutze, "Where Does the Money Go? Best and Worst Practices in Foreign Aid," *Journal of Economic Perspectives*, vol. 22, no. 2 (Spring 2008). For more on foreign aid reform, also see: CRS Report R40 102, *Foreign Aid Reform: Studies and Recommendations*, by Susan B. Epstein and Matthew C. Weed and CRS Report R40756, *Foreign Aid Reform: Agency Coordination*, by Marian Leonardo Lawson and Susan B. Epstein.

[15] Ibid.

[16] U.S. Congress, Senate Committee on Foreign Relations, *The International Financial Institutions: A Call for Change*, 111th Cong., 2nd sess., March 10, 2010, http://foreign.senate.gov/imo/media/doc/55285.pdf.

[17] World Bank, *New Data Show 1.4 Billion Live On Less Than US$1.25 A Day, But Progress Against Poverty Remains Strong*, August 26, 2008, http://go.worldbank.org/F9ZJUH97T0.

[18] Jeffrey Sachs, The End of Poverty: Economic Possibilities for Our Time (Penguin Books, 2006), p. xvi.

[19] William Easterly, *The White Man's Burden* (New York: Penguin Press, 2006), pp. 176-177.

[20] For more on the choice between bilateral and multilateral aid, see, for example: Helen Milner and Dustin Tingley, "The Choice for Multilateralism: Foreign Aid and American Foreign Policy," Working Paper, February 10, 2010 and Helen Milner, "Why Multilateralism? Foreign Aid and Domestic Principal-Agent Problems," in *Delegation and Agency in International Organizations*, eds. Darren Hawkins et al. (New York City: Cambridge University Press, 2006), pp. 107-139.

[21] See the note in **Figure 8** for explanation of OECD DAC data. DAC data does not, for example, include military assistance provided by the United States or the callable capital committed by the United States to the MDBs.

[22] Available at http://gbk.eads.usaidallnet.gov/.

[23] For the Administration's request for FY201 1, see U.S. Department of Treasury, *International Programs: Justification for Appropriations, FY2011 Budget Request*, http://www.treas.gov/offices/international-affairs/intl/fy201 1/FY%20201 1%20CPD%20for%20web.pdf.

[24] For the Administration's requests for appropriations to the MDBs and the final appropriations to the MDBs since 1999, see CRS Report RS20792, *Multilateral Development Banks: U.S. Contributions FY1998-FY2009*, by Jonathan E. Sanford.

[25] The World Bank (IBRD), the IFC, the AfDB, and the EBRD have also requested capital increases for their non-concessional lending windows. Any U.S. participation in these capital increases are expected to be included in the FY20 12 budget, although hearings on the capital increases could be held as early as 2010.

[26] For more on the GEF, see CRS Report R41 165, *Global Environment Facility (GEF): An Overview*, by Richard K. Lattanzio.

[27] For more on HIPC, see CRS Report RL34644, *Debt Relief for Poor Countries*, by Jonathan E. Sanford and Martin A. Weiss.

[28] Sec. 570(a)(2) of the Omnibus Consolidated Appropriations Act, 1997 (P.L. 104-208). Also on human rights more broadly, see 22 USCS § 262d.

[29] 22 USC § 2291j(a)(2).

[30] 22 USC § 262g.

[31] 22 USC § 262p-4r(a).

[32] 22 USC § 262p-4m.

[33] 22 USC § 262s-1.

[34] 22 USC § 262r-6(b)(2).

[35] Sec. 7086 of the Consolidated Appropriations Act, 2010 (P.L. 111-117).

[36] World Bank Contracts Award website (http://go.worldbank.org/GM7GBOVGS0) reports firm nationality for only a fraction of total contracts awarded.

[37] Sec. 299d of the Foreign Operations, Export Financing, and Related Programs Appropriations Act, 2006 (P.L. 109- 102).

[38] Christopher L. Pallas and Jonathan Wood, "The World Bank's Use of Country Systems for Procurement: A Good Idea Gone Bad?," *Development Policy Review*, vol. 27, no. 2 (2009), pp. 215-230.

[39] World Bank, *Strengthening World Bank Group Engagement on Governance and Anticorruption: Second-Year Progress Report*, October 20, 2009, p. viii, http://go.worldbank.org/CJL9TZH330.

[40] Christopher L. Pallas and Jonathan Wood, "The World Bank's Use of Country Systems for Procurement: A Good Idea Gone Bad?," *Development Policy Review*, vol. 27, no. 2 (2009), pp. 215-230.

[41] World Bank, Operations Policy and Country Services, *Use of Country Procurement Systems in Bank-Supported Operations: Proposed Piloting Program*, R2008-0036/5, May 20, 2008, http://siteresources.worldbank.org/INTPROCUREMENT/Resources/UseOfCountrySystemsFinalApprovedVe rsionFor Disclosure-June20-2008.pdf.

[42] Christopher L. Pallas and Jonathan Wood, "The World Bank's Use of Country Systems for Procurement: A Good Idea Gone Bad?," *Development Policy Review*, vol. 27, no. 2 (2009), pp. 215-230.

[43] Ibid.

[44] The G-20 nations include 19 large developed and emerging-market countries (Argentina, Australia, Brazil, Canada, China, France, Germany, India, Indonesia, Italy, Japan, Mexico, Russia, Saudi Arabia, South Africa, South Korea, Turkey, the United Kingdom, and the United States), as well as the European Union. For more on the G-20, see CRS Report R40977, *The G-20 and International Economic Cooperation: Background and Implications for Congress*, by Rebecca M. Nelson. The report also discusses the G-20 proposal to reform voting at the IMF.

[45] G-20, *Leaders' Statement: The Pittsburgh Summit*, September 24-25, 2009, http://www.pittsburghsummit.gov/mediacenter/129639.htm.

In: Multilateral Development Banks and International Finance
Editor: Leah M. Groffe
ISBN: 978-1-61728-883-8
© 2010 Nova Science Publishers, Inc.

Chapter 2

THE AFRICAN DEVELOPMENT BANK GROUP[*]

Martin A. Weiss

SUMMARY

The African Development Bank (AfDB) Group is a regional development bank currently based in Tunis, Tunisia. It comprises three lending facilities: the market rate facility, the AfDB; a concessional lending facility, the African Development Fund; and a trust fund established by Nigeria to lend to low-income African countries. The Bank has 53 African members, as well as 24 non-regional members, including the United States.

INTRODUCTION

The African Development Bank (AfDB) Group is a regional development bank (RDB) "dedicated to combating poverty and improving the lives of people of the continent."[1] In February 2003, the Bank temporarily relocated to Tunis, Tunisia from its permanent location in Abidjan, Côte d'Ivoire due to political instability in that country.

STRUCTURE

The AfDB Group comprises three lending facilities:

- The **African Development Bank** (the Bank), created in 1964, is a regional development bank that provides grants, loans and technical assistance. It seeks to promote sustainable economic growth and reduce poverty in the Bank's 53 African

---

[*] This is an edited, reformatted and augmented version of a CRS Report for Congress publication, Report #RS22690, dated January 30, 2009.

member countries.[2] The Bank also participates in a wide variety of international programs including the Heavily Indebted Poor Country (HIPC) Debt Relief Initiative, the more comprehensive Multilateral Debt Relief Initiative (MDRI), and the New Partnership for Africa's Development (NEPAD).[3] As of May 2007, total subscribed capital is U.S. $33 billion.

- The **African Development Fund** (AfDF, the Fund) is a concessional lending/grant making facility for low-income African member countries created in 1972. There are currently 38 AfDF borrower countries. The AfDF is primarily financed by 24 non-regional countries including the United States, Canada, and several European and Asian countries. Every three years, donors agree on a replenishment agreement for the next three fiscal years. In December 2007, negotiations concluded for the eleventh replenishment of AfDF resources (AfDFVI) that will provide financing of $8.9 billion during 2008 to 2011.

- The **Nigeria Trust Fund** is a fund, created by Nigeria in 1976, to provide financing on terms between those of the AfDB and the AfDF to low-income regional member countries. Although the Fund expired in 2006, the Nigerian government agreed to extend the fund for an additional 10 years.

In FY2008, the Bush Administration requested $2.0 million to clear the outstanding arrears on U.S. payments to purchase shares of the most recent global capital increase (GCI) of AfDB resources in 1998. For the AfDF, the Bush Administration requested $135.7 million for the final installment of a three-year commitment under the agreement for the tenth replenishment of the AfDF (AfDF-10) and $4.9 million to pay a portion of outstanding U.S. arrears to the AfDF. The U.S. total three-year commitment for AfDF-10 is $407 million, which contributes to a $5.4 billion total replenishment. P.L. 110-161, the *Consolidated Appropriations Act, 2008*, provides the full request of $135.7 million to the AfDB.

For FY2009, the Administration has requested that Congress authorize U.S. participation in the three years of AfDF 11 (2009-2011) and contribute $1 56.055 million in budget authority for the first of three installments of the U.S. contribution to the eleventh replenishment (AFDF-1 1) covering the period 2009-2011. The Administration is again requesting $2 million to clear arrears to the AfDB general capital.

BACKGROUND

The Bank was founded in 1964 as an exclusively African institution. Most African countries had just become independent amid great optimism about the continent's economic prospects. However, poor African economic performance during the Bank's early years soon made it clear that an exclusively African membership would be unable to achieve a level of creditworthiness for AfDB bonds sufficient to generate adequate resources. Consequently, in 1973, the United States and other donor countries from outside Africa were invited to join the Bank's concessional lending facility, the AfDF. The non-concessional lending facility, the AfDB, was still restricted to African countries. The United States declined to join the AfDF until 1976. For several years, Canada was the largest donor country.

The African Development Bank Group

Table 1. Composition of the AfDB Group Executive Boards

Total Number of EDs		Number of African EDs	Number of Non-African EDs
AfDB	18	12 (60%)	6 (40%)
AfDF	12	6 (50%)	6 (50%)

In 1980, the AfDB opened itself to membership by countries outside Africa. Today, the Bank has 53 African members, including both the North African and the sub-Saharan countries, and 24 non-regional members. The latter include all of the major donors of development aid to Africa. The Fund has 27 contributing members, including 25 non-African countries and South Africa.

VOTING

In the AfDB Group, every member state is represented on the Board of Governors, typically by the state's finance minister. The Board of Governors is the highest decision-making body. Day-to- day management of the AfDB Group is handled by the Boards of Directors. The Board of Directors (also known as the Executive Board) of the AfDB is composed of 18 Executive Directors (EDs). Twelve members are elected by the Governors of regional countries and six by the Governors of non-regional member countries. Directors are elected for three years terms that are renewable once.

The Board of Directors of the AfDF is composed of twelve EDs. Non-regional donor nations select six EDs. Thus, while African EDs hold a majority of the votes on the AfDB board, 12 of 18 (60%), in the AfDF, voting is evenly split between the six African and six non-African EDs.

Members' voting power within the AfDB and AfDF Boards of Directors is largely determined by the size of their contribution to the Bank's financial resources. In the AfDB, Nigeria is the largest shareholder, with 8.76% of the vote on the Executive Board. In the AfDF, the United States is the largest country shareholder, with 6.5% of the vote, followed by Japan, with 6.8%. Executive Directors, with the exception of the United States, represent more than one country on each Board. However, unlike at the World Bank, where U.S. voting power exceeds 16% and is much larger than any other ED and can thus veto major reforms, each ED at the AfDB Group has roughly equal voting weight.

CRISIS IN THE MID-1990S AND U.S. FUNDING

In the mid-1990s, the African Development Bank faced what has been called a "mid-life crisis," after non-regional members lost confidence in its lending policies and management practices. Many African countries had experienced severe economic and budgetary problems for years, resulting in part from inappropriate economic policies and also from external factors, including high oil prices and low prices for their commodity exports. African countries were becoming increasingly uncreditworthy; yet the AfDB had continued to extend non-concessional loans to them. By 1994, AfDB arrears had reached $700 million, twice their level in 1992.[4] Short of resources, the AfDB Group made virtually no loans in 1994.

In April 1995, the U.S. General Accounting Office issued a report that called the Bank "solvent but vulnerable" and criticized an AfDB governance system that allowed borrowers to control decision-making.[5] From 1993 to1999, the United States made almost no contributions to the AfDB Group. In the mid-1990s, the United States led other non-regional members in a decision to suspend negotiations on a new AfDF replenishment for the AfDF until the Bank agreed to sweeping institutional reforms. Congress rescinded half of the FY1995 appropriation for the AfDF.

In August 1995, after nine rounds of voting, Bank members elected Omar Kabbaj, a Moroccan financial official who advocated management and fiscal reforms at the Bank. In May 2000, Kabbaj was unanimously re-elected for a second five-year term. During his tenure, Kabbaj won widespread praise from financial analysts and non-regional governments for his success in implementing promised reforms. Non-regional endorsement of Kabbaj's reform agenda came at the May 1998 annual meeting, when the Board of Governors agreed to the fifth general capital increase (GCI-V) of the AfDB, representing a 35% boost in the Bank's resources. The increase will, if fully funded, increase the non-regional share in the Bank's capital from 33% to 40%, thus giving non-regional members 40% of the votes on the Bank's Board of Governors.[6] Moreover, at the insistence of the non-regional members, decisions on Bank operations are to be taken by a 66% majority, while "crucial" decisions (such as increasing the AfDB quota) would require the approval of 70% of shareholders.[7] Thus, there would have to be at least some non-regional support for major Bank actions. These modifications to the Bank's "African character" were initially opposed by some regional members, but eventually won enough support from regional member nations to pass. U.S. contributions to the African Development Fund resumed in FY1998, and the funding levels in recent years have made the Fund a small, but important component of the overall U.S. economic assistance program for Africa.

In 2003, the U.S. Office of Management and Budget (OMB) completed a Program Assessment Rating Tool (PART) examination of the AfDF.[8] While OMB gave the Fund high scores in Program Management (100%) and Program Purpose and Design (80%), lower scores were recorded for Strategic Planning (63%) and Program Results (33%), leading to a total program score of 59% and an overall rating of "Results Not Demonstrated." The U.S. Department of the Treasury points out in its FY2008 budget request, however, that the PART evaluation was completed prior to the Bank's introduction of a new results measurement framework, which incorporates into all country strategy papers and projects indicators to better measure results. Improvement of weak systems for measuring the effectiveness of multilateral development bank (MDB) projects has been a core focus of the Bush Administration's MDB reform agenda.[9]

THE AfDB GROUP'S FUTURE ROLE

The African Development Bank Group is one of many development agencies active in Africa, and it loans smaller amounts than the World Bank and the major bilateral donors. Furthermore, the Bank has long been considered to be the least capable of the regional development banks. The future effectiveness of the AfDB largely rests on its ability to delineate its role in a crowded aid field populated by larger multilateral donors, the United Nations and the World Bank, regional donors such as the European Union and the bilateral programs of the major donors.

In order to define a clearer AfDB mission, in October 2006, current AfDB Group President Donald Kabaruka appointed an eminent persons group to advise him on the Bank's future. The group, chaired by former Mozambican President Juaquim Chissano and former Canadian Prime Minister Paul Martin, released its final report in fall 2007. The panel commends the Bank for moving in this direction by increasing its work in recent years in areas where it has proven expertise, primarily infrastructure construction (including transportation, water, and energy services), while leaving other issues, such as HIV/AIDS policy to the World Bank or single sector funds such as the Global Fund to Fight AIDS, Tuberculosis, and Malaria.

A key concern of President Kaberuka and the Chissano-Martin report is that the "AfDB has excess capacity and the AfDF has excess demand," meaning that the rift between African countries performing well and those performing poorly is growing.[10] Thus, the AfDB is sitting on large under-utilized reserves for the 15 countries that qualify for AfDB financing. At the same time, there is insufficient funding for AfDF borrower countries. To address this, Kaberuka and the Panel propose merging the regular and concessional lending facilities into a single fund. Any attempt to merge the lending facilities would require the approval of the Executive Board.

A further complication is the temporary status of the Bank's headquarters. Although legally based in Abidjan, Côte d'Ivoire, civil war in that country prompted the Bank to temporarily move its headquarters to Tunis, Tunisia in 2003. Lack of a final settlement of the Ivorian political crisis has to date prevented the Bank from returning to its permanent location. At the same time, while the Tunisian government would reportedly be happy to have the Bank permanently relocate to Tunis, the Ivorian government has blocked the move. Until a settlement is reached on the Bank's permanent home, continued tension will likely make staff recruitment more challenging given the wealth of alternative opportunities for well-trained development economists.

Lastly, some observers question if there is a need for a regional development bank for Africa, or if the United States should contribute to such an institution. In their view, the United States might better focus its funding on bilateral assistance programs, or perhaps the World Bank's concessional aid facility, the International Development Agency (IDA), where U.S. influence as a shareholder is greater than at the AfDB. In 2006, IDA committed $3.5 billion in loans and $1.1 billion in grants to Africa, a doubling of aid from 2000 levels. At the same time, the AfDB Group approved a total of $1.4 billion in loans, grants, and investments. Advocates of a continued role for the AfDB group argue that even though it cannot match other donors in the sum of total loans provided, the AfDB, "Africa's Bank," with an African president, has a unique understanding of African needs. They contend that African governments more readily accept the Bank's advice. They also argue that it is useful for the United States to be seen in Africa as a supporter of a homegrown African development institution. Others contend, however, that non-regional aid donors can be just as effective as a local institution. Furthermore, they may be less susceptible to corruption and nepotism, charges that have plagued the AfDB group in the past.

In December 2008, AfDB Board of Directors approved a medium-term strategy that incorporates several of the recommendations of the high level panel. The new strategy will run till 2012; a key component is a decentralization of AfDB operations that has led to the proliferation of Bank offices throughout the continent. There are currently 23 AfDB local offices compared to only three in 2002. Another component of the new strategy is a significant increase in lending activity with projected loan activity increasing by 50% between 2008 and 2012. This increase is to be driven by several factors including: a 50% increase in the size of the next replenishment round for the the AfDF and increased focus on private sector lending for the AfDB.

End Notes

[1] More information is available at the Bank's website: https://www.afdb.org.

[2] Like the market rate facilities of the World Bank and the other RDBs, AfDB's funds are raised on the international capital markets and then re-lent at a small premium to member countries. Countries borrow from the World Bank and the RDBs for a variety of reasons including their extensive technical assistance and advisory capability.

[3] For more information, see CRS Report RL33073, *Debt Relief for Heavily Indebted Poor Countries: Issues for Congress*, by Martin A. Weiss; CRS Report RS22534, *The Multilateral Debt Relief Initiative*, by Martin A. Weiss.

[4] E. Philip English and Harris M. Mule, *The African Development Bank* (Boulder, Colorado: Lynne Rienner, 1995), p. 29.

[5] *Multilateral Development Banks: Financial Condition of the African Development Bank* (GAO/NSIAD-95-143BR).

[6] While most analysts agree that the reforms introduced by Kabbaj were successful, not all donors have completed their contributions to GCI-V. As of the end of AfDB Group FY2006, arrears to the Bank were around $4,783,680.

[7] *Africa Research Bulletin, Economic Series*, May-June, 1998, p.13455-13456.

[8] For more information on the OMB PART program, see http://www.whitehouse.gov/omb/part/.

[9] Statement of Assistant Secretary Clay Lowery before the Senate Foreign Relations Committee on the Multilateral Development Banks and the Fight Against Corruption, March 28, 2006.

[10] "Investing in Africa's Future: The ADB in the 21st Century" Report of the High Level Panel. Available at http://www.oxan.com/display.aspx?StoryDate=20080215&ProductCode=OADB&StoryType=DB&StoryNumber=

In: Multilateral Development Banks and International Finance   ISBN: 978-1-61728-883-8
Editor: Leah M. Groffe   © 2010 Nova Science Publishers, Inc.

Chapter 3

MULTILATERAL DEVELOPMENT BANKS: U.S. CONTRIBUTIONS FY1998-FY2009·

Jonathan E. Sanford

SUMMARY

This chapter shows in tabular form how much the Administration requested and how much Congress appropriated during the past 11 years for U.S. payments to the multilateral development banks (MDBs). It also provides a brief description of the MDBs and the ways they fund their operations.

U.S. PARTICIPATION IN THE MDBS

The United States is a member of five MDBs: the World Bank, African Development Bank (AfDB), Asian Development Bank (AsDB), European Bank for Reconstruction and Development (EBRD), and Inter-American Development Bank (IDB). It also belongs to two similar organizations, the North American Development Bank (NADBank) and the International Fund for Agricultural Development (IFAD). For FY2009, the Administration proposed and Congress appropriated funds for U.S. participation in two new World Bank facilities, the Clean Technology Fund (CTF) and the Strategic Climate Fund (SCF).

THE MDBS AND THEIR PROGRAMS

The MDBs have similar programs, though they all differ somewhat in their institutional structure and emphasis. Each has a president and executive board that manages or supervises

---

* This is an edited, reformatted and augmented version of a CRS Report for Congress publication, Report #RS20792, dated February 3, 2010.

all of its programs and operations. Except for the EBRD, which makes only market-based loans, all the MDBs make both market-based loans to middle-income developing countries and concessional loans to the poorest countries. Their loans are made to governments or to organizations having government repayment guarantees. In each MDB, the same staff prepares both the market-based and the concessional loans, using the same standards and procedures for both.[1] The main differences between them are the repayment terms and the countries which qualify for them.[2]

The MDBs also have specialized facilities which have their own operating staff and management but report to the bank's president and executive board. The World Bank's International Finance Corporation (IFC) and the IDB's Inter-American Investment Corporation (IIC) make loans to or equity investments in private sector firms in developing countries (on commercial terms) without government repayment guarantees. The AsDB makes similar loans from its market-rate loan account. The World Bank's Multilateral Investment Guarantee Agency (MIGA) underwrites private investments in developing countries (on commercial terms) to protect against noneconomic risk. At the IDB, the Multilateral Investment Fund (MIF) helps Latin American countries institute policy reforms aimed at stimulating domestic and international investment. It also funds worker retraining and programs for small- and micro-enterprises. The MIF originated as part of President Bush's 1990 Enterprise for the Americas Initiative (EAI.)

The NADBank was created by the North American Free Trade Agreement (NAFTA) to fund environmental infrastructure projects in the U.S.-Mexico border region. The International Fund for Agricultural Development, created in 1977, focuses on reducing poverty and hunger in poor countries through agricultural development. The Global Environment Facility (GEF) funds projects dealing with international environmental problems. The GEF's assistance program is managed by the World Bank.

FUNDING MDB ASSISTANCE PROGRAMS

The MDBs' concessional aid programs are funded with money donated by their wealthier member country governments. Loans from the MDBs' market-rate loan facilities are funded with money borrowed in world capital markets. The IFC and IIC fund their loans and equity investments partly with money contributed by their members and partly with funds borrowed from commercial capital markets. The MDBs' borrowings are backed by the subscription s of their member countries. They provide a small part of their capital subscriptions (3% to 5% of the total for most MDBs) in the form of paid-in capital. The rest they subscribe as callable capital. Callable capital is a contingent liability, payable only if an MDB becomes bankrupt and lacks sufficient funds to repay its own creditors. It cannot be called to provide the banks with additional loan funds.

Countries' voting shares are determined mainly by the size of their contributions. The United States is the largest stockholder in most MDBs. Japan has provided more to the AsDF and AfDF, while Nigeria and Egypt have subscribed larger shares in the AfDB. Periodically, as the stock of uncommitted MDB funds begins to run low, the major donors negotiate a new funding plan that specifies their new contribution shares.

Table 1 shows the U.S. contribution share and voting share for all MDB programs. In most banks, countries get a few votes because they are members, regardless of the size of their capital subscription. Thus, for banks with a large number of small members, the voting share of large subscribers such as the United States may be a little smaller than their share in providing the bank's resources. Voting shares are the same for both market-based and concessional loans in the AsDB and IDB.

In IDA, by contrast, the donors have separated the issues of voting power and contributions. In recent decades, they have chosen not to expand their voting share as they contribute new funds to IDA. Thus, while the United States, Canada, Japan, the countries of the European Union, and the wealthy Arab oil states have donated 99% of IDA's resources, they have 65% of the vote. This is more than enough to protect their interests, as decisions are reached by majority vote. The arrangement diffuses possible tensions by giving the developing countries a sense that their voices are heard.

Before 1976, the United States was the only significant contributor to the IDB's Fund for Special Operations. Non-regional countries have since joined the IDB and the FSO has become a much smaller program and he U.S. share has declined substantially. The African Development Bank controls 50% of the vote in the AFDF, though it has contributed only about 1% of the concessional loan program's resources. This maintains a semblance of African control. The interests of the donors are protected by the fact that a three-quarters majority is required to approve AFDF loans.

U.S. APPROPRIATIONS FOR MDBs

Table 2 shows the amounts the Administration has requested and Congress has appropriated (budget authority) annually since FY1998 for U.S. contributions and subscriptions to the multilateral banks. The numbers in parentheses are subscriptions to MDB callable capital. Since 1981, the United States no longer appropriates money to back its callable capital subscriptions to the MDBs. Rather Congress sets annual program ceilings in the Foreign Operations Appropriations Act specifying the amount of callable capital the United States may subscribe in each MDB during the current fiscal year.

Table 1. U.S. Contribution and Voting Shares in the MDBs

	Contribution Share	Voting Share		Contribution Share	Voting Share
World Bank Group			**Inter-American Dev Bank**		
IBRD	16.8%	16.4%	IDB	30.3%	30.0%
IDA	22.1%	12.9%	FSO	50.5%	30.0%
IFC	24.1%	23.6%	IIC	25.5%	25.1%
MIGA	18.9%	15.1%	MIF	39.4%	29.1%
Asian Development Bank			**African Development Bank**		
AsDB	15.6%	12.8%	AfDB	6.4%	6.4%
AsDF	12.6%	12.8%	AfDF	12.7%	6.1%
EBRD	10.1%	9.8%	**IFAD**	13.6%	13.6%
NADBank	50.0%	50.0%			

Table 2. U.S. Contributions or Subscriptions to Multilateral Development Banks, Millions of U.S. Dollars (Includes Recisions)

	2000 Request	2000 Approp.	2001 Request	2001 Approp	2002 Request	2002 Approp	2003 Request	2003 Approp
WORLD BANK GROUP								
Int'l Bank for Reconstruction & Development (IBRD)								
—IBRD capital, paid in	-.-	-.-	-.-	-.-	-.-	-.-	-.-	-.-
—(IBRD capital, callable)	-.-				-.-	-.-	-.-	-.-
Int'l Development Association (IDA)	803.4	775.0	836.0	775.0	803.0	792.4	874.3	844.5
Int'l Finance Corporation (IFC)	-.-	-.-	-.-	-.-	-.-	-.-	-.-	-.-
Multilateral Investment Guarantee Agency (MIGA)								
—MIGA paid in capital	10.0	4.0	16.0	10.0	10.0	5.0	3.6	1.6
—(MIGA capital, callable)	(50.0)	(20.0)	(80.0)	(50.0)	(50.0)	(25.0)	(18.0)	(8.0)

Table 2. (Continued)

	2000 Request	2000 Approp.	2001 Request	2001 Approp	2002 Request	2002 Approp	2003 Request	2003 Approp
Global Environmental Facility (GEF)	143.3	35.8	176.0	108.0	100.0	100.5	177.4	146.9
ASIAN DEVELOPMENT BANK								
—AsDB ordinary capital, paid in	13.7	13.7	-.-	-.-	-.-	-.-	-.-	-.-
—(AsDB ordinary capital, callable)	(672.7)	(672.7)	-.-	-.-	-.-	-.-	-.-	-.-
Asian Development Fund (AsDF)	177.0	77.0	125.0	72.0	103.0	98.0	147.4	97.2
AFRICAN DEVELOPMENT BANK								
—AfDB ordinary capital, paid in	5.1	4.1	6.1	6.1	5.1	5.1	5.1	5.1
—(AfDB ordinary capital, callable)	(80.0)	(64.0)	(64.0)	(64.0)	(80.0)	(80.0)	(80.0)	(80.0)
African Development Fund (AfDF)	127.0	128.0	100.0	100.0	100.0	100.0	118.1	107.4
INTER-AMERICAN DEVELOPMENT BANK GROUP								
—IDB ordinary capital, paid in	25.6	25.6	-.-	-.-	-.-	-.-	-.-	-.-
—(IDB ordinary capital, callable)	(1,503.7)	(1,503.7)	-.-	-.-	-.-	-.-	-.-	-.-
Fund for Special Operations (FSO)	-.-							
Inter-American Investment Corp (IIC)	25.0	16.0	34.0	25.0	25.0	18.0	30.3	18.2
Multilateral Investment Fund (MIF)	28.5	-.-	25.9	10.0	-.-	-.-	29.6	24.4
EUROPEAN BANK FOR RECON & DEVELOP								
—EBRD paid in capital	35.8	35.8	35.8	35.8	35.8	35.8	35.8	35.6
—(EBRD capital, callable)	(123.2)	(123.2)	(123.3)	(123.3)	(123.3)	(123.3)	(123.3)	(123.3)
INTL FUND FOR AGRICULTURAL DEVELOP			-.-	5.0	20.0	20.0	15.0	14.9
NORTH AMERICAN DEVELOPMENT BANK								
—NADBank capital, paid-in	-.-	-.-	-.-	-.-	-.-	-.-	-.-	-.-
—(NADBank capital, callable)	-.-	-.-	-.-	-.-	-.-	-.-	-.-	-.-
TOTAL MDB APPROPRIATION	**1,494.4**	**1,115.0**	**1,434.8**	**1,146.9**	**1,230.1**	**1,174.8**	**1,437.1**	**1,295.8**

Table 2. (Continued)

	2004 Request	2004 Approp	2005 Request	2005 Approp	2006 Request	2006 Approp.	2007 Request	2007 Approp.
WORLD BANK GROUP								
Int'l Bank for Reconstruction & Development								
—IBRD capital, paid in	-.-	-.-	-.-	-.-	-.-	-.-	-.-	-.-
—(IBRD capital, callable)	-.-	-.-	-.-	-.-	-.-	-.-	-.-	-.-
Int'l Development Association (IDA)	976.8	913.2	1061.3	843.2	950.0	909.1	950.0	940.5
Int'l Finance Corporation (IFC)	-.-	-.-	-.-	-.-	-.-	-.-	-.-	-.-
Multilateral Investment Guarantee Agency								
—MIGA paid in capital	4.0	1.1	-.-	-.-	1.7	1.3	-.-	-.-
—(MIGA capital, callable)	(20.0)	(4.5)	-.-	-.-	-.-	-.-	-.-	-.-
Global Environment Facility					107.5	79.2	80.0	79.2
ASIAN DEVELOPMENT BANK								
—AsDB ordinary capital, paid in	-.-	-.-	-.-	-.-	-.-	-.-	-.-	-.-
—(ordinary capital, callable)	-.-	-.-	-.-	-.-	-.-	-.-	-.-	-.-
Asian Development Fund (AsDF)	151.9	144.4	112.2	99.2	115.3	99.0	115.3	99.0
AFRICAN DEVELOPMENT BANK								
—AfDB ordinary capital, paid in	5.1	5.1	5.1	4.1	5.6	3.6	5.0	3.6
—(AfDB ordinary capital, callable)	(80.0)	(79.6)	(79.5)	(79.5)	(88.3)	(88.3)	78.6	(88.3)
African Development Fund (AfDF)	118.1	112.7	118.0	105.2	135.7	134.3	135.7	134.3
INTER-AMERICAN DEVELOPMENT BANK GROUP								
—IDB ordinary capital, paid in	-.-	-.-	-.-	-.-	-.-	-.-	-.-	-.-
—(IDB ordinary capital, callable)	-.-	-.-	-.-	-.-	-.-	-.-	-.-	-.-
Fund for Special Operations (FSO)					-.-	-.-	-.-	-.-
Inter-American Investment Corp (IIC)	30.9	-.-	-.-	-.-	1.7	1.7	-.-	-.-
Multilateral Investment Fund (MIF)	32.6	25.0	25.0	10.9	1.7	1.7	25.0	1.7

Table 2. (Continued)

	2004	2004	2005	2005	2006	2006	2007	2007
	Request	Approp	Request	Approp	Request	Approp.	Request	Approp.
EUROPEAN BANK FOR RECON & DEVELOP								
—EBRD capital, paid in	35.4	35.4	35.4	35.2	1.0	1.0	-.-	-.-
—(EBRD capital, callable)	(123.3)	(122.0)	(122.0)	(122.0)	(2.3)	(2.3)	-.-	-.-
INT'L FUND FOR AGRICULTURAL DEVELOP	15.0	14.9	15.0	15.0	15.0	14.9	18.0	18.0
NORTH AMERICAN DEVELOPMENT BANK								
—NADBank capital, paid-in	-.-	-.-	-.-	-.-	-.-	-.-	-.-	-.-
—(NADBank capital, callable)	-.-	-.-	-.-	-.-	-.-	-.-	-.-	-.-
TOTAL MDB APPROPRIATION	1,534.8	1,386.5	1,492.7	1,219.2	1,335.3	1,245.8	1,329.0	1,273.2
	2008	**2008**	**2009**	**2009**	**2010**	**2010**	**2011**	**2011**
	Request	**Approp**	**Request**	**Approp**	**Request**	**Approp.**	**Request**	**Approp.**
WORLD BANK GROUP								
Int'l Bank for Reconstruction & Development								
IBRD capital, paid in	-.-	-.-	-.-	-.-				
(IBRD capital, callable)	-.-	-.-	-.-	-.-				
Int'l Development Association (IDA)	1,060.0	942.3	1,277.0	1,115.0	1,320.0	1,263.0	1,285.0	
Int'l Finance Corporation (IFC)	-.-	-.-	-.-	-.-				
Multilateral Investment Guarantee Agency								
MIGA paid in capital	1.1	-.-	-.-	-.-				
Int'l Clean Technology Fund			400.0	-.-	400.0	300.0	400.0	
Strategic Climate Fund					100.0	75.0	235.0	
Global Food Security Fund							408.0	
Global Environmental Facility (GEF)	106.8	81.1	80.0	80.0	86.5	86.5	175.0	
ASIAN DEVELOPMENT BANK								
AsDB ordinary capital, paid in	-.-	-.-	-.-	-.-			106.6	
(ordinary capital, callable)	-.-	-.-	-.-	-.-			(2,558.0)	

Table 2. (Continued)

	2008 Request	2008 Approp	2009 Request	2009 Approp	2010 Request	2010 Approp.	2011 Request	2011 Approp.
Asian Development Fund (AsDF)	133.9	74.5	115.3	105.0	115.3	105.0	222.0	
AFRICAN DEVELOPMENT BANK								
AfDB ordinary capital, paid in	2.0	2.0	-.-	0.8				
(AfDB ordinary capital, callable)	-.-	-.-	-.-	-.-				
African Development Fund (AfDF)	140.6	134.6	156.1	150.0	159.9	155.0	155.9	
INTER-AMERICAN DEVELOPMENT BANK								
IDB ordinary capital, paid in	-.-	-.-	-.-	-.-				
(IDB ordinary capital, callable)	-.-	-.-	-.-	-.-				
Fund for Special Operations (FSO)	-.-	-.-	-.-	-.-				
Inter-American Investment Corp (IIC)	-.-	-.-	-.-	-.-	4.7	4.7	21.0	
Multilateral Invest. Fund (MIF)	29.2	24.8	25.0	25.0	25.0	25.0	25.0	
EUROPEAN BANK FOR RECON & DEVELOP								
EBRD capital, paid in	-.-	-.-	-.-	-.-	-.-	-.-	-.-	-.-
(EBRD capital, callable)	-.-	-.-	-.-	-.-	-.-	-.-	-.-	-.-
INTL FUND FOR AGRICULTURAL DEVELOP	18.1	17.9	18.0	18.0	30.0	30.0	30.0	
NORTH AMERICAN DEVELOPMENT BANK								
—NADBank capital, paid-in	-.-	-.-	-.-	-.-	-.-	-.-	-.-	-.-
—(NADBank capital, callable)	-.-	-.-	-.-	-.-	-.-	-.-	-.-	-.-
TOTAL MDB APPROPRIATION	**1,499.0**	**1,277.3**	**2,071.3**	**1,493.8**	**2,341.3**	**2,044.2**	**3,013.5**	

Source: Derived from the annual appropriation legislation and Treasury Department budget presentation documents. Figures in parentheses are callable capital, which is not actually appropriated. (See text.) Dashes show that no U.S. contribution or subscription was requested and/or approved by Congress that year.

End Notes

[1] The International Development Association (IDA) is the World Bank's concessional loan affiliate. The Asian Development Fund (AsDF), African Development Fund (AFDF), and Fund for Special Operations (FSO) are the comparable programs at the AsDB, AfDB, and IDB.

[2] MDB market-based loans cost a little more than the rate the banks pay to borrow funds commercially. IDA and AFDF charge about 3/4 of 1% annually. The IDB charges 1% to 4% annually, depending on the project and the borrower. Most borrowers from the concessional programs have per capita incomes of less (often much less) than $900 annually.

In: Multilateral Development Banks and International Finance	ISBN: 978-1-61728-883-8
Editor: Leah M. Groffe	© 2010 Nova Science Publishers, Inc.

Chapter 4

THE INTERNATIONAL FINANCIAL INSTITUTIONS: A CALL FOR CHANGE[*]

A Report to the Committee on Foreign Relations

LETTER OF TRANSMITTAL

UNITED STATESSENATE,
COMMITTEE ON FOREIGN RELATIONS,
Washington, DC, March 10, 2010.

Dear Colleague: The International Monetary Fund, World Bank, African Development Bank, Asian Development Bank, European Bank for Reconstruction and Development, and Inter-American Development Bank are foreign policy tools that allow the United States to leverage the contributions of other countries to promote our national security and humanitarian interests in alleviating poverty and promoting progress around the world. For this reason, the U.S. Congress regularly supports appropriations for subsidized loan and grant programs through the multilateral development banks and recently provided a loan to the IMF. As one of the largest shareholders in these institutions, the United States enjoys an opportunity to influence their policies and programs. We must be cautious about forfeiting our leadership positions at these institutions.

Seven years ago, I began an oversight project on the multilateral development banks, focused on ensuring that their financing reached the intended people and projects. I chaired six Senate Foreign Relations Committee hearings that included reviews of individual projects and policies of the respective development banks. I met with international financial institution leaders and my staff examined projects in many countries. The attached report provides fifty recommendations for eight different organizations to improve the accountability, transparency and effectiveness of the World Bank, the IMF and the other development banks. The

---

[*] This is an edited, reformatted and augmented version of a U. S. Government Printing Office publication, Report#111-43, dated March 10, 2010.

American people must have confidence that our funds will be managed effectively, efficiently, and transparently. Given our domestic budget and employment situation, it is all the more critical that we ensure that our contributions successfully promote United States interests.

The United States and the G-20 are evaluating changes to the relative power countries wield at the international financial institutions while considering requesting billions in additional funds for the multilateral development banks this spring. This chapter suggests that contributions to the development banks should be a consequence of, not a precursor to, needed reforms given that financial flows to development countries are rebounding sharply from their 2009 lows.

This Senate Foreign Relations Committee report, written by Nilmini Gunaratne Rubin with significant contributions from Jay Branegan, Shellie Bressler, Keith Luse, Kezia McKeague, Carl Meacham, Michael Phelan, and Dorothy Shea, as well as assistance from Erin Baggott, Cory Gill, Katie Lee, Marik String, and Alexandra Utsey, synthesizes important recommendations to transform the international financial institutions. I hope it will inform a vital debate about these institutions before we make agreements on how to reallocate leadership power and decide whether to provide them with additional funding.

Sincerely,
RICHARD G. LUGAR,
Ranking Member.

INTRODUCTION

Beginning in 2003, Senator Richard Lugar directed his staff on the Senate Foreign Relations Committee to undertake an examination of the international financial institutions[1] to determine how they could better serve American interests and more effectively achieve their missions of alleviating poverty, hunger and disease in poor countries, promoting sustainable development, economic growth, and good governance, and ensuring financial stability. This staff report brings together the results of much of the oversight since that time. As detailed in the pages that follow, key conclusions emerge:

- The international financial institutions too often focus on issuing loans rather than on achieving concrete development results within a finite period of time;
- They should concentrate more clearly on "putting themselves out of business" by creating stable, self-sustaining economic growth in their client countries;
- For the institutions that are currently seeking major capital increases, the Administration and the other donor countries of the G-20 should be firm in demanding that needed reforms are secured before committing additional funds; and
- The international financial institutions should redouble their efforts, including increasing resources for internal controls, to battle the invidious corruption that has thwarted so many development projects.

EXECUTIVE SUMMARY

The international financial institutions (IFIs) have traditionally been an important element of U.S. foreign policy. They support the broad U.S. foreign policy goals of promoting stability and development and ending poverty; they leverage U.S. taxpayer dollars and support a large corps of development experts and international economists to supplement the U.S. government's own expertise; they provide fora where the U.S. can cooperate with friends and allies; they are emblems of U.S. economic and diplomatic leadership; and owing to the United States' position as the largest, or one of the largest, donors in each institution, they are able to help influence specific regions and countries in ways that are favorable to U.S. interests.

But, they are also international bureaucracies, answerable to no one government or constituency, yet subject to influence and suasion by many, including donors, borrowers, and other political actors. They often operate with little public scrutiny, and many times in challenging environments, where bureaucratic obstacles, corruption, civil or military strife, and governmental incapacity can harm the success of their work. Most significantly, the two largest and most important IFIs, the World Bank and the International Monetary Fund (IMF), were created more than fifty years ago, in the aftermath of World War II, when one country, the United States, towered over the rest financially, global exchange rates were fixed, international financial flows were tiny, trade was burdened with steep tariffs and quotas, private sector investment and lending in developing countries were negligible, and the principle of free-market capitalism was not widely accepted. All that has changed, but have the IFIs kept pace?

As the world struggles to emerge from the worst economic crisis since World War II, it is an appropriate time to ask whether the IFIs are performing optimally and doing the jobs they should be doing. Does the world really need the IMF, World Bank, African Development Bank, Asian Development Bank, European Bank for Reconstruction and Development, and Inter-American Development Bank today? Can they be changed to better address our needs? How should we re-design them? What could the international financial institutions have done to keep the crisis from occurring in the first place? What can they do now to best mitigate the fallout from the crisis? Do they achieve their various missions of promoting stability, fighting poverty, encouraging growth, and promoting democracy?

Such questions are particularly timely because nearly all the IFIs have sought, or will soon seek, major new infusions of money from their donors, including the taxpayers of the United States. Congress will have to approve the amount and the form of these new contributions. Congress must be able to assure taxpayers that the money is needed, and that it will be used efficiently. It must ask whether the new money is being requested primarily to respond to the financial crisis, and if so, whether it should be advanced on a temporary basis. The crisis should not be used as an excuse to win increases that could not otherwise be justified. As the requests for capital are negotiated with the international donor community, there is a window of opportunity for significant reform. Given a 2009 signing statement from the administration, indicating that the President did not recognize an obligation to pursue Congressionally mandated reforms at the IMF contained in authorizing legislation, Congress may have an interest in securing the reforms before authorizing funds for the capital increases.[2]

Soon after he became Chairman of the Senate Foreign Relations Committee (SFRC) in 2003, Senator Richard Lugar launched a multi-faceted project designed to answer many of the questions cited above. Under his chairmanship, the SFRC held six hearings into the operations of the World Bank and the other multilateral development banks (MDBs), his staff conducted numerous oversight trips to the various banks' headquarters and to bank-funded projects, and Sen. Lugar met personally with the head of each MDB. The committee produced a major piece of legislation, which was enacted into law in 2005. The oversight activity continued as Sen. Lugar assumed the role of ranking member of the committee and as staff continued to make site visits, hold briefings with IFI personnel and others, attend MDB annual meetings, and conduct inquiries regarding various IFI issues.

This project, initially focused on the IFIs' efforts to battle corruption, has expanded to include other issues of institutional management, personnel, and aid effectiveness. During the period of the project, improvement occurred in certain areas that have come under intense staff scrutiny or Congressional mandate, but most IFI operations and thinking continue to be characterized by inertia and a reluctance to reform. In particular, the regional MDBs look to the World Bank to set the standard of practice, failing to move if the World Bank does not, even though significant problems may be evident. And even once the World Bank does change, the regional MDBs are often slow, in some cases extremely slow, to adopt corresponding policies of their own. One of the key recommendations of the report is that the IFIs work much more closely together to share experience and information and to collaborate on policies.

In general, staff found that the IFIs still serve U.S. policy interests and leverage American taxpayer dollars. Therefore, the U.S. should retain a leadership role in the institutions. However, in the current fiscal environment, the institutions themselves and the Obama administration will have to make a strong and compelling case if further U.S. tax dollars from an already-overstretched federal budget are to be made available. Any new capital increase should be approved only after the relevant institution has formally agreed to a reform agenda and begun to implement it. The Obama administration should conduct an authoritative review of the IFIs' practices and policies leading up to the financial crisis to learn what, if anything, they could have done to prevent it. Steps should be taken to integrate lessons learned into future IMF and development bank activities. In normal times, the World Bank and the regional banks focus on long-term development and not, for instance, on disaster relief and other short-term events. The review should examine whether the MDBs need, or should have, new authorities to deal with financial crises. Further, to garner public support, the Treasury Secretary should consult closely with Congress as talks on new funding proceed, and he should strive to ensure that any funding required for the crisis should be temporary in nature, while the institutions themselves should conduct a rigorous review to find costs savings in their own operations. The institutions should commit to rigorous budgetary discipline to make sure that as many resources as possible are being used to fight poverty and maintain financial stability. The IFIs will only succeed if they are seen as part of the solution to the crisis, not part of the problem.

Regarding the politically fraught issues of governance, voting rights, and citizenship directives, U.S. voting shares and veto authority should be maintained, and that having an American as head of the World Bank helps maintain domestic public support for the institution. Any changes to these arrangements should be considered on a system-wide basis, including the IMF, the World Bank, and the regional MDBs. Staff does not underestimate the difficulty in achieving such changes. Throughout the course of this project, staff has repeatedly encountered evidence that U.S. citizens are discouraged from working at the regional MDBs because of U.S. tax law burdens which nationals of other countries do not face. Because the presence of U.S. citizens materially improves the performance and accountability of the institutions, staff recommends that Congress fix the tax disincentives that penalize Americans working abroad.

The IFIs suffer from a lack of transparency regarding loan decisions, environmental impact, inspection panels, project assessment, etc., which hurt both public perceptions and their effectiveness. The most recently issued public disclosure policies of the World Bank and the European Bank for Reconstruction and Development (EBRD), for instance, improved somewhat on the previous versions but fell far short of what was optimal. The report makes a number of recommendations for improved public disclosure of policies and decisions, at both the board and management level, and for more parliamentary consultation in borrowing countries.

Nearly all the IFIs suffer from a "pressure-to-lend" culture that places more emphasis on signing project agreements and getting loans out the door than on actually improving the development level of the borrowing country. There must be a systemic re-orientation to focus on outcomes instead of outputs. That will require putting in new incentive structures within the banks and new evaluation mechanisms. The banks should focus more clearly on the effort to "put themselves out of business" by graduating countries from their "soft loan" windows and, eventually, out of borrowing completely. When the World Bank reaches the milestone of being in a country for fifty years, it should not be a cause for celebration. Specifically, the executive boards of the development banks should require presentation of projects and programs at their completion to put an emphasis on results and to incentivize development bank professionals to focus on the results of projects rather than the amounts. Currently, board review of projects and programs is only done at the approval stage. In addition, the development banks need to install meaningful staff evaluation systems so that professionals are rewarded for good project design and implementation rather than for promoting large projects in important countries. To that end, the banks should develop a common evaluations framework so that results of the different development banks can be compared across the board and within countries. Projects should be designed with clear indicators so that results can be measured, and the indicators should be published so civil society can track the projects' progress. Also, the development banks should sell advisory services to interested countries rather than requiring that countries borrow in order to receive advice from the development banks.

Regarding lending to resource-rich developing countries, which has been of particular interest to the SFRC, banks should focus on Extractive Industry Transparency Initiative (EITI) principles of revenue transparency and fighting corruption, with an emphasis on acting before resource revenues start flowing in large amounts. Relatively small amounts of aid money could thus help channel large amounts of countries' own funds toward poverty reduction. Because corruption has been shown to be a decisive factor in hobbling development, all the banks should embed oversight funds into project and program financing so that an adequate percentage of the funds can be used by borrowing countries to support monitoring, investigations, prosecutions, and technical assistance for oversight.

Prior to the global economic crisis that struck in 2008, many had begun to question the need and rationale for the IMF. Lending was down sharply, very few countries were enrolled in IMF programs, its credibility and popularity were badly damaged by both the Russian financial collapse and the Asian financial crisis, and the organization was forced to institute a 20 percent cut in personnel. However, early in 2009 as the financial crisis swept the globe, it was evident that the IMF was best-suited for crisis management, and the G-20 voted to triple IMF resources. This abrupt reversal of fortune could be oversimplified into the question, "What do you do with the firemen when there is no fire?," as one IMF official put it. Congressional debate over the Obama administration's request for Congress to authorize the U.S. portion of the new funds would have been a good opportunity to explore the role and function of the IMF in crisis and non-crisis situations. Unfortunately, that debate did not happen. The process for authorization of the IMF funds did not follow the usual procedures and proved unnecessarily partisan. As U.S. legislative action was critical for many of the issues related to IMF reform and enhanced funding, the rushed legislative process, as described in more detail in the report, denied Congress the opportunity to thoughtfully promote needed changes at the IMF. In the meantime, there are a number of obvious reforms the IMF should undertake, many of them related to improved transparency and consultations with the parliaments of borrowing countries, providing the significant requirements for reform that come with IMF programs. The IMF should also develop guidelines to ensure that its financing will not exacerbate conflict or underlying hostilities when lending to a post-conflict or current conflict country, and it should explicitly judge a country's appropriate level of military spending as an indicator of financial health.

Staff have visited the headquarters of each IFI, and repeatedly interviewed Treasury and IFI officials about the policies and operations of each bank. A number of recommendations have emerged related to IFIs in general and to specific institutions. They are detailed in the following section.

RECOMMENDATIONS

Committee staff developed specific recommendations for the administration, Congress, and the international community to reform the international financial institutions and help them adjust to the changing needs and evolving standards of a post-economic crisis world.

The Obama administration should:

1) *Focus on the ultimate goal of the international financial institutions succeeding in their development and economic missions and thereby putting them out of business.* Push the institutions to pay closer attention to the steps needed for governments to generate their own revenue and access capital markets on a favorable basis. Encourage the institutions to set up clear graduation guidelines for a country to move from being a borrower to becoming a donor.

2) *Undertake a review to determine what, if anything, the international financial institutions could have done to prevent the recent global financial crisis.* Steps should be taken to integrate lessons learned into future IMF and development bank activities.

3) *Consider delaying a G-20 commitment for capital increases for the multilateral development banks until it is clear that capital infusions are necessary, needed reforms are underway, and upcoming elections of leadership positions at some development banks are completed.*

4) To the extent possible, *the administration should pursue temporary capital increases* given that the impact of the global financial crisis will eventually wane.

5) *Commission a review of potential cost savings at the international financial institutions.* Opportunities to reduce spending at these organizations must be examined and the institutions should commit to rigorous budgetary discipline to make sure that as many resources as possible are being used to fight poverty and maintain financial stability.

6) *Preserve United States leadership of the World Bank and senior level positions at the other IFIs.* Having an American at the helm of the World Bank helps ensure continued U.S. support for the institution and facilitates communication with the World Bank. Historically, the President of the World Bank has been a United States citizen, the Managing Director of the IMF has been European, the President of the European Bank for Reconstruction and Development has been European, the President of the African Development Bank has been African, the President of the Asian Development Bank has been Japanese and the President of the Inter-American Development Bank has been from Central or South America. Should the administration choose not to follow this recommendation, any deal to loosen the citizenship directives on leadership at the IMF or World Bank should include loosening the citizenship directives at the regional development banks.

7) *Maintain United States voting shares and veto rights at the international financial institutions.* As talks continue at the G- 20 on reallocating shares at the IFIs, the administration should not agree to a deal where the United States' voting share declines or where the United States loses its veto over certain policies, given the size of the United States economy and the importance of the IFIs to United States policy interests.

8) *Clearly post summaries of U.S. votes on international financial institution projects* and programs on the International page of the Treasury Department website. The Bush administration began posting whether it abstained from voting, voted no or voted yes on development bank projects, but it is very difficult to find the web page.

9) *Reveal additional U.S. Executive Director positions that are delivered at the international financial institutions.* Current United States statute calls on the U.S. Directors to share their statements with Congress on inspection panel cases, operational policies, and projects with significant environmental impacts. The administration should voluntarily release the detailed U.S. positions on projects in countries of specific foreign policy interest such as Iraq and Afghanistan and on projects in areas of particular sensitivity such as energy and post-conflict reconstruction.

10) *Press the international financial institutions to work together.* Close collaboration is critical because the mandates of the development banks and the IMF, development, and financial stability are inherently connected and impact each other. For example, when development banks provide budget support loans to countries, they should

work with the IMF and obtain an assessment letter. The IMF should utilize development bank tools such as conflict filters when lending to post-war countries.

11) *Encourage the international financial institutions to systematically factor in the role of conflict to ensure that their financing does not inadvertently exacerbate conflict.* The World Bank developed a conflict filter for Sri Lanka, a series of questions to be asked at each stage of project development, which should be expanded for use in other countries and by the other international financial institutions.

12) *Promote parliamentary approval of international financial institution projects and programs.* The executive branches of few developing countries are required to seek parliamentary approval of international financial institution loans or grants. Few developing countries have parliaments that set a ceiling within which the executive branch can conclude individual agreements with the international financial institutions.

13) *Review any connection between the misuse of funds and debt relief.* Debt relief has been provided to countries that cannot afford to pay back their loans, it has not been provided for loans made knowingly to countries with corrupt leaders who misused or stole the funds.

14) *Designate an Ambassador-at-Large for Global Transparency* to promote disclosure at the international financial institutions that is consistent with efforts within the United States government and at other international organizations including the United Nations.

15) *Actively recruit U.S. citizens for positions at the international financial institutions and help applicants navigate the hiring process.*

Congress should:

16) *Consider supporting capital increases for multilateral development banks that have successfully implemented needed reforms.*

17) *Consider providing funds to clear United States' current arrears (unmet commitments) to the development banks, the existence of which* undermines United States influence at these entities.

18) *Fix tax disincentives which penalize Americans working abroad.*

The International Monetary Fund should:

19) *When providing loans to resource rich countries, take steps to account for the billions in revenues that are streaming into the country.* Specifically, the IMF should implement the recommendations from its own Guide to Resource Revenue Transparency; obtain a commitment to not censor individuals who raise concerns about oil revenue management; require disclosure of public official conflicts of interest in companies bidding for oil and gas rights; and call for an independent audit of the Ministry of Finance and Petroleum. Macroeconomic reform, economic development, and participatory governance all rely upon dissemination of information in order for the government to be more effective and to enable civil society to play a productive role in increasing accountability of government officials.

20) *Require countries to take anti-corruption measures,* reveal their budgets, and implement public financial management guidelines on budget transparency for loans to the government's budget, such as the flexible credit line[3] that was created in 2009.

21) *Provide grants rather than loans to countries that clearly cannot repay their loans,* such as Haiti after the January 2010 earthquake.

22) *Utilize proceeds in excess of projections from gold sales to fund grants and debt relief for the poorest countries.*

23) *Engage with Parliaments in the course of developing an IMF program.* While IMF programs include significant reforms, sometimes requiring legislative action, parliaments are rarely consulted by the IMF.

24) *Develop guidelines to ensure that IMF financing will not exacerbate the conflict or underlying hostilities* when lending to a post-conflict or current conflict country.

25) *Not shy away from making recommendations on the appropriate level of military expenditures* as they can be a significant determinant of a country's financial health.

The multilateral development banks (the World Bank, African Development Bank, Asian Development Bank, European Bank for Reconstruction and Development, and the Inter-American Development Bank) should:

26) *Plan for the future, not just the present.* Projects should be designed with a long-term view. For example, agricultural projects should be designed to withstand climate change and roads projects should be developed to accommodate pedestrians in areas projected to become densely populated.

27) *Strengthen anti-corruption efforts.* Increase resources for internal controls and anti-corruption efforts. Embed oversight funds into project and program financing so that a small percentage of the funds can be used by borrowing countries to support monitoring, investigations, prosecutions, technical assistance to Parliamentarians, government audit agencies, and ombudspeople, promoting better oversight.

28) *Refocus attention on the impact, rather than the size and goals, of development bank projects and programs.* Executive boards of the development banks should require presentation of projects and programs at their completion to put an emphasis on results and to incentivize staff to focus on the results of projects rather than the amounts. Currently, board review of projects and programs is only done at the approval stage. In addition, the development banks need to install meaningful staff evaluation systems so that staff are rewarded for good project design and implementation rather than for promoting large projects in important countries.

29) *Design a common evaluations framework* that includes the collection of shared baseline data to save money and avoid repetition. Baseline data is important in determining whether or not the development bank project made an impact.
   a) Produce comparable indicators and data dissemination standards so that results of the different development banks can be compared across the board and within countries.
   b) Projects should be designed with clear indicators so that results can be measured.
   c) Publish indicators so civil society can track the projects progress.
   d) Evaluate all projects and publish evaluations of all projects.

e)   Integrate lessons learned into project design.

30) *Better coordinate activities,* particularly food security assistance, starting with agreements on development principles and working with host governments to adhere to national development plans.

31) *Increase grants and subsidized loans for the poorest countries and create a predictable system to transfer profits to their grant-making and subsidized lending windows for poor countries* from the development banks' lending operations.

32) *Integrate the principles of the Extractive Industries Transparency Initiative into extractive industry project design.* All the MDBs now endorse the EITI, but when providing financing to resource rich countries, the development banks should focus their efforts on improving revenue management and fighting corruption, conditioning loans on revenue disclosure and contract transparency, and promoting transparency before the revenues actually start flowing from extractive industries. Relatively small amounts of aid money could thus help channel large amounts of countries' own funds toward poverty reduction.

33) *Revamp inspection panels and other inspection mechanisms so that people and communities negatively affected by development bank projects have clear access to redress.* Current mechanisms allow complaints to be made about failures to follow development bank policy but the only beneficiary is the bank itself, which learns of its mistakes. The affected people simply remain affected and are rarely compensated or made whole.

34) *Lending to the private sector should be focused on regions and sectors that truly need additional funding*to allow for the best use of scarce resources and to not crowd out the commercial lenders.

35) *When lending money directly to a country's budget, require publication of the budget and implementation of adequate public financial management standards.* Consult with the IMF on major budget support loans.

36) Since some emerging market countries are more interested in receiving advice than money from the development banks,*consider charging for advisory services.* Currently, most development banks only provide advisory services as part of a financing package.

37) *Minimize the environmental impact of projects, including increasing awareness of greenhouse gas emissions.*Develop and implement a strategy to lower greenhouse gas emissions trajectories while enhancing access to affordable energy services. Develop a best practice protocol for greenhouse gas accounting.

The World Bank should:

38) *Allow the Government Accountability Office to commence the two reviews requested by Senator Lugar, Senator Bayh,* Senator Leahy, and then-Senator Biden. One review would examine the goals, criteria for success, and ability to fight corruption and implement procurement procedures of the World Bank's subsidized loan and grant window, the International Development Association. The other review would scrutinize the World Bank's process for conducting environmental assessments, the impact of environmental assessments on project design, and the process for assessing environmental impact after a project is completed.

39) *Revise its public information policy to allow Executive Directors to release their Executive Board statements to their constituencies and to the public.* The World Bank's new public information policy makes significant strides towards transparency and presumes disclosure. However, the Executive Directors who are representatives of country members are not allowed to release their statements to the Board on policies and projects.

The African Development Bank should:

40) *Revamp its website to disclose what the African Development Bank is doing in each recipient country,* noting how much is going to what project, linking relevant documents and providing information on inspection panel cases. The current website provides limited information about the Bank's activities.
41) *Increase pursuit of misconduct by staff, contractors, and procuring companies and publish the list of debarred individuals and companies.* Compared to the other development banks, the African Development Bank has far fewer cases under investigation.

The Asian Development Bank should:

42) *Publish the names of the companies that it debars due to fraud or other misconduct.*
43) *Reform its human resources system,* including the selection of staff on the basis of transparent recruiting process and external recruiting at all levels.
44) Ensure that lending to *middle-income countries is focused on poverty alleviation.*

The European Bank for Reconstruction and Development should:

45) *Spread its lending across the region and not continue concentrating its portfolio in one country.* Currently, 41 percent of its lending goes to one borrower, Russia. The bank's limited resources clearly should be directed at countries with fewer of their own resources. A corollary, the Nunn-Lugar program initially invested heavily in Russia, but over time has shifted to other countries and Russia's contributions have increased. As Sen. Lugar noted in an August 2009, letter to the Wall Street Journal, "the Russian share of total Nunn-Lugar spending has dropped from 88 percent in 2001 to 37 percent as construction projects conclude and Moscow assumes more of the cost." No such weaning process is evident for the EBRD and Russia-instead, the trend has been going in the opposite direction.
46) *Focus lending to sectors and projects that lack access to market financing.*Currently, some loans are reportedly going to Russian oligarchs and projects that could obtain private capital, including the oil sector.
47) *Make additionality criteria more transparent and more explicit,* both as a statement of policy and on individual investments.
48) *Develop local currency lending and local capital markets.*

The Inter-American Development Bank should:

49) *Fully implement financial management reforms.* The Inter- American Development Bank is taking initial steps to reform its investment strategy, credit risk management, capital adequacy policy, and operational risk framework following an unrealized loss of $1.9 billion from its liquid portfolio of cash management instruments.

50) *Provide more grants and subsidized loans for the poorest countries* in the Western Hemisphere, including Haiti.

DISCUSSION

The world has changed drastically since the international financial institutions were created. Private capital flows to developing countries dwarf official donor assistance to those countries. Most exchange rates float under market pressures while they were previously fixed under the gold standard. Markets for goods, services, and finance are connected. We have seen the growth of sovereign wealth funds, fluctuations in energy prices, and multiple financial crises.

The recent financial crisis, which began in industrialized countries, quickly spread to emerging market and developing economies.[4] Most industrialized countries (except for Iceland) have been able to finance their own rescue packages, but many poor countries have insufficient sources of capital and have turned to help from the international financial institutions.

As we emerge from the worst economic crisis since the Great Depression, we must ask ourselves if we are content with the structure of the international financial institutions. Does the world really need the IMF, World Bank, African Development Bank, Asian Development Bank, European Bank for Reconstruction and Development, and Inter-American Development Bank today? How should we design them? Can they be changed to address our needs? What could the international financial institutions have done better to keep the crisis from occurring in the first place? What can they do now to best mitigate the fallout from the crisis? Do they achieve their various missions of promoting stability, fighting poverty, encouraging growth, and promoting democracy?

Some of these questions are being addressed by the international community. In November 2009, G-20 Finance Ministers said that "the International Financial Institutions will play an important role in supporting our work to secure sustainable growth, stability, job creation, development, and poverty reduction. It is therefore critical that we continue to increase their relevance, responsiveness, effectiveness, and legitimacy."[5]

The G-20 is examining changes to the allocation of voting power at the World Bank Executive Board, which "primarily reflects countries' evolving economic weight and the World Bank's development mission."[6]

In addition, the G-20 called for a review of World Bank and regional development bank capital to "ensure they have sufficient resources"[7] to be completed by the first half of 2010. The G-20[8] asked "the World Bank to play a leading role in responding to problems whose nature requires globally coordinated action, such as climate change and food security, and agreed that the World Bank and the regional development banks should have sufficient resources to address these challenges and fulfill their mandates."[9]

Senator Lugar's Ongoing Oversight Effort

At the direction of then-Chairman Richard G. Lugar, the Republican staff of the Senate Foreign Relations Committee in 2003 began a study of the international financial institutions, following whistleblower reports of corruption related to the development banks. Staff tested the viability of policy recommendations through meetings, document reviews, and site visits to projects in Africa, Asia, Europe and Central Asia, Latin America, and the Middle East. Staff asked if the international financial institutions were the tools needed to solve the problems of today's world, were the IFIs capable of needed changes, and what those changes would be.

As Chairman of the Senate Foreign Relations Committee, Senator Lugar held six hearings in the 108th and 109th Congress to probe how the banks could become more effective, accountable, and efficient. As Senator Lugar noted, "We are living in an era when threats posed by terrorism, weapons proliferation, international communicable diseases, increasing competition for energy supplies, and other factors have enlightened many of the world's people to the need to ensure that poor nations are not left behind. But these same threats also place competing demands on national budgets. If development projects are transparent, productive, and efficiently run, I believe that they will enjoy broad support. If they are not, they are likely to fare poorly when placed in competition with domestic priorities or more tangible security related expenditures."[10]

Numerous reforms were implemented following Senator Lugar's advocacy, particularly improvements to MDB anti-corruption efforts. These reforms include: creation of a joint MDB framework for combating fraud and corruption in their activities and operations; movement towards cross-debarment by barring companies that violate one development bank's policies from contracts with the other development banks; a new anti-corruption and governance strategy at the World Bank; two new codes of conduct at the European Bank for Reconstruction and Development, replacing codes adopted in 1991; an amended Public Communications Policy at the Asian Development Bank to allow the Integrity Division discretion to publicly disclose project procurement-related audit reports; a strong and comprehensive Whistle-blowing and Complaints Handling Policy approved by the African Development Bank in 2007; and a new Code of Ethics and ethics training for all staff implemented by the Inter-American Development Bank (IADB). However, much more needs to be done.

Hearings

With the intent of strengthening reforms at the multilateral development banks (MDBs), particularly reforms related to corruption, Senator Lugar chaired six Senate Foreign Relations Committee hearings in the 108th and 109th Congress on September 28, 2004, July 21, 2004, May 13, 2004, April 21, 2005, March 28, 2006, and July 12, 2006. The hearings heard testimony by representatives from the Treasury Department, the United States Executive Directors to the MDBs, academics, non-governmental organizations, and members of civil society. These hearings contributed to the committee's understanding of both the value of the MDBs' work and problems with their operations.

The hearings before the Foreign Relations Committee demonstrated that:

- Significant multilateral development bank funding has been lost to corruption and it is difficult to ascertain such amount precisely, in part because the multilateral development banks have not implemented procedures to calculate such amounts, either in the aggregate or on a country basis;
- The multilateral development banks are taking action to address fraud and corruption but additional measures remain to be carried out;
- The capability of anticorruption mechanisms, including investigations, reporting, and disposition, are not consistent among the multilateral development banks and divergences in anticorruption policies exist that may hinder coordination on fighting corruption;
- Weaknesses in whistleblower and reporting policy and practice exist at the multilateral development banks, to varying degree, that impede antifraud and anticorruption efforts;
- Greater transparency and investigative independence is necessary to provide effective development aid;
- The Secretary of the Treasury encourages anticorruption efforts at the multilateral development banks and reviews loans made by such banks, however, the United States has limited ability to investigate the misuse of funds from such banks; and
- In some cases, the countries bearing the cost of prosecuting corruption related to the multilateral development banks are the countries that can least afford such costs, for example, the Government of Lesotho incurred considerable expense, despite competing priorities, such as those arising from an HIV/AIDS rate of more than 25 percent in that country, to investigate and prosecute fraud and corruption related to a project that received funding from the World Bank and the World Bank did not contribute money towards the prosecution or investigation.[11]

A number of recommendations arose from the testimony of over 20 witnesses. These include:

- Establish an international auditing body responsible for rooting out corruption and waste at all MDBs
- Reform the "pressure to lend" incentive system in the MDBs that emphasizes lending volume, not effectiveness
- Re-examine legal immunity for employees of international organizations
- Develop best practice procurement procedures for use by all the MDBs
- Strengthen whistle-blower protections
- Automatically disclose bank-imposed sanctions of contractors and individuals
- Establish mutual recognition of blacklists across all MDBs

Legislation

S. 1129. The hearings also formed the basis for the Development Bank Reform and Authorization Act of 2005, which was approved unanimously by the Senate Foreign Relations Committee. The full text of the bill is in Appendix VII. The bill was introduced by Senator Lugar and had eleven co-sponsors (Senators Alexander, Biden, Clinton, Cochran, Coleman, Hagel, Isakson, Martinez, Obama, Stevens, and Thune). Significant portions of the bill became law in November 2005 in H.R.3057. With passage of this legislation, Congress made a strong statement that it recognizes the critical role of the MDBs in achieving development goals around the world, but also that the operations of these banks must be transparent, efficient, and free of corruption. The legislation contained many reforms aimed at achieving more transparency and accountability in the banks' operations. It requires the Secretary of the Treasury and the United States Executive Directors to the MDBs to support clear and public anti-corruption procedures that are coordinated across all the MDBs. It promotes staff financial disclosure procedures, whistleblower protections, and the establishment of independent ethics and auditing offices. It also encourages transparent budget processes for countries that receive budget support from the MDBs and additional disclosure requirements for natural resource extraction projects.

Since the introduction of S. 1129, many of the measures it promoted have made progress. For example, the MDBs have now developed common definitions of fraud and corruption and are working to create consisted debarment policies so that a person that is debarred by one multilateral development bank is ineligible to conduct business with the other multilateral development banks during the specified ineligibility period. Many of the MDBs have strengthened their auditing, accounting and evaluations processes.

They have also made some embraced the need for extractive industry project transparency. While much more still needs to be done, it is important to recognize that positive changes have been made since the 2005 introduction of the Development Bank Reform and Authorization Act was introduced.

S. 954. The World Bank International Development Association Replenishment Act of 2009, which was introduced with Senator Kerry and co-sponsored by Senator Kaufman, passed out of Committee on July 16, 2009, and directs the Secretary of the Treasury to seek to ensure that multilateral development banks: (1) implement greenhouse gas accounting in analyzing the benefits and costs of individual projects; and (2) expand their climate change mitigation activities.

S.955. The African Development Fund Replenishment Act of 2009, which was introduced with Senator Kerry and co-sponsored by Senator Kaufman, passed out of Committee on July 16, 2009, and directs the Secretary of the Treasury to: (1) seek to ensure that each multilateral development bank discloses to member countries the banks' operating budget, including expenses for staff, consultants, travel, and facilities; (2) require that the U.S. Executive Director of each multilateral development bank use U.S. influence to ensure that the bank endorses and integrates the principles of the Extractive Industry Transparency Initiative; (3) submit related reports to Congress.

Amendments to H.R. 2346 and H.R. 1105. Provisions suggested by Senator Lugar that were included in H.R. 2346 require the Secretary of the Treasury to ensure that the multilateral development banks make timely, public disclosure of their operating budgets including expenses for staff, consultants, travel, and facilities.

Senator Lugar offered an amendment to H.R. 2346, which was included in H.R. 1105 and co-sponsored by Senators Leahy and Kerry, that would require standard public disclosure of documents of the IMF presented to the Executive Board of the Fund and summaries of the minutes from Board meetings, as recommended by the Independent Evaluation Office, not later than two years after the document was presented or meeting occurred. It also directs the U.S. Executive Director at the IMF to promote: 1) transparency and accountability in the policymaking and budgetary procedures of governments of members of the Fund; 2) the participation of citizens and nongovernmental organizations in the economic policy choices of those governments; and 3) the adoption by those governments of loans, agreements, or other programs of the Fund through a parliamentary process or another participatory and transparent process, as appropriate.

S.2961. The Haiti Recovery Act of 2010, which was introduced with Senator Dodd and co-sponsored by Senators Durbin and Kerry, urges the Secretary of the Treasury to direct the U.S. Executive Director to each international financial institution to advocate the cancellation of all remaining debt obligations of Haiti and the treatment of any debt service payments as well as the use of some of the realized windfall profits that exceed the required contribution to the Poverty Reduction and Growth Trust (as referenced in the IMF Reforms Financial Facilities for Low-Income Countries Public Information Notice (PIN) No. 09/94) from the ongoing sale of 12,965,649 ounces of gold acquired since the second Amendment of the Fund's Article of Agreement, to provide debt stock relief, debt service relief, loan subsidies, and grants for Haiti.

Investigations and Reports

Site Visits. Between 2005 and 2009, Senate Foreign Relations Committee staff observed development bank financed projects or met with development bank officials in a range of countries including Bangladesh; Cambodia; Chile; China; Ghana; India; Indonesia; Lebanon; Lesotho; Paraguay; Peru; the Philippines; Rwanda, Senegal; South Africa; Sri Lanka; Tanzania; Tunisia; and Yemen.

SFRC Food Security Report. In the February 2009 staff report entitled "Global Food Insecurity: Perspectives from the Field," Senate Foreign Relations Committee staff asserted that "the international donor community must come together at the country level to better coordinate aid activities, starting with agreements on development principles and working with host governments to adhere to national development plans."

SFRC Extractive Industries Report. In the October 2008 Senate Foreign Relations Committee report entitled "The Petroleum and Poverty Paradox: Assessing U.S. and International Community Efforts to Fight the Resource Curse," staff recommended that "international donors who give aid to resource-rich countries should focus their efforts on improving revenue management and fighting corruption. Relatively small amounts of aid money could thus help channel large amounts of countries' own funds toward poverty reduction." Specific recommendations included:

- The World Bank and the IMF, which make regular assessments of countries' performance, should be consistent in the assessment of countries' progress on transparency compared to their own professed benchmarks. They also should ensure that their staffing at key posts reflects commitments made to those governments in technical assistance on improved financial governance.
- The regional development banks should integrate EITI into their operations, now that all of the regional development banks have endorsed EITI principles in their projects. (The IDB was the last to do so.) The regional development banks should condition loans on revenue disclosure and contract transparency.
- Multilateral development banks should condition loans on progress in implementing transparency measures and they should promote transparency before the resource revenues actually start flowing from extractive industries.

Commissioned GAO Report on the World Bank. On May 14, 2008, Senators Lugar, Bayh, and Leahy, citing the importance of good stewardship of U.S. taxpayer dollars, called on the Government Accountability Office to study whether the World Bank has taken adequate steps to combat corruption and effectively govern programs designed to fight global poverty. In their letter, the Senators stated that "the use of public funds to help improve the lives of the world's poor carries with it a responsibility to ensure that the Bank is effectively run and its efforts produce tangible results."[12]

The Lugar-Bayh study would examine whether the World Bank is:

- Establishing clear goals for projects financed by the International Development Association;
- Establishing clear criteria for measuring the success of IDA projects;
- Working effectively to reduce corruption within governments that receive IDA funding; and
- Effectively implementing procedures for procurement of IDA goods and services.

In March 2009, GAO staff stated that "we cannot begin this work because of challenges we recently faced in gaining access to World Bank officials to discuss these types of questions. We are continuing to negotiate access with World Bank officials but this process is likely to take at least several months." Senator Lugar's staff continues to press the World Bank and GAO to begin this chapter during the first half of 2010.

United States Benefits from Involvement

The international financial institutions present the United States with an opportunity to maintain its influence, address national security issues, and provide global leadership in an era when the American economy may not be the overwhelming source of power it once was. The Treasury Department's recent justification for appropriations asserts that "our funding through the MDBs leverages substantial amounts of additional money both directly, through co- financing, guarantees, and insurance of investment projects, and indirectly, through pro-investment infrastructure improvements and policy reforms."[13]

Each dollar that the United States contributes to the World Bank's concessional window (International Development Association) yields $11 of grants or low-interest loans to developing countries and each dollar contributed to the World Bank's regular lending window (International Bank for Reconstruction and Development) yields over $26 of lending to developing countries.[14] Our bilateral assistance, through the United States Agency for International Development, the State Department, and other agencies, allows the United States to maintain direct control over its funding. While U.S. funding through the international financial institutions forces us to relinquish some control, it does allow us to influence how collective donors address large scale issues.

As the largest contributor to most of the multilateral development banks, the United States has the largest voting shares at the World Bank, Inter-American Development Bank, and European Bank for Reconstruction and Development. The United States ties with Japan as the largest shareholder at the Asian Development Bank, while Nigeria and Egypt have subscribed larger shares in the African Development Bank.[15]

Table 1 in Appendix V shows the U.S. contribution share and voting share for all MDB programs.[16] In most banks, countries get a few votes because they are members, regardless of the size of their capital subscription. Thus, for banks with a large number of small members, the voting share of large subscribers such as the United States may be a little smaller than their share in providing the banks' resources. Voting shares are the same for both market-based and concessional loans in the AsDB and IDB.

The American people must have confidence that our contributions to the international financial institutions will be managed effectively, efficiently, and transparently. Given our domestic budget and employment situation, it is all the more critical that we ensure that our contributions promote U.S. interests.

More Money for the Development Banks?[17]

The international financial institutions, namely the IMF,[18] the World Bank,[19] the African Development Bank,[20] the European Bank for Reconstruction and Development,[21] and the Inter-American Development Bank[22] are asking the United States and other donor countries for billions of dollars to be used for additional capital. The Obama administration has already agreed to the Asian Development Bank's proposal to request more than $500 million from Congress for a 200 percent capital increase. Negotiations continue on the requests from the other development banks. From the United States alone, the Inter-American Development Bank is seeking $2.4 billion, the World Bank is seeking $1.1 billion, the African Development Bank is seeking $270 million, and the European Bank for Reconstruction and Development Bank is seeking $150 million.[23]

Secretary Geithner indicated that the Treasury Department is "currently reviewing requests for capital increases at a number of the MDBs and will move forward only on commitments where we are confident that they represent the best use of U.S. taxpayer funds within the context of our overall global development goals.[24] For example, we need to be satisfied that each MDB is fully employing its available resources efficiently and effectively and that each is committed to implementing needed reforms that will focus their missions and improve their effectiveness in accordance with the core principles . . . including an increased commitment to transparency, accountability, and good corporate governance; an increased capacity to innovate and achieve demonstrable results; and greater attention to the needs of the poorest populations." Since the fall of 2009, Treasury staff has regularly updated staff of the Senate Foreign Relations Committee on their review of capital increase requests.

As the requests for capital are negotiated with the international donor community, there is a window of opportunity for significant reform. Given the administration's signing statement that accompanied last year's supplemental appropriations bill, indicating that the administration may not pursue legislatively-mandated reforms at the IMF, Congress may have an interest in securing the reforms before authorizing funds for the capital increases.[25] Of serious concern is the speed at which the international community is moving forward with the capital increases—the G-20 expects to finalize decisions on the capital commitments this spring.

Before committing to providing additional funds to the multilateral development banks, the United States and the G-20 must rethink the role of the international financial institutions that provide crisis support and assistance to developing countries and emerging markets.

It also is imperative that our government examine the capital increases for each bank as a unique request. Each financial institution has distinct management challenges. For example, capital increases for the European Bank for Reconstruction and Development must be accompanied by much more information concerning whether wealthy Russian business interests are benefiting from the 41 percent of bank funds that flow to that country. Similarly, capital increases for the Inter-American Development Bank must address how that Bank is reforming its practices after its unrealized loss of $1.9 billion in 2008 from its liquid portfolio of cash management instruments. The World Bank, for its part, has been a leader in addressing concerns about corruption and governance. Among other steps, it regularly publishes the names of contracting companies and individuals that have violated World Bank policies.

The United States and other major donor countries have unwisely and unnecessarily linked the timing for general capital increase decisions to each individual Bank's annual or spring meeting, beginning with the Inter-American Development Bank in March 2010, the World Bank in April 2010, and the African Development Bank and European Bank for Reconstruction and Development in May 2010. This is an artificial deadline. The G-20 communiqué links the general capital increases to: (1) a review of capital needs, given the four lending priorities articulated in the communiqué; and (2) key institutional reforms. Rather than applying an arbitrary deadline, fulfillment of the G-20 criteria should be the guide to timing. The development banks must not just commit to a reform agenda—ideally, those reforms should be underway before donors pledge millions, if not billions, in funds.

Many of the general capital increase requests were initiated on an emergency basis at the height of the global financial crisis under the direction of the G-20 in early 2009. Now private capital flows are returning to many developing markets and varying levels of economic recovery are emerging in the regions serviced by the MDBs. It is therefore appropriate to take a measured and thoughtful approach to General Capital Increase (GCI) decisions that can take into account the real lending demands and longer-term strategies of the relevant MDBs before permanently increasing their operations (Table 9).

Delay is particularly appropriate in cases where the current leadership of a bank is about to end its term and a new leader is to be chosen. The U.S. will want to make sure that the newly elected leadership is committed to a reform agenda. The granting of a new GCI should be a consequence, not a precondition, of new bank management accepting and beginning to implement the important changes sought by the U.S. and other donors. Gaining buy-in at the most senior level of the MDBs is essential to ensure that implementation of reforms takes place. With no clarity about who will be leading several of these MDBs moving forward, a commitment of substantial sums in capital immediately prior to elections would be an unnecessary leap of faith.

United States in Arrears to the Development Banks

Over the years, Congress has not funded the administration's requests to fulfill commitments made to the multilateral development banks during the course of international negotiations through which the United States has extracted numerous reforms. The arrears status of the United States has already reduced slightly the U.S. shares at the African Development Bank, for example, undermining the ability of the United States to leverage the development banks for our foreign policy interests.

As noted by Secretary Geithner, the United States has over $1 billion in unmet commitments to the multilateral development banks. The bulk of the unmet commitments are to the concessional windows, which provide grants and subsidized loans to the poorest countries.[26] The large arrears weaken U.S. leadership at these institutions, due to significant skepticism of the willingness of the United States to deliver on any initiatives that require significant funding.

In particular, the United States' pledges for debt relief through the development banks have not been fully funded by Congress. Because the United States has fallen far behind in fully funding for World Bank IDA replenishments, the United States will not be able to earn sufficient credits to meet current international debt relief commitments under the Multilateral Debt Relief Initiative (MDRI). Without full funding for arrears to the Inter-American Investment Corporation (IIC) at the Inter-American Development Bank as scheduled, the United States will fail to clear longstanding arrears and will permanently lose capital shares in the institution.

Linkage between Corruption and Debt

World Bank economists Craig Burnside and David Dollar asserted in the *American Economic Review* that "in the presence of poor policies. . . . aid has no positive effect on growth." Similarly, the World Bank web site identifies corruption as "the single greatest obstacle to economic and social development." Corruption associated with MDB loans not only squanders development funds and enriches dishonest officials and contractors, it leaves impoverished nations with the burden of the resulting debts.[27]

Corruption impedes development efforts in many ways. Bribes can influence important bank decisions on projects and contractors. Misuse of funds can inflate project costs, deny needed assistance to the poor, and cause projects to fail. Stolen money may prop up dictatorships and finance human rights abuses. Moreover, when developing countries lose development bank funds through corruption, the taxpayers in those poor countries are still obligated to repay the development banks. "When projects intended to boost economic development are derailed by corruption, the poorest suffer and are cheated of projected benefits in quality health care, clean water, and education," Senator Lugar said.[28]

In 1999, the United States and other industrialized nations established the Highly Indebted Poor Countries Initiative in response to crippling levels of debt combined with anemic economic growth in dozens of developing countries. This was followed several years later by the more comprehensive Multilateral Debt Relief Initiative. These initiatives allowed poor countries with unsustainable debt levels to receive debt relief in exchange for adopting economic policy reforms and channeling their debt savings to poverty reduction activities. However, countries that were managing their debts but had their development bank funds siphoned off by corrupt officials did not benefit from these rounds of debt relief. These debts remain.

The most important way to combat the need for future debt relief is to ensure that development loans are implemented effectively and ethically.

Monitoring and Evaluations Vary

Currently, the development banks vary in their evaluations processes and findings, and it is important that each project and program be evaluated. For example, the World Bank is developing outcome and output indicators, the Asian Development Bank has created operational effectiveness and efficiency indicators and the Inter-American Development Bank is creating indicators covering the effectiveness of its priorities. They should share project and program effectiveness data throughout their banks and the other banks.

Moreover, the findings from those evaluations must be incorporated in future programming. To paraphrase Professor David Levine of the University of California at Berkeley—project evaluations have a cost but it is much costlier to fund ineffective projects over and over again.

The development banks rarely develop baseline data so that they can demonstrate the impact of their projects and programs. In contrast, the United States' Millennium Challenge Account has procured baseline data for some of its projects. Where appropriate, the development banks should establish baseline data and share that data with other donors to avoid unnecessary overlap.

The IMF's Independent Evaluation Office (IEO) has been heralded not only for its autonomous findings but because its recommendations are often included in the development of new IMF programs. The IEO was formed after most of the evaluation offices of the other international financial institutions, and some argue that its later development has been an advantage.

The African Development Bank is taking steps to evaluate all projects—currently less than one-quarter of projects were evaluated according to interviews held in May 2009. AfDB staff has determined that the success of development programs is most highly correlated with (1) the commitment of the borrowing country to fully implement the program; and (2) the quality of the project design. AfDB staff noted that if a project is designed poorly, it cannot be fixed during implementation and that it was imperative to get it right at the beginning. The AfDB is committing to posting its project ratings. Officials talked about the need for "virtuous circles" to be developed so that evaluations lead to accountability which leads to better projects which are then evaluated.

Need More Focus on Transparency

Most pressing international issues are spearheaded by specific offices in specific agencies. However, the responsibility for promoting transparency is not delegated to a particular part of the U.S. government. Some argue that all parts of our government are responsible for transparency but without a clear office responsible for promoting transparency with international organizations and development financing, these issues do not receive the consistent attention that they deserve. The creation of an Ambassador at Large for Global Transparency would allow for the full vetting of transparency issues and press for consistent transparency measures at the international financial institutions and other international organizations with which the United States works.

Across the board, the international financial institutions have a tradition of secrecy and opacity that may be typical of certain private sector financial institutions and politically sensitive international organizations. It is not, however, appropriate for public sector institutions that are funded by the taxpayers of democratic countries and that make decisions affecting the lives of millions in the developing world. Steps toward greater transparency that have been undertaken by the development banks in recent years make for better accountability, greater effectiveness, and ultimately stronger public support. But much more needs to be done.

The World Bank instituted a new information disclosure policy which significantly improves the ability of the institution to disclose information to the public. Nevertheless, it does not allow World Bank Board Executive Directors to release their statements on projects and policies. Disclosure of U.S. Executive Director votes and statements at the development banks would help enable Americans to understand what policies the United States is promoting at the development banks. Should a development bank preclude an Executive Director from releasing his or her statements, a summary of the U.S. position on the policy or project should be revealed.

During the Bush administration, the Treasury Department did begin posting on its website how the U.S. executive directors voted on a project or policy. However, on the current version of the website it is difficult to locate the voting records.

In 2004, Senator Lugar sent then-President Kabbaj a letter about the AfDB's website. Staff discussed the need for an improved AfDB website with multiple AfDB officials. It is important for the public to know what projects the AfDB is funding in each country. All officials agreed but stated that the AfDB did not have the staff or the capacity to produce such a website soon. They noted that the World Bank's communications staff was substantially larger than the AfDB's communications staff.

Coordination Could Be Improved

As the Report of the External View Committee on Bank-Fund Collaboration asserts, "close collaboration is vital because, while the Bank and the Fund have separate mandates, they are inherently linked. For instance, macroeconomic stability (a major Fund concern) will not be sustained unless linked to supply side measures and improved quality of public spending (a major Bank concern). Similarly, global monetary stability (a Fund concern) will have a direct bearing on overall development prospects (a Bank concern)."[29]

While the development banks have recently agreed on a shared definition of fraud and corruption and are considering cross-debarment, they do not share a policy on investigation. When development banks provide budget support loans to countries, they should work with the IMF and obtain an assessment letter to ensure that the economic policy conditions are appropriate for such a loan. In Argentina and Botswana, the Inter-American Development Bank and African Development Bank respectively did not obtain IMF letters prior to lending significant loans to those governments' budgets.

Similarly, the IMF should utilize development bank tools such as conflict filters when lending to post-conflict countries. In Sri Lanka, the IMF provided a large loan without utilizing the conflict filter that had been developed by the World Bank for that country.

Questions around Budget Support

Following the global financial crisis, international financial institutions have been increasing their provision of budget support or loans that go directly to the government's budget and are not targeted to a specific project. In May 2009, the IMF announced a new flexible credit line, to lend directly to a government's budget rather than solely to a country's central bank, the normal recipient of IMF loans.[30]

Some are concerned that the international financial institutions are lending large amounts as budget support without a corresponding budget management and fiscal transparency framework to ensure that the funds are not misused. For example, the AfDB has issued sizeable loans that do not appear to be fully coordinated with the other international financial institutions such as the IMF. Usually, it is the IMF that provides short and medium-term support while the development banks, such as the AfDB, provide long- term support.

In June 2009 the AfDB approved a large $1.5 billion loan for Botswana, an amount more than 13 percent of the country's GDP. The AfDB website noted that Botswana is "one of the best managed economies in Africa." The AfDB's press release noted the following:

> The loan falls within the framework of the recently approved strategy by the Bank to provide support to member countries affected by the financial crisis and is the largest such facility ever granted by the Bank. The Budget Support Loan is designed to fill part of the gap in the government's 2009/ 2010 budget deficit currently estimated at 13.5 percent of GDP caused by falling commodity prices, particularly diamonds.
>
> "The case of Botswana illustrates the impact that the financial crisis is having on even the best managed economies in Africa. I am delighted that the Bank has been able to respond quickly and flexibly in this 'unique case' within the Bank's framework of response to the financial crisis," said Donald Kaberuka, the President of the Bank.

The crisis which is affecting African countries through different channels is increasing demands for support from the international financial institutions including the Bank.

This is the first such borrowing from the Bank by Botswana in 17 years. Previously Botswana had in fact several times contributed to the replenishment of the African Development Fund (AfDF), the soft window of the Bank Group.[31]

Focus on Low-income Countries

The international financial institutions vary in their focus on serving the poorest countries and the poorest communities in middle income countries. The World Bank has a formal system to transfer profits from loans to middle-income countries made by the International Bank for Reconstruction and Development into a grant and subsidized lending window for low-income countries through the International Development Association. Going forward, it will be important for the African Development Bank and the Inter-American Development Bank to increase transfers to their respective grant and subsidized lending windows.

The IMF has made significant efforts to address the needs of low income countries through debt relief and to increase its subsidization of low-income country borrowing. In July 2009, the IMF Executive Board agreed to lower concessional interest rates to zero for at least the next two years. One tool that the IMF does not employ is to provide direct grants. While some would argue that IMF is not well suited to provide grant financing, it is something that should be considered when lending to countries with a history of debt relief and dire economic conditions. For example, when the IMF provided Haiti with a $114 million emergency loan in January 2010, Managing Director Dominique Strauss-Kahn stated that "if we succeed—and I'm sure we will succeed—even this loan will turn out to be finally a grant, because all the debt will have been deleted. And that's the very important thing for Haiti now." It would appear that, in these cases, offering grants would be more efficient and provide more policy clarity.

The IMF has been selling gold to fund its new income model to pay for staff salaries and ongoing operations as well as to subsidize borrowing for low-income countries. It appears that the earnings on the sale of gold are significantly higher than initially expected. The IMF has not determined how to use these excess proceeds. Given the demand by low-income countries, it would be helpful if the excess proceeds were directed to a fund for those low-income countries to be used for grants, subsidization of loans, and technical assistance.

Ability to Do Independent Investigations Uneven

Each development bank has an independent investigation mechanism to "address the concerns of the people who may be affected by Bank projects and to ensure that address the concerns of the people who may be affected by Bank projects and to ensure that the Bank adheres to its operational policies and procedures during design, preparation and implementation phases of projects."[32] The level of independence enjoyed by each mechanism varies, as does the quality of their investigations. The IDB recently approved a new independent investigation policy, following assertions that its mechanism was cumbersome

CASE STUDIES

Chile and the Inter-American Development Bank Lessons from the Transantiago

In February 2006, Santiago, Chile, replaced its previous transportation network of competing, privately-owned buses with what was proclaimed as a new state-of-the-art public transportation system, Transantiago. The purpose of the costly project was to shorten passenger waiting and travel time and reduce levels of vehicle emissions. Instead, the public heavily criticized Transantiago for increasing congestion and commuting delays for Santiago's population of six million people, although these problems have been diminishing consistently as operational performance has improved.

Regulated by the Ministry of Transportation, the new public transit system has also been plagued by financing problems. As of August 2009, its total deficit reached $1.42 billion, with a monthly average of $49 million. The Chilean Congress refused to include the Bachelet administration's request for a subsidy to Transantiago in the 2008 Budget Law due to the system's implementation problems. This denial of funding led the administration to seek two loans in 2008: $400 million from the Inter-American Development Bank (IDB) and $10 million from the state-owned Banco Estado.

The IDB loan became the subject of contentious debate in Chile because the funding was requested by the Chilean government to support the system, which is privately operated and financially managed by the Transantiago Financial Administrator (AFT). For the IDB, it was unusual to provide a private sector loan with a negative cash flow; Transantiago had already been operating on a deficit for over a year. The purpose of the loan was to ensure the system's operations while a new sustainable financial framework was implemented, including a permanent subsidy established by law.

A group of legislators challenged the decrees authorizing the IDB loan before Chile's Constitutional Court, claiming that the administration did not have the authority to request and guarantee a loan between the IDB and the AFT without appropriate legislation. In September 2008, the Court declared the decrees authorizing the IDB loan unconstitutional. As Chile entered a period of technical default on the IDB loan, the administration attempted to negotiate a solution to Transantiago's funding, as well as the outstanding IDB debt, with the Chilean Congress. In August 2009, the Congress approved repayment of the IDB loan as well as a subsidy for public transport throughout Chile, which would also cover Transantiago's operating deficit.

In many countries, IFI loans require legislative approval or ratification. Though each country will develop the appropriate procedure to include broad input, this case study exemplifies what can happen without meaningful consultation between the IFIs and the legislative branches of government. In a March 2009 report on the IDB loan, an Investigative Commission established by the Chilean House of Representatives not only criticized the Chilean executive branch for bypassing the legislature, but also judged the performance of the

IDB to be "careless and irresponsible" in granting a loan that violated Chile's constitution. [33] While IDB officials defended the decision by detailing the feasibility and environmental impact studies that preceded the granting of the loan, it is clear that opposition to the project should have been recognized.

India and the World Bank: the Detailed Implementation Review (DIR) Fallout

After a 2005 World Bank investigation revealed systematic fraud and corruption in the Indian health sector, the World Bank and the Government of India agreed to conduct a Detailed Implementation Review (DIR). A DIR is not a traditional audit of specific allegations; the DIR raises "red flags" on how fraud and corruption could affect the outcome and the effectiveness of the project. Disconcertingly, the DIR strained relationships between the World Bank and the Government of India (GOI)—not only due to the findings of the report, but also because of the nature in which the report was conducted and released.

The GOI was disappointed with several aspects of the report. The DIR was released publicly at the same time the Minister of Finance was given a copy to review. Prior to public release, the GoI was given no opportunity to respond. The GOI felt that the DIR did not seek participation of program divisions within the Ministry of Health & Family Welfare while finalizing the report, which "resulted in an avoidable lop-sidedness and occasional erroneous interpretation of data."[34] The GOI also contended that fraud and corruption were terms too broadly used, for example, to inaccurately describe certain instances of inadequate supervision or maintenance.

The report, though, included many legitimate concerns regarding fraud, corruption and the effectiveness of programs that the GOI and the World Bank have subsequently sought to address through a joint action plan. The World Bank acknowledged feedback from the GOI regarding concerns about the DIR process and has made revisions to internal policies. The World Bank plans to address detailed comments from the GOI during the implementation of the joint action plan to ensure that future reports are reviewed by host countries prior to being released publicly and that names of people or companies are not published until indicators of fraud and corruption are confirmed.

This case study reveals the challenges that IFIs face in terms of how they interact with national governments. When conducting reviews and audits of development projects within a certain country, many times these institutions must simultaneously cooperate and preserve a good relationship with the government while maintaining an independent and responsible evaluation. To protect this balance, IFIs must develop a framework in which to conduct reviews like the DIR. As evidenced by this case study, the lack of a framework can lead to a deteriorating relationship with the national government and the potential for a less successful review and subsequent implementation of necessary reforms.

The International Monetary Fund in Indonesia

International Monetary Fund-Indonesia relations had a difficult beginning in the 1950s and 1960s. While the IMF offered assistance to Indonesia under President Sukarno, he rejected the offer as contrary to communism.[35] In 1963, the government devalued the Rupiah in an effort to gain IMF support for its overdue foreign debt payments.[36] IMF, World Bank and American loans soon followed.[37] However, Britain established the Malaysian Federation the same year, which Sukarno strongly opposed and countered by nationalizing British firms in Indonesia. Consequently IMF loans in Indonesia were cancelled, ending cooperation.[38] In 1965, Sukarno formally severed relations with the IMF and the World Bank, choosing to instead ally with communist Asian countries.[39]

In 1966 after the 1965 military coup, new Indonesian President Suharto requested the IMF to return to Indonesia. In 1967, Indonesia formally joined the IMF.[40] Suharto implemented IMF recommended policies including budget deficit reduction and movement towards an export economy.[41] The 1960s were characterized by "a very close relationship.between the staff of the Bank and the Fund and their interlocutors in the Indonesia government—a group of young U.S.-trained economists . . . who were brought into government by General Suharto."[42]

While scholars concluded that "The relationship between Indonesia's 'New Order' government and the IMF over the last 30 years was excellent," serious strains appeared during the IMF's management of the 1997-1999 Asian Financial Crisis.[43] (Prior to the crisis, both the IMF and the World Bank had issued reports that were positive about the Indonesian economy.) [44]

Although controversial and considered by some to be incessantly meddling, the IMF package, in the short-term, had successful results. The rupiah strengthened and market confidence returned.[45] From late 1997 into January 1998, the economy took a turn for the worse and political events began to move quickly. Facing economic chaos, President Suharto relented to IMF pressure and moved to cut government spending by postponing several subsidized projects.

A new IMF-Indonesia program was announced to restore confidence in the rupiah through tight monetary policy and structural reforms such as eliminating monopolies and state subsidies. The photograph from the signing ceremony of this agreement, with IMF Managing Director Michel Camdessus standing over President Suharto, became an infamous and inflammatory symbol of Indonesia's subjugation to the West. Ongoing turmoil led to President Suharto's resignation.

Indonesia has largely graduated from the IMF program. The beginning of the post-crisis era was marked by lingering and considerable resentment of the IMF in Indonesia and a desire to move the country away from IMF advice by quickly repaying debts. In 2003, the Indonesian government, "under pressure from its legislators, declared that it wanted to break free of its commitments to the IMF," and Chief Economics Minister Dorodjatun Kuntjoro-Jakti said that "the government did not wish to extend the existing \$4.8 billion loan package with the Fund."[46] By October 2006, Indonesia had announced its intention to pay all of its outstanding \$3.2 billion IMF debts early.

There has been significant criticism of IMF policy in Indonesia from a range of economists including Jeffrey Sachs, Martin Feldstein and Robert Rubin. In the ultimate analysis, Indonesia was the country hardest hit by the 1997-1999 Asian Financial Crisis. Its

GDP fell by 13 percent in 1998, compared to 11 percent in Thailand, 7 percent in the Republic of Korea and Malaysia and 1 percent in the Philippines. These losses were worse on a per capita basis: Indonesia's per capita GDP fell by 34 percent over 1997- 1999, Thailand's by 13 percent and the rest of the region in single digits.[47]

The IMF-Indonesia recently reported to the Senate Foreign Relations Committee that "since there has not been a formal IMF-supported program for several years, IMF policy advice and recommendations for Indonesia are formulated in the context of bilateral surveillance. In this context, IMF economists visit member countries regularly to discuss with the authorities the risks to domestic and external stability that may argue for adjustments in economic or financial policies. During their mission, the IMF staff often meet with stakeholders (parliamentarians and representatives of business, labor unions and civil society) to help evaluate the country's economic policies and direction. Upon its return to headquarters, the mission submits a report to the IMF's Executive Board for discussion. The comments and recommendations of the Board are communicated to the authorities and form the basis for follow up discussions."

Based on this statement from the IMF, it appears officials of the institution discuss economic policy with Indonesian officials and provide nonbinding recommendations, a very different role from its active and interventionist participation of the past with Indonesia. The IMF and its activities in Indonesia have evolved with the emergence of democracy and the ongoing battle for strengthened institutions intended to support a growing economy.

Development Banks in Kenya: Monitoring and Procurement Challenges

The first loan by the World Bank to Kenya was in 1960 for an agriculture project. Since then there have been close to one hundred credits and grants by the International Development Association (IDA) with a total net commitment of about US$ 4.5 billion. The assistance provided over the years has been interrupted at regular intervals due to financial scandal, gross corruption, and political and social instability. Invariably, progress is halting and gains are easily reversed. The Bank has determined that the 2008-2009 political instability and additional concurrent economic and environmental crises have increased the poverty headcount by 22 percent and severe poverty has increased by 38 percent, thus reversing the gains made over the past five years.

The Bank's own reviews over the years have offered blistering assessments of the effectiveness of its loans and monitoring as well as that of Kenya's own partnership in achieving program goals. According to the World Bank Country Assistance Evaluation for Kenya of November 20, 2000, "Kenya qualified for nearly $3 billion in assistance from 1980 to 1996 but was unable to meet conditionality in implementation and reforms, . . . and that OED overall satisfactory outcome ratio of 57 percent for Kenya was lower than that for the Africa region (63 percent) and Bank-wide (75 percent). Sustainability was likely in 21 percent, and institutional development was substantial in only 6 percent of commitments."

In an effort to explain some of the deficiencies in the Kenya program, auditors said that "some of the factors adversely affecting outcomes at the sectoral level were deficient Bank monitoring and evaluation systems, inadequate ministerial financial systems, reluctance of the Government to consult widely with the potential target communities, and difficulties in observing IDA guidelines on procurement." Further, "high Bank managerial turnover, particularly for human resource development projects, and barely acceptable quality at entry of two infrastructure projects approved in FY96 were also noteworthy." The review identified the necessity for greater emphasis on governance, income distribution, and gender opportunities while elevating the Bank's own comparative advantage to other donors. The role of the resident representative was also deemed as too limited, a concern some Kenyan officials reject and claim far too political an involvement This self-critical evaluation by the Bank placed part of the blame for the failure upon its own institutional shortcomings.

Kenya opened its portfolio with the African Development Bank Group in 1964. An AfDB official indicated that poverty reduction was the chief priority for the organization. According to this official, the bulk of current AfDB loans, approximately 75 percent, are dedicated to infrastructure projects, especially highways, international transport routes, and energy infrastructure. The AfDB also provides resources for agriculture and social sector investments. A limited amount of some five percent is dedicated to institutional support such as public finance management. Approximately 95 percent of loans are concessional, 40 year loans. The total portfolio currently allocated for Kenya is $600 million.

The African Development Bank is considered the lender of last resort by some observers in Kenya. Its reputation is that of a lender with more lenient rules for its financing arrangements. According to the Bank Information Center, the AfDB group operates with a degree of opacity that has raised the concern of observers in civil society. Staff also heard from donors that the AfDB, although an important donor in Kenya and the region, is the least constrained in its programming with the Kenyan government. Officials at the Kenyan Ministry of Finance lauded the AfDB as having an advantage in dealing with the government given its regional knowledge and ease of cooperation. AfDB officials indicate that their Bank is closer to the ground and its funding is "more flexible and consistent, so its predictability provides incentives as each three-year commitment is made clear at least a year ahead of time."

Although it brings considerable resources to Kenya, its staffing size naturally limits the degree to which it is able to conduct regular monitoring and oversight. The World Bank is much bigger and brings considerable technical assistance and knowledge to its headquarters in Nairobi, while the AfDB has a much smaller footprint. Nonetheless, the AfDB indicated that the organization's Country Policy and Institutional Assessment (CPIA), is done annuallyand informs a final measure of eligibility for funding.

An area in which the AfDB seeks to mitigate risk is also an area of significant fraud and misappropriation in Kenya—the procurement agencies. AfDB's insistence on the use of its procurement process may well relieve considerable risk from the Kenyan equation. Nonetheless, the Mars Group indicated that significant inconsistencies existed in the procurement of materials and services surrounding the transport sector in which the AfDB was engaged. There is also the AfDB requirement that Kenya must perform audits on its programs even as the Bank does them itself based on internally selected risk factors. Finally, AfDB officials indicated that their resources were provided and listed in the government budget but were ring-fenced until the project task manager clears their disbursement.

As it is, the AfDB official in Nairobi claimed that there were few if any problems with any of their projects—"there have been no major corruption events." This seemed remarkable given the extent of confirmed corruption throughout the government and especially across donor project finance.

Lebanon: Manipulation of Crises[48]

Lebanon is still recovering from the 2006 war between Israel and Hezbollah, which left much of southern Lebanon and other parts of the country in ruins. The 2007 fighting between Lebanese Armed Forces and Fatah al-Islam at the Nahr al-B arid Palestinian refugee camp led to further casualties and damage. According to the State Department, over \$3.7 billion in civilian infrastructure was destroyed in both conflicts and thousands were displaced.

In 2009, a lengthy period of negotiations to form a national unity government followed the June 7th elections and resulted in five months of inertia, as the caretaker government was not empowered to make any significant decisions, including on security assistance and international financial institution lending. Further complicating matters, the Parliament has not passed a budget for the past five years. Official guidance allows Ministries to spend 1/12 of the previous year's expenditures each month, but a widening deficit suggests that more is being spent. Moreover, the substantial off- budget aid that the Government of Lebanon (GOL) is believed to receive is not accounted for, contributing to a general lack of fiscal accountability.

The problem of official corruption was a recurring theme during a recent staff visit, with several interlocutors pointing to an overall lack of transparency, fueled by a lack of accountability in the official budget process, as well as off-budget revenues and expenditures. Many observers also perceive an unhealthy influence of the country's confessional political system on the apportionment of state resources. Speaking to the specific problems of corruption in the management of international donor assistance, one official charged that, "The entire system is corrupt and inefficient." He attributed some of the problems to a "shopping list approach" to foreign aid, and the absence of national priorities or a commitment to exploiting synergies.

Another interlocutor with whom staff met opined that, in the face of a succession of crises, the GOL has become a master at manipulating international donors, relying on hand-outs rather than taking on much-needed structural reforms. "The whole international community has been blackmailed for ages. We don't need more money. We need to change the rules of the game. We need to change the structure. We need to break our dependence on foreign aid."

Without minimizing the seriousness of the crises that Lebanon has confronted in recent years, IFIs should guard against missing opportunities for change that crises present. While crises can be used as an excuse for inaction, they can also be catalysts for addressing difficult issues. Against the backdrop of Lebanon's recent political and economic difficulties, the IFIs should press for reforms that address Lebanon's current economic development challenges and help prevent future crises. In addition, as in any post-conflict or current conflict country, the IFIs should utilize a conflict screen to ensure that their financing will not exacerbate the conflict or underlying hostilities.

Lesotho: Demonstrating the Need to SupportInvestigations and Prosecutions

Many in Lesotho felt that the World Bank gave an inadequate response to corruption related to the Lesotho Highlands Water project (LHWP), to which the World Bank provided more than $150 million. In 2004, the World Bank debarred one company, Acres International, for three years as well as one individual. Two years later the World Bank debarred Lahmeyer International, for up to seven years, after the Senate Foreign Relations Committee invited Guido Penzhorn to testify about his conviction of companies and individuals for bribing the head of LHWP.

Several members of civil society and government officials were dissatisfied with the length of the Acres International debarment. They were concerned that the World Bank mitigated the debarment because "Acres had already been ordered to pay a criminal fine by the Lesotho courts and that the relevant persons involved in Acres' work on the LHWP are no longer in positions of responsibility in the company." They noted that Acres was the only convicted company that had not yet paid its complete fine.

While the World Bank allowed the companies convicted of bribery to attend their Sanctions Committee hearing, they did not allow the government of Lesotho to send a representative or prosecutor to attend the hearing and summarize the volumes of evidence that were presented at trial according to the Chief Justice of Lesotho, the Attorney General of Lesotho, and the chief prosecutor in the LHWP bribery cases.

Lesotho spent a significant amount of money to prosecute a number of companies for bribery related to the LHWP. However, despite an earlier assertion by World Bank staff that the World Bank could contribute to the cost of prosecution because the "bank has deep pockets," the World Bank did not provide any funding to assist the government in addressing the bribery allegations. The World Bank did not provide funding because it did not have a mechanism to loan or grant money to pay for a prosecution, according to World Bank staff.

The U.S. Embassy was praised by the Chief Justice of Lesotho for its assistance during the period of the trials for providing funding for internet access and Lexis-Nexis (a web-based legal research tool) so that the judiciary could access the most recent and relevant legal research. This information tool was not biased towards or against a conviction, it simply allowed the government of Lesotho access to important international legal information.

When visiting the Katse Dam in Lesotho in August 2004, Committee staff met with a number of villagers that were not satisfied with the compensation they received for the impact of the dam on their livelihood. Compensation packages are determined by the implementing agency in a country and are designed to meet World Bank safeguard policies. In addition to involuntary resettlement safeguard policies, the World Bank applies safeguards policies regarding indigenous peoples, cultural property, dam safety, pest management, environment, forests, natural habitat, waterways and disputed areas to project lending. However, policy-based lending (also called budget support or adjustment lending), does not incur safeguards.

If an affected person is not satisfied with the compensation package they are assigned, they must appeal to the implementing agency. If the implementing agency does not act, the affected people do not have recourse through the project. An instrument for recourse is not a requirement of the World Bank safeguards. The implementing agency suggested that affected people can appeal to the Ombudsman. The Office of the Ombudsman did not receive funds or additional staffing through the LHWP project. The Ombudsman said that a project tribunal to hear the complaints of affected people would have been helpful.

Near the Katse Dam, Committee staff visited a number of villages that were impacted by the Lesotho Highlands Water project. The agreement between Lesotho and South Africa stipulates that no person be made worse off by the Lesotho Highlands Water Project. Nevertheless, there are a number of impacts on the villagers that are difficult to address.

Reportedly, the HIV/AIDS rate in the project area is higher than the 29 percent HIV/AIDS rate in the rest of Lesotho because the disease was transmitted by dam construction workers to the villagers.

The dam created a barrier that hampers access of villages like Mapeleng to Katse town where there are medical, social and economic resources. Affected villagers said that they must now either pay to cross the dam, pay for a taxi or walk for many hours to reach Katse. Villagers expressed concern about a Lesotho Highlands Development Authority-imposed licensing fee for people who want to fish on the Katse dam. As many villagers are subsistence farmers, raising cash to fish or for transportation is a significant challenge. Finally, some villagers complained that the springs that they used to depend on dried up after the construction and filling of the Katse dam. They noted with irony that they had a view of clean mountain water destined for South African taps but that they lost their access to safe water.

The Asian Development Bank's Lackof Success in the Philippines

The AsDB did a review of its portfolio in the Philippines, a country with, by many accounts, a major corruption problem, and found that of projects begun since 1986, following the fall of dictator Ferdinand Marcos, fewer than one-third had been judged successful, one of the worst success rates of the AsDB. The report enumerated a number of causes for this poor performance, but corruption was not explicitly or even implicitly cited. When asked if this was because the bank didn't want to offend the Philippines or if it was indeed the fact that no corruption was involved in any of the 36 cases, officials said they were convinced it was the latter. They said that while there is corruption in AsDB projects in other countries, there was none in the Philippines. Said one, "Has the effectiveness been affected by corruption? Yes. Has the money leaked out? No."

He contended that corruption, inefficiency, lack of capacity, etc., in various Philippine government institutions, at the national and local level, might delay or impede projects, and there might be losses of Philippine government counterpart funds, which are not as well protected. "It's not our funds, it's the other players'," he said. (The problems in the portfolio, which has subsequently been cleaned up, were caused by a rush of money to support the post-Marcos democracy, resulting in the AsDB attempting "too many projects, which were too complicated, too quickly," officials said. In a letter to the SFRC, the Philippine government likewise listed a number of reasons other than open corruption for the poor performance of the projects. Both sides outlined steps that have been taken to improve the situation, one of which is to be much more careful about approving projects. The AsDB says it now starts only about one new project per year in the Philippines.)

It may well be that the AsDB is correct and there was no corruption involving AsDB funds in any of the failed programs, or it may be that by taking an overly restrictive view of what constitutes corruption, ignoring the great difficulty in detecting it, the AsDB is able to claim a better record on corruption than is warranted.

The European Bank for Reconstruction andDevelopment's Overexposure to Russia

Russia receives by far the largest amount of money from the EBRD. As part of the 2006 Capital Resources Review (CRR), the EBRD's five year strategy said Russia should get up to 41 percent of its business volume by the end of the period (up from 31 percent at the start). The advanced countries' share would drop from 15 per cent to 6 percent, reflecting the intent to graduate most of them, and the share for the others (Central Asia, the Balkans) would be largely unchanged at about 53 percent. It is generally understood that this large share for Russia (which was set before the 2007-08 spike in energy prices greatly enriched Russian coffers) was accepted by the Americans in the CRR, at the behest of the Europeans, because the Americans chose to concentrate their efforts on obtaining graduation of the EU-8. In 2008, the EBRD's business volume in Russia was 36 percent, and by the end of 2009 it was expected to be in a similar range, although at the end of August 2009 the figure was 28 percent.

As Russia's commodity-based economy surged in recent years and its large conglomerates, often dominated by persons with apparent political connections, consolidated and expanded their operations, the office of the U.S. Executive Director (USED) began to express growing concern about volume of lending to Russia and the appropriateness of some of the EBRD's clients there. Senator Lugar, upon returning from an "energy tour" of several Central Asian countries, wrote to the EBRD in early 2008 asking if the large volume of lending to prospering Russia was shortchanging the former Soviet republics in Central Asia that were far less developed, and whether the bank was devoting sufficient staff resources to generating projects in these more difficult environments. Outsiders, too, were raising questions about the need for so much lending to Russia, the world's largest energy exporter and holder of the third largest foreign exchange reserves. A November 2007, Wall Street Journal op-ed noted, "With a significant chunk of the EBRD's funds now directed toward financing for companies controlled by the Russian state, Kremlin-friendly oligarchs and large public companies such as Lukoil, it is increasingly difficult to see how these investments are consistent with the bank's goal of furthering pluralism, multiparty democracy or market economics. Russia doesn't need the money—at least, not from the EBRD. .[It] is increasingly wealthy, boasting more than $440 billion in foreign reserves, including over $110 billion allocated to its sovereign wealth funds. This summer, Russia even announced the creation of its own $10 billion Russian Development Bank to invest in the same types of projects as the EBRD itself." At the same time, many observers have noted, the gusher of income from oil and gas sales was reducing the pressure on the Russian government to continue with the wide-ranging economic and governance reforms it had embarked upon after the1998 economic collapse. "You only reform when you feel the pain," one IFI manager said.

EBRD officials insist that the nearly 250 projects they have signed with Russia over the past three years are helping reform the economy, expand markets, diversify the product mix, and bring better governance and competition to a host of sectors. "When we invest in Russia, we get something back in terms of transition impact," one top official told staff. Another said, "We invest in Russia for the same reason the Nunn-Lugar program spends money in Russia-to get them to do things they would not otherwise do because it is in our interest that they do them." They say that contrary to the characterization, few loans go to the firms of the so-called oligarchs, only 14 percent go to state companies, and that increasingly the money is going to regions outside Moscow and St. Petersburg, where needs are greatest. (From 2005 to 2008, annual investments outside those two centers rose from 68 percent of the total to 94 percent, according to the bank's figures.) The EBRD has been a big player in the railways, ports, and power sector. Where critics might view this as propping up state-linked monopolies, the bank sees this activity as implementing large scale reform by investing in commercial subsidiaries, private rail operators, and improving corporate governance and transparency in transportation, and by helping privatize generating companies, and investing in safer, cleaner and more efficient power plants. A restructured, more flexible power sector has follow-on benefits throughout the economy in terms of transition, one official explained: "One of the biggest problems facing a start-up small or medium enterprise is getting access to the electricity grid."

The EBRD is investing significantly in the Russian energy sector, hardly one that is unable to attract capital. But after gorging on cheap oil and gas for years, many Russian energy users are highly inefficient. The bank says that "Russia has been the largest single recipient of EBRD sustainable energy investment during Phase I of the bank's Sustainable Energy Initiative, representing 28.3 percent of the total cumulative SEI investments." This includes what the bank calls a "landmark" loan of 600 million euro to Severstal, a Soviet-era steel and mining behemoth that was privatized in the hectic early days of post-Communist Russia and is headed by Alexei Mordashov, a one-time Soviet-era manager of the plant who is now reputed to be one of Russia's richest so-called "oligarchs." Severstal employs 92,000 people worldwide; has operations in France, Britain, Italy and the United States (where it is the fourth largest American steelmaker); and is listed on the London Stock Exchange. The loan helped finance the company's "strategic energy efficiency program." The U.S. voted to abstain (the only naysayer) on this 2007 loan because, while it supported the goals of improving energy efficiency in the region, it felt that a company of Severstal's strength could have obtained private financing, and the company was already pursuing an energy efficiency strategy. (In fact, the U.S. has voted "abstain" or "no" on the other three Severstal-linked loans made since 2002.) The bank also makes loans in the small business sector, and about a third of the portfolio is in the banking sector. Roughly a third of the EBRD's Russia investments in 2008 were equity or quasi-equity stakes.

The EBRD's own annual indices provide a mixed picture of accomplishment at the macro level in Russia. While some areas are already at the top of the scale-the index of small-scale privatization and the index of price liberalization-others have stubbornly refused to improve, or have even worsened slightly. For instance, the index of large-scale privatization fell from 3.3 in 2002 to 3.0 in 2005, where it remains today. The index of competition policy has remained stuck at 2.3 since 2002, as have the "roads" component of infrastructure reform and the enterprise reform index. The index for railways, where the EBRD has put in much effort, has steadily improved from 2.3 to 3.0, and the power sector index has done even better, from 2.3 to 3.3.

The EBRD is aware, of course, that Russian tycoons control many corporate assets that were formerly state-owned in Russia (and similarly, if to a lesser degree, in other former Soviet republics), and that the stories of how they obtained control are not always clear. But bank officials have essentially decided that whatever happened in the murky past, right after the Soviet Union collapse when the World Bank and western governments were urging rapid privatization, should stay in the past. They have in effect drawn a line in history and judge their clients from that point forward. The EBRD says it does due diligence integrity checks on that basis and only does business with oligarchs who have proven their bona fides as legitimate corporate chieftains and entrepreneurs.

To better understand the issues regarding Russian lending, staff looked at loans not supported by the U.S. at Executive Board meetings, including one for 120 million euro in July 2009, to the conglomerate Sistema, controlled by Vladimir Evtoushenkov, listed by one account as Russia's 18th richest billionaire. A chemical engineer by training with a doctorate in economics from Moscow State University, he created the company in the 1990s by cobbling together a bunch of telecommunications, technology, and retail firms, the Soviet travel agency Intourist, as well as some oil interests. It now bills itself as "the largest public diversified financial corporation in Russia and the Commonwealth of Independent States (CIS), which manages companies serving over 100 million customers in the sectors of telecommunications, high-tech, oil and energy, radio and aerospace, banking, real estate, retail, mass-media, tourism and healthcare services." It is the largest mobile phone operator in Russia and the CIS, and its mobile company, Mobile TeleSystems (MTS), was listed on the New York Stock Exchange in 2000. Sistema itself is listed on the London Stock Exchange. Mr. Evtoushenkov, who is active on corporate governance issues, is credited by one British newspaper as having built the "most western" Russian conglomerate. The loan, billed in the EBRD's press release as "a shot in the arm for the high-tech sector at a time of tight credit," in part financed the sale of the EBRD's own equity interest in Sitronics, Sistema's electronic chips subsidiary, back to Sistema, and provided liquidity for Sitronics, which was facing a crisis-related credit squeeze. The U.S. voted to abstain, citing a lack of transition impact and the fact that 60 percent of the loan would be used to pay for EBRD's exit. (The loan went to Sistema because Sitronics itself couldn't qualify.)

This was actually the sixth investment that the EBRD had made in Sistema or its subsidiaries since 2004. The U.S. supported three of the other five, and abstained on the other two, in both cases arguing that a $17 billion a year company like Sistema could easily obtain commercial financing for the deals. The three it supported were to MTS for expanding or upgrading mobile phone service to underserved areas in rural Russia and the CIS countries. The bank said the Sitronics loan was part of its larger effort to help Russia diversify away from over-reliance on raw materials and develop "a knowledge economy" and that it was riding to the rescue of a long- time client, a solid company that ran into crisis-related trouble.

Staff interviewed Mr. Evtoushenkov, 61, at his offices near Red Square in Moscow. He said he was grateful for the loan and that his firm has developed good relations with the EBRD over the years. "They believe we are a very reliable partner," he said. He stated he has known all the EBRD presidents, and said he has never had any disputes or disagreements with the bank. Staff asked why he would seek financing from the EBRD, which doesn't offer concessional rates and often makes more demands than normal banks. "Some people may find it difficult to get a loan from them, but for us it is not difficult," he said. Prior to the crisis, he said, "We had no difficulties getting money," with about 40 percent of his company's financing coming from within Russia, the rest from foreign sources, including Asian banks. He said he was unaware that the U.S. had voted against some of the Sistema loans. He praised the EBRD's other work in Russia, especially its support for small and medium businesses, which, he said, have difficulty getting regular bank financing. Asked if he had any suggestions for improving the EBRD or changing the way it operates, he said he was quite satisfied with current arrangements, and urged that there be no changes until the current crisis is over. "Maybe after 2010 they could reconsider their strategy, but not today," he said.

Given Russia's size and importance, it is probably inevitable that it would receive a large portion of the EBRD's loans. It is also inevitable that there will be a political dimension to the bank's lending strategy. Given the EU's proximity to Russia, its much broader commercial engagement with the country, its heavy reliance on Russian gas to keep warm in the winter, and its member countries' tradition of state-backed investment programs, the Europeans are naturally more predisposed than the Americans (and others) toward an expansive view of the EBRD's involvement in the Russian economy. These two views will never be completely reconciled, but staff believes that by applying a more rigorous and transparent standard for lending decisions to Russia and adopting a principle similar to graduation for the Russia lending program the bank could come closer to a consensus on a way forward that would more equitably distribute its resources around the region and enhance its credibility among donor country taxpayers.

Additionality is the prime source of skepticism about the EBRD's activities in Russia. If the EBRD is doing things in Russia that "they would not otherwise do," (to quote the EBRD official above), taxpayers are reasonable in asking just why Russia isn't doing it and why the bank is. The EBRD should be especially transparent when it is lending to large state-owned or controlled enterprises like the railroads, or to the oligarchs. As Mr. Evtoushenkov said, during normal times he, and presumably most of Russia's tycoons, has ready access to commercial capital. It strains public credulity on additionality when the bank lends money to a private firm controlled by a man whose net worth is greater than the bank's annual profit in a good year. The bank should issue a detailed public policy statement on the additionality criteria and a step-by-step explanation of how the determination is made, and with each Russian investment include a statement on how the criteria were applied and the procedures followed.

Sri Lanka: The Need for Concerted Conflict Sensitivity[49]

Sri Lanka's economy suffered from the high cost of fighting its separatist war with the Liberation Tigers of Tamil Eleem (LTTE). Expensive purchases of war-related equipment and ammunition, often on longer-term contracts and using up valuable foreign reserves, coupled with a drop in exports due to the global economic downturn, pushed Sri Lanka to request a $2.6 billion stand-by arrangement from the IMF in early 2009 which was approved in July. The overall defense budget has yet to see any sort of "peace dividend." Longer-term contracts with foreign suppliers of military equipment, particularly China, continue to weigh heavily on the budget, and the military has pushed for an expansion of bases and personnel in the North. Some contend that a continued high level of troops is required in the formerly LTTE-held areas to hunt down remaining LTTE forces, seize hidden caches of weapons, and prevent any resurgence of violence. At the same time, military and civilian officials stressed to staff that the bulk of the requested increase of about 15 percent in the defense budget is due primarily to the government's need to pay down military debts incurred during the final stages of the war.

Donors have responded to the war's end by shifting their portfolios to the North and East of Sri Lanka. However, there is a chance that this could breed resentment in the South where there is still much poverty. While some international donors seemed to be artfully calibrating their operations in Sri Lanka so as not to exacerbate underlying tensions, others chose to ignore the conflict outright. U.S. government assistance has focused on conflict sensitivity and economic equity among all ethnic groups—Sinhalese, Tamil, and Muslim—and on addressing the regional economic imbalances in conflict-affected areas that have been amplified by the conflict.

World Bank staff in Sri Lanka, including Country Director Naoko Ishii and Senior Country Economist Claus Pram Astrup, should be commended on their development of a "conflict filter to enhance effectiveness and reduce reputational risks" at the concept design and implementation stages of projects. As laid out in the World Bank Sri Lanka Country Assistance Strategy Paper 2009- 20 12, the filter asks:

- Have sufficiently broad stakeholder consultations been conducted?
- Have adequate impartial grievance mechanisms been established?
- Are project management and administration adequately sensitive to inter-ethnic issues?
- Are conflict-generated needs adequately identified?
- Have opportunities to strengthen reconciliation and inter-ethnic trust been adequately identified?

World Bank staff noted that the filter had been a useful engagement tool. The Asian Development Bank as well as other international donors factor in conflict though in less formal ways.

However, the IMF does not officially consider conflict sensitivity at all and almost prides itself on its tunnel focus on financial indicators, although the IMF's mandate is macroeconomic stability— and a key factor to economic stability is resolution of war and conflict. On July 24, 2009, the IMF approved a $2.6 billion loan to support the Government of Sri Lanka's "ambitious program. to restore fiscal and external viability and address the significant reconstruction needs of the conflict-affected areas, thereby laying the basis for future higher economic growth." The IMF did not examine the possible impact of its program on the conflict in Sri Lanka. The IMF reportedly did not provide its Executive Board with a copy of the government's reconstruction program, a program which had not been shared publicly in Sri Lanka and received no input from civil society. Though the World Bank consults IMF assessment letters when it does significant budget support, the IMF did not reciprocate the consultation and incorporate the results of the World Bank's conflict filter.

IMF Resident Representative Koshy Mathai argued that although the government had used the IMF Letter of Intent as a vehicle to clarify its own reconstruction plans and humanitarian assistance and despite IMF staff interest in those issues, it was outside the IMF's mandate to have conditionality in political and military areas. He suggested that other international fora were more appropriate for addressing those concerns. The first of eight tranches (roughly $330 million each) of the loan was in the reserves at Central Bank as prescribed and the second tranche was also approved.

In addition, the IMF did not fully engage with Sri Lanka around issues of military spending. In October 1991, the IMF Executive Board discussed Military Expenditure and the Role of the Fund. While most Directors indicated that military expenditures "can have an important bearing on a member's fiscal policy and external position,. national security, and judgments regarding the appropriate level of military expenditures required to assure that security, were a sovereign prerogative of national governments and were not in the domain of the work of the Fund." [50] This is a discussion that should be revisited by the IMF Executive Board.

The Asian Development Bank's Inspection Panels

Two projects reviewed by AsDB inspection panels are illustrative of the bank's attitude. One, the $500 million Samut Prakarn wastewater project in Thailand outside Bangkok, led to numerous corruption-related charges by the Thai government against many senior officials of the project. (None of them were AsDB employees). The project is not only notorious in Thailand, where the Prime Minister at the time was quoted in the local press as saying, "This project is riddled with corruption" related to major, unapproved changes in the plans for the huge sewage treatment facility, land speculation, political influence peddling, gross overcharging, and selection of a site that posed major environmental hazards. It is also famous within the AsDB, which provided a portion of the financing. As one bank official explained to staff, "It became a very hot issue within the AsDB. Half the staff said nothing was wrong, half said there was. It paralyzed the board, which refused to find the bank at fault."

Aside from the many failures to follow AsDB procedures which led to the corruption, the bank's response to the corruption once discovered also has been found wanting. According to the Bank Information Center (BIC) report, a management mission to Thailand in 2000 "did not take the allegations seriously and was more concerned with defending management's previous decisions." As the case went on, the bank kept citing various bureaucratic and legalistic reasons why its various units could not tackle the corruption issues head-on. "Management's review of the project failed to find any evidence of corruption," the BIC report concludes, "and both the Inspection Panel and the Anticorruption Unit of the Office of the Auditor General declined to consider the issue at all. Moreover, the AsDB has never publicly commented on the results of the investigations by the Thai authorities, or the fact that the government has instituted criminal proceedings against so many senior officials on the project. Nor has AsDB taken any action in light of those findings, or launched a wider investigation of corruption on the project."

Bank officials noted that one major result of the controversy was to completely revamp the so-called "accountability mechanism" and replace the cumbersome Inspection Panel system with a more streamlined and user-friendly "accountability mechanism" that has an ombudsman—called a Special Project Facilitator (SPF)—and a Compliance Review Panel (CRP). An issue that bears monitoring is borrowing country cooperation with AsDB investigations: at the beginning of this controversy, the Thai government refused to admit members of the Inspection Panel into the country. This provoked protests from the U.S. representative and others, as well as formal expressions of concern from the board. The issue may have been resolved by the change in the Inspection Panel system (which was done with the site access issue very much in mind). At the time, the Panel was composed of outsiders, like the World Bank's Panel. Under the new system instituted in 2004, the Special Project

Facilitator is considered bank staff, and as such has a clear right to visit AsDB project sites. The Compliance Review Panel, while they are now also bank employees, are considered agents of the board and have to ask the host country for permission to enter.

A second revealing case was the outcome of a 2004 Inspection Panel on a large irrigation project in Pakistan, the Chasma Right Bank Irrigation Project Stage III, which found a number of areas where the bank failed to follow its own procedures regarding environmental impact and community consultation, among others. No allegations of corruption have so far surfaced. The panel found that AsDB management believes "the provisions of the 'internal laws' of the bank are not mandatory" and in this case chose to ignore them because they would cause delays. As the panel notes, "An internal law of the bank may be amended or repealed by the board" but not ignored at management's whim. "As long as it remains, there must be strict compliance.to hold otherwise would result in uncertainty and undermine the authority of the Board." Equally illustrative is management's response to the panel report, which was defensive and at times dismissive. Said one compliance official of the bank's response: "They shouldn't be in total denial of wrongdoing. It gives a very bad impression of the bank."

This accountability mechanism-the SPF and the CRP—is overdue for a required five-year review, with some saying there isn't enough data to review (which itself raises questions). Since 2004, only 25 cases have been brought to the SPF, but all except nine have been ruled ineligible. The SPF is supposed to act as a mediator to help resolve problems between the bank and the complainants, not as a tribunal. Requests to the CRP for compliance review must be preceded by the filing of a complaint with the SPF. Only three compliance requests have actually been filed with the Compliance Review Panel: one was determined by the CRP to be ineligible (a water supply project in Nepal), one is being reviewed by the CRP (an environmental project in Fuzhou, China, filed in June 2009), and in the third, a transport project in Sri Lanka, the AsDB was found to be non-compliant and the remedial action has been under "monitoring" by the CRP for four years. (The CRP also took over the monitoring of the Chasma project in Pakistan mentioned above. That monitoring was completed in 2009, and a final report is due in early 2010.) The new mechanism apparently suffers some of the same problems of access as the old one. In November of 2009, China denied the CRP consent to visit the Fuzhou project site to continue its review. According to the CRP's website, "the CRP then attempted to obtain further evidence via translator-assisted teleconferences with the Requesting Parties." Considering the significant amounts of money China has received from the Asian Development Bank (and the World Bank) over the years, it is disturbing that officials would block an investigation into the use of AsDB funds, and raises questions about whether they are trying to protect individuals who may have acted improperly. This development is all the more reason why the AsDB should commence an independent review of the accountability mechanism without further delay.

The office of the USED, which has been pushing hard against management inertia and working with Board colleagues to get the review underway, continues to encourage greater bank engagement with a range of stakeholders and noted to staff that, "according to some observers, it seems that Affected Persons (APs) still find it difficult to access the Accountability Mechanism; the Accountability Mechanism is not regarded as responsive to the concerns of APs, who are the intended beneficiaries of AsDB interventions; livelihoods are still considered to be at risk under some AsDB projects, especially infrastructure projects; and some stakeholders are still skeptical as to the Bank's commitment to governance and accountability and the 'independence' of the SPF and the CRP." Similar problems have been raised at the inspection panels of other banks.

Whenever (and if) the review is started, it will not be completed until after publication of this chapter. However, the USED's office and other stakeholders have raised a number of issues that should be addressed in the review, and Congress may want to use them as a checklist to help gauge how thorough the review process was and how effective it was in addressing concerns.

- Has the Accountability Mechanism achieved its 2003 ambition: i.e. has it become a less complex, transparent, independent, more efficient forum to handle complaints and consider compliance? And is it contributing to improved development effectiveness or has it enhanced the quality of AsDB projects?
- The AsDB has a dual phase system requiring APs to go through the consultation/problem-solving phase before requesting an investigation under the compliance review phase-is this two-step system appropriate; or should it be collapsed into a consolidated system (perhaps following the IFC/MIGA model)?
- Is the Accountability Mechanism truly "independent?" The SPF reports to the President, and the CRP reports to the Board, but the President is the Chairman of the Board. Many commentators questioned this arrangement and consider that this does not represent best practice.
- Independence also raises issues of budget, staffing, performance assessment, access to independent legal advice (not dependent on obtaining legal advice from the AsDB's General Counsel) and the right to engage experts and consultants (not dependent on processing by Central Operations Services Office.)
- The Accountability Mechanism policy requires at least two affected persons to initiate a complaint and compliance request (or for representatives to have clear authority to represent them), but an AsDB project may affect natural habitats, heritage sites, endangered species and so forth, where there may be no "affected persons," as such, to trigger the AM. Nevertheless, the AsDB must still be accountable and compliant in such cases. What can be done to guarantee the AsDB's accountability and compliance in such cases?

Yemen: Empowering Reform from within[51]

The World Bank has about $1 billion in existing projects in Yemen. The Bank's objective in Yemen is to facilitate Yemen's further progress toward the Millennium Development Goals. These goals, in turn, are in sync with the stated goals of the Republic of Yemen Government (ROYG), as articulated in the National Reform Agenda, the focus of which is on human development, including education and health; water resource management; and good governance. The National Reform Agenda, however, was developed with substantial input from the international donor community.

Although successful projects can be externally driven, the potential for success increases when IFIs support "locally owned" initiatives. Locally owned reform processes entail participation—and buy-in—from the local community and government in development projects. When there are in-country efforts to solve endemic problems, IFIs should foster and support these endeavors. An examination of the current situation in Yemen reveals that IFIs have opportunities to incorporate these types of locally owned initiatives into their planning and implementation strategies.

One potential opportunity to engage with the ROYG is through locally owned development and poverty reduction planning. Unhappy with the slow pace and uneven results of ROYG reform efforts, a small group of largely Western-educated and well-connected intellectuals and technocrats, under the auspices of the President's son, developed a targeted action plan to focus the government's short- to medium-term reform efforts. This group took into consideration the Government's Third Five-Year Plan for Poverty Reduction, as well as other existing plans and strategies, but determined that these various plans sought to take on too many challenges at once.

Therefore, the group independently developed 10 priorities on which the ROYG should focus for the next year. The 10 points are not perfect; they do not address head on the need to eliminate government subsidies for diesel, for example, relying instead on a strategy of seeking lower prices on the international market to reduce costs. That said, because this plan is "locally owned," in the words of one of its drafters, it stands a greater chance of success than reforms mandated by foreign donors. IFIs and the international donor community should work to empower and support this model and invest in similarly structured endeavors.

Another opportunity to support locally owned initiatives is by encouraging investment in the private sector. Increased foreign direct investment (FDI), as well as domestic investment, will be critical if Yemen is to create needed jobs—and hope for the future—among its increasing population of young job seekers. According to the 2009 report of the UN Conference on Trade and Development, Yemen is experiencing a downward trend in FDI inflows. Gross domestic investment as a percentage of GDP has also declined over the past two years.

In the face of falling oil revenues and its rapidly depleting oil sector, the ROYG had been putting its hopes in the development of the liquefied natural gas (LNG) sector. As the Country Director for the International Finance Corporation put it, however, the slump in the international market for LNG renders this strategy no longer viable. He made the case that, "If Yemen's economic development prospects are to have any success, it will be as the result of very time-consuming, hard-slogging micro-financing." There are no quick fixes. Right now, he said, there is no coordination among donors on private sector development. Nor were there any micro-finance banks based in Yemen, although one—al-Amal—has announced plans to open there.

To the extent that micro-finance banks need to be induced to enter the Yemeni market, IFIs should provide incentives. The IFIs should work in conjunction with the ROYG to focus more attention—and resources—on private sector development. The International Finance Corporation (IFC) has thus far provided business education training to 26,000 graduates, many of whom will become trainers themselves. Such activities should be expanded and built upon on a national and local level to realize reform and development goals.

Transparency and the European Bank forReconstruction and Development

At the EBRD, which lends almost exclusively to the private sector, officials have sometimes defended non-disclosure practices as being necessary to protect a firm's competitively significant data. Staff appreciates this concern, but believes that it is used to justify keeping far too much information from public scrutiny. Staff has looked at some internal EBRD documents and believes that in many cases it would be a simple matter to "scrub" the documents of commercially sensitive information. The EBRD in 2006 updated its Public Disclosure Policy, the cornerstone of its transparency efforts, yet the U.S. abstained when the policy came up for board approval. The USED felt, as did a number of NGOs, that while an improvement over the previous policy, the new one did not go far enough, perhaps reflecting the strong desire of the bank's private sector client base for maximum confidentiality. The new public information policy didn't require disclosure of board votes, for instance, and it maintained a poor appeal process for those who feel they were wrongly denied access to information. The exercise demonstrated, as one NGO member put it to staff, "The EBRD is not willing to accept a presumption of disclosure."

The EBRD should take a number of concrete steps to improve transparency. First, the bank should develop and publicize an explicit set of criteria for the advanced countries to "graduate" from EBRD lending. Currently, the only former EBRD client to graduate is the Czech Republic, which did so in 2007. Seven other EU clients were also expected to graduate by 2010, but that was put off when the financial crisis hit-yet there were no public benchmarks to justify the decision. (Why, for instance, didn't Poland graduate, since it escaped the recession that hit other Central European countries?). Making the graduation criteria public and clearly defined would help mobilize public opinion within client countries to press for change. Once graduation is understood in the markets to be a rigorous and objective standard, countries that meet the criteria would be rewarded with improved risk ratings and better access to global capital markets. From the point of view of taxpayers and legislators in donor countries, having an explicit graduation goal and orienting all the bank's operations toward reaching it would make clear that the EBRD is not trying to build an empire or perpetuate its existence, but rather working conscientiously to put itself out of business. This would help clear up questions about the bank's long-term mandate.

Second, the EBRD should be more transparent about the potential "transition" impact of it loans and investments, since its mandate is to hasten the implementation of capitalist structures, not to be just another commercial lending fund. Staff recommends more transparency and detail in how the potential transition impact ratings are disclosed for each project. Currently on the website there is a brief, two-line description of the transition impact, but more specific information available to those inside the bank, such as a rationale for the loan, its additionality, the downside transition risks, etc., is not disclosed, apparently because "commercially sensitive" information might be revealed. Likewise, staff recommends that the U.S. (and other donors, for that matter) give more detailed explanations for their "abstain" or "no" votes, especially on large or controversial projects. For instance, the U.S. recently abstained on the largest single loan in EBRD history-$500 million to the Russian railway-without public explanation. Treasury officials said this policy of reticence has to do with internal board dynamics, but staff believes the taxpayer would be better served by bringing these debates out into the open.

Third, the EBRD should be more transparent regarding one of its other key mandates, namely, additionality, the principle that the bank should lend only to clients who cannot get reasonable financing elsewhere. The additionality criteria should be more transparent and more explicit, both as a statement of policy and on individual investments. (This is in addition to the earlier recommendation regarding more transparency in transition impact.) If EBRD is making loans to a resource-rich country like Russia because the government or private investors won't, taxpayers are reasonable in asking just why they aren't and why the bank is. The EBRD should be especially transparent when it is lending to large state-owned or - controlled enterprises like the railroads, or to the so-called oligarchs, the billionaires who control many business groups. It strains public credulity on additionality when the bank lends money to private firms controlled by very wealthy people.

The Inter-American Development Bank's Needto Strengthen Financial Management

Inter-American Development Bank is in the process of reforming its practices after its unrealized loss of $1.9 billion in 2007/2008 from its liquid portfolio of cash management instruments. After detecting the losses, Senator Lugar's staff has meet regularly with the Inter-American Development Bank to promote needed changes to the IDB's financial management to ensure that the losses do not recur.

Joshua Goodman of Bloomberg wrote an article "IDB's Losing Bets in U.S. Mortgages May Weaken Case for Funding" on March 21, 2009, excerpted below, which describes the issues around the financial losses:

> The Inter-American Development Bank failed to rein in managers who made losing bets in the U.S. mortgage market, including investments in securities issued by Countrywide Financial Corp., according to an outside consultant's findings reviewed by the IDB board today.
>
> The Washington-based bank, the biggest lender for infrastructure projects in Latin America, took a nearly $1 billion loss last year after plowing as much as 60 percent of its cash reserves into mortgage-backed securities, an unusually aggressive investment strategy that went "largely undetected" by agency officials, according to the review by Oliver Wyman, the consulting unit of Marsh & McLennan Cos.
>
> The weaknesses allowed the IDB to risk twice as much of its cash portfolio in asset-backed securities as the World Bank does, and 10 times as much as the Asian Development Bank, the consultant's review found.
>
> "You can't run these things like a hedge fund," said Morris Goldstein, a former deputy director of the International Monetary Fund's research department and senior fellow at the Peterson Institute for International Economics in Washington. "Portfolios of official lenders have to be very conservative."
>
> Wyman recommended possibly hiring outside financial managers, the "urgent" improvement of oversight and the establishment of guidelines so assets have a "high probability of being liquid in the most adverse market conditions."
>
> IDB Chief Financial Officer Ed Bartholomew disputed the consultant's findings, saying the mortgage and asset-backed securities peaked at 42 percent, not 60 percent, of its investment portfolio. After writing down the securities by an average 25 percent, the figure

fell to 26 percent at the end of 2008, he said. More than 99 percent continue to perform and about 85 percent carry the top AAA credit ratings, he said.

'No Material Effect'

"The magnitude of these unrealized losses has no material effect" on the bank's ability to lend, Bartholomew said in an interview today. "Any capital increase would be driven by a long-term vision about the kind of lending we want to support."

The IDB's bets were fueled by pressure to increase returns on what were supposed to be highly liquid investments, the consultant's review found. That led to the purchase of two Countrywide Financial mortgage-backed securities in October 2007, after the collapse of the subprime mortgage market had already caused the mortgage lender's shares to plunge more than 50 percent, according to the review.

"It's surprising how far they invested in these toxic assets," said Claudio Loser, former director of International Monetary Fund's Western Hemisphere department and now a fellow at the Inter-American Dialogue in Washington. "In hindsight it was a stupid decision."

Lugar's Concern

Senator Richard Lugar of Indiana, the ranking Republican on the Foreign Relations Committee, said the strategy was of "grave concern" and sought explanations in a Feb. 5 letter to IDB President Luis Alberto Moreno. A copy was provided by Lugar's office.

"It would be premature to consider a capital increase before Congress is assured that the IDB's financial structures and controls are robust and that necessary reforms have been implemented," Lugar said in an e-mailed statement today.

"The IDB is making a 'tremendous effort' to increase donations from members this year so it can approve a record $18 billion in loans," Moreno, 55, said in a March 5 interview published on the IDB website. A commission of outside experts headed by former Peruvian finance minister Pedro Pablo Kuczynski will present its recommendations at the annual meeting.

"The IDB faces an uphill battle," Clay Lowery, a former assistant U.S. Treasury secretary for international affairs who is now a managing director of the Glover Park Group in Washington, said in an interview today. "They are asking for a capital increase, which is important to Latin America, at a time when it appears that they had taken significant risks in their trading book."

Lowery said the Treasury first raised concerns about the IDB's investment strategy in late 2007.

Funding Needs

Bartholomew said he couldn't discuss any plans for the capital increase request until they were discussed by the IDB's board.

The IDB needs more funding because Latin American and Caribbean countries are increasingly turning to the lender as the credit crisis deepens. Jamaica, on Jan. 16, became the third country following Costa Rica and El Salvador to tap a $6 billion emergency liquidity line the bank created last October.

Remittances to Latin America and the Caribbean from migrant workers are forecast to fall this year for the first time on record, as unemployment rises in wealthier nations. If the crisis persists two years, poverty could swell by as much as 12.7 million people, according to IDB estimates.

To help relieve some of the strain on social services, the IDB is aiming to approve a record $18 billion in loans, compared with last year's previous record of $11.1 billion.

"The IDB is very worried," said Loser. "For the first time in seven years, credit markets are closed to Latin America. They know they'll be called on to increase lending for the next two to three years."

APPENDIX I. U.S. ENGAGEMENT

Although the international financial institutions (IFIs) are run by their own managements, the member governments exercise policy direction and oversight responsibility. A board of governors for each IFI, representing all member countries, meets once a year to make policy decisions, while boards of executive directors meet more frequently to approve projects and supervise operations of the institutions.

As the largest shareholder in all of the IFIs except the Asian Development Bank, the United States takes an active oversight role. The U.S. Governor of all six institutions is the Secretary of the Treasury. The Treasury Department is the lead agency in charge of operational policy and the day-to-day conduct of U.S. participation in the IFIs.

The State Department also follows policy on the IFIs as it relates to U.S. political relationships. The Under Secretary of State for Economic, Energy, and Agricultural Affairs is the U.S. Alternate Governor for the multilateral development banks. For the International Monetary Fund (IMF), however, the Alternate Governor is the Chairman of the Federal Reserve.

The U.S. Executive Directors are appointed by the President and confirmed by the Senate. The Alternate Executive Directors are subject to Senate approval only for the IMF, the World Bank, and the Inter-American Development Bank (IDB). The Executive Directors and Alternates represent the United States at executive board meetings and report to the Secretary of the Treasury through the Assistant Secretary of International Affairs.

Other U.S. government agencies are also involved in oversight of the IFIs. The Working Group on Multilateral Assistance (WGMA) meets weekly to coordinate agency views on all loan proposals scheduled for consideration by the executive boards of the multilateral development banks during the following two weeks. Chaired by the Treasury Department, these meetings include representatives from the State, Agriculture, and Commerce Departments, USAID, Federal Reserve Board, and the Export-Import Bank.

In addition to the confirmation of Executive Directors through the Senate Foreign Relations Committee, the Congress determines the level of U.S. contributions to the IFIs. It can also pass legislation directing U.S. policy towards the IFIs. For instance, Congress has adopted laws requiring the Executive Directors to seek specified improvements in the institutions' treatment of environmental issues. In this regard, USAID reports to Congress on the environmental impact of IFI loans. Congress also requires the Treasury Department to report to the appropriate congressional committees on the actions taken by each IFI to implement the policy goals specified in legislation.

APPENDIX II. THE INTERNATIONAL FINANCIAL INSTITUTIONS

International Monetary Fund

The International Monetary Fund (IMF) was created at the 1944 Bretton Woods Conference in New Hampshire to prevent a return of the international financial chaos that preceded World War II. Its formal mission is to "foster global growth and economic stability," provide "policy advice and financing to members in economic difficulties," and work "with developing nations to help them achieve macroeconomic stability and reduce poverty."[52]

The IMF has three principal functions and activities: (1) surveillance of financial and monetary conditions in its member countries and of the world economy, (2) financial assistance to address major balance of payments problems, and (3) technical assistance and advisory services to member countries.[53] Based in Washington, D.C., the IMF currently employs about 2,600 staff.

The IMF has developed various loan instruments, or facilities, that are tailored to address the specific circumstances of its diverse membership. The majority of IMF loans come from the General Resources Account (GRA), using one of two facilities: Stand-By Arrangements (SBA), which address short-term balance of payments problems, or the Extended Fund Facility (EEF), which focuses on longer-term difficulties with external payments.[54]

Low-income countries may borrow at a subsidized interest rate under new concessional financing facilities. Approved by the IMF Executive Board on July 23, 2009, these new facilities are intended to make financial support more flexible and tailored to the diversity of low-income countries. They replace the existing Poverty Reduction and Growth Facility (PRGF) and the Exogenous Shocks Facility (ESF), and will be organized under the umbrella of a new Poverty Reduction and Growth Trust. The three new lending windows are the Extended Credit Facility (ECF), which provides medium-term support; the Standby Credit Facility (SCF), which addresses short-term and precautionary needs; and the Rapid Credit Facility (RCF), which offers rapid low-access financing with limited conditionality to meet urgent balance of payments needs.[55]

The United States' total IMF quota is $337.2 billion. The United States is the largest shareholder with a quota of 37.15 billion Special Drawing Rights (SDRs),[56] worth approximately $57.7 billion, and a 16.77 percent voting share.[57]

In response to the global economic crisis, the G-20 nations agreed in April 2009 to triple the IMF's lending capacity to $750 billion, based on contributions from member countries. In June 2009, the U.S. Congress approved $108 billion in new loan authority for the IMF. Several other countries have pledged contributions to increase IMF resources, including, as of July 2009, Japan ($100 billion), European Union ($100 billion), Norway ($4.5 billion),

Canada ($10 billion), Switzerland ($10 billion), Republic of Korea ($10 billion), Australia($7 bilion), Russia (up to $10 billion), China (up to $50 billion), and Brazil (up to $10 billion).[58]

World Bank

Like the IMF, the World Bank was created as a result of the 1944 Bretton Woods Conference. Its initial purpose of rebuilding post-war Europe grew to encompass worldwide poverty alleviation and sustainable economic development. Currently focused on the achievement of the Millennium Development Goals, the World Bank aims to "fight poverty" and "to help people help themselves and their environment by providing resources, sharing knowledge, building capacity, and forging partnerships in the public and private sectors."[60]

The World Bank pursues these objectives through the provision of financial and technical assistance. More than 10,000 employees from over 160 countries work at the World Bank. Two-thirds are based at the headquarters in Washington, D.C., while the remaining third work in more than 100 country offices in the developing world.[61]

The World Bank divides its lending between the International Bank for Reconstruction and Development (IBRD) and International Development Association (IDA). The IBRD assists middle- income countries with loans at near-market rates using funds raised on the international capital markets. Established in 1960 due to concerns that low-income countries could not afford to borrow at near-market rate terms, the IDA provides concessional loans to the world's poorest countries. The IDA's highly discounted assistance is funded with contributions from donors and transfers from the IBRD and is increasingly provided as grants.[62]

As of June 30, 2008 (the end of the World Bank's fiscal year), total subscriptions to the IBRD were $157.43 billion. The United States is the largest contributor, having subscribed to $31.96 billion of the IBRD's capital stock. Of this amount, $2.0 billion is paid-in and $29.96 billion is subject to call.[63] The United States has a 16.36 percent voting share.[64]

As of June 30, 2008, total contributions to the IDA were $177.5 billion. The United States is also the largest contributor to the IDA, having subscribed or contributed $38.98 billion. The United States has a 12.71 percent voting share.[65]

The last general capital increase of the IBRD was agreed to in 1988, and the United States provided its final installment to the IBRD's capital in FY 1996. The most recent round of IDA replenishment negotiations (IDA-15) concluded on December 14, 2007.[66] At the meeting, donors agreed to provide $41.6 billion, an increase of $9.5 billion over the previous replenishment (IDA-14) ($32.1 billion). The United Kingdom pledged donations of $4.3 billion over three years, making it the largest single donor to IDA-15. The United States increased its pledge by 30 percent to $3.7 billion and will see its share rise from 13.8 percent to 14.7 percent. Several countries are contributing to IDA for the first time: China; Cyprus; Egypt; Estonia; Latvia; and Lithuania.[67]

Since their creation, cumulative IBRD lending is $446 billion and IDA commitments are $193 billion.

Table 1. International Monetary Fund Disbursements[59]
Billions of U.S. Dollars

	2000	2001	2002	2003	2004	2005	2006	2007	2008	2009
GRA	11.13	36.86	39.14	31.52	6.47	3.55	3.67	1.49	20.82	18.43
PRGF-ESF	0.76	1.35	2.09	1.32	1.26	0.63	0.78	0.51	0.99	1.42

Note: 2009 data as of June 30, 2009

Inter-American Development Bank

The Inter-American Development Bank (IDB) Group was co- founded by the United States and 19 other member countries in 1959 in response to social and political turmoil in Latin America and the Caribbean in the context of the Cold War. Based in Washington, DC, the IDB now has 26 borrowing members and employs approximately 2,000 staff.

The IDB aims to "combat poverty and promote social equity,"[69] providing loans and grants and offering policy advice and technical assistance. The IDB's primary lending window is non-concessional Ordinary Capital (OC). The Fund for Special Operations (FSO) is the concessional window of the IDB and focuses on economic development in the hemisphere's poorest nations: Bolivia, Guyana, Haiti, Honduras, and Nicaragua. The FSO makes subsidized loans with interest rates of 1 percent to 2 percent and maturities of up to 40 years.

As of December 31, 2008 (the end of the IDB's fiscal year), total subscriptions to the IDB were $100.9 billion. The United States is the largest contributor, having subscribed to $30.31 billion of the IDB's capital stock. Of this amount, $1.3 billion is paid-in and $29.01 billion is subject to call. The United States has a 30.01 percent voting share.[70]

The most recent general capital increase for the ordinary capital account and the FSO was in 1994. The U.S. contribution of $153.7 million was contributed in six equal installments over the 1995- 2000 period.[71] At a meeting on July 2, 2009, the IDB Board of Governors set a December 2009 deadline for technical discussions on a proposed capital increase and a replenishment of the FSO.[72]

Between 1961 and December 2008, the IDB approved $149.00 billion of operations from its Ordinary Capital and $18.52 billion from the FSO.

Table 2. World Bank Operations.[68]
Billions of U.S. Dollars

	2000	2001	2002	2003	2004	2005	2006	2007	2008	2009
IBRD	10.92	10.49	11.45	11.23	11.05	13.61	14.14	12.83	13.47	32.90
IDA	4.36	6.76	8.07	7.28	9.04	8.70	9.51	11.87	11.23	14.00

Note: 2009 data as of June 30, 2009

The International Financial Institutions: A Call for Change

Table 3. IDB Operations.[73]
Billions of U.S. Dollars.

	2000	2001	2002	2003	2004	2005	2006	2007	2008
IDB	4.969	7.411	4.143	6.232	5.468	6.448	5.632	8.577	11.085
FSO	0.297	0.443	0.406	0.578	0.522	0.41	0.605	0.152	0.138

African Development Bank

The African Development Bank (AfDB) Group was founded in 1964 "to help reduce poverty, improve living conditions for Africans and mobilize resources for the continent's economic and social development." It employs 1,491 employees in its headquarters in Tunis, Tunisia, and in 23 field offices.[74]

The AfDB Group comprises two main lending facilities. The African Development Bank provides grants, loans, and technical assistance. The African Development Fund (AfDF) is a concessional facility for low-income African member countries created in 1972. There are currently 38 AfDF borrower countries. The AfDF is primarily financed by 24 non-regional countries including the United States, Canada, and several European and Asian countries.[75]

The United States is the second largest shareholder after Nigeria. At current exchange rates, total U.S. paid-in capital through December 31, 2008 is approximately $220.4 million. Total callable capital is approximately $1.95 billion.[76] The United States has a 6.33 percent voting share.

The most recent general capital increase for the AfDB was in 1998. The total capital increase was approximately $7 billion, the U.S. share of which is 5.8 percent. The total U.S. paid-in capital commitment of $40.8 million was paid over 8 years ending in FY 2007. In December 2007, negotiations concluded for the eleventh replenishment of AfDF resources (AfDF-VI) that will provide financing of $8.9 billion during 2008 to 2011. The U.S. total three- year commitment for AfDF-11 is $468.2 million. In the current AfDF-11 replenishment, the U.S. share is 8.7 percent (behind the United Kingdom, Germany, and France).[77]

Between its inception in 1967 and December 2008, the AfDB approved approximately US$38.2 billion of operations and the AfDF approved approximately $28.0 billion.

Table 4. African Development Bank Group Operations.[78]
Billions of U.S. Dollars

	2000	2001	2002	2003	2004	2005	2006	2007	2008
AfDB	0.63	1.24	1.36	1.16	1.25	1.16	1.45	2.30	2.36
AfDf	1.01	1.46	1.08	1.54	1.42	1.54	2.13	1.70	2.55

Table 5. Asian Development Bank Group Loans.[80]
Billions of U.S. Dollars

	2000	2001	2002	2003	2004	2005	2006	2007	2008
AsDB	4.01	3.98	4.01	4.73	4.05	4.40	5.99	8.07	8.70
AsDF	1.57	1.36	1.65	1.38	1.24	1.36	1.27	1.89	1.79

Asian Development Bank

Founded in 1966, the Asian Development Bank (AsDB) aims "to help its developing member countries reduce poverty and improve the quality of life of their people." With headquarters in Manila, Philippines, and 27 field offices, it employs approximately 2,5C00 staff.[79] The AsDB's primary activities are extending project loans and grants, making equity investments, and providing technical assistance to its developing member countries.

The Asian Development Fund (AsDF), the AsDB's concessional facility, was created in 1972 to provide loans to Asia's poorest countries. The AsDF is funded principally through periodic replenishments by donor nations. There have been seven replenishments since the AsDF was created in 1972.

The United States and Japan are the largest shareholders, each owning $8.5 billion worth of shares in the institution. This ownership stake corresponds with a voting share of 12.76 percent. As of December 31, 2008, the United States has contributed $3.42 billion to the AsDF. Voting shares in the AsDF are the same as in the AsDB.

The most recent capital replenishment, AsDF-9, covers the years 2005 to 2008. Donors agreed to contribute $7 billion over the four- year period, an increase from the $5.7 billion provided during AsDF-8 (200 1-2004). Japan maintains its position as the leading AsDF contributor in AsDF-9 with $1.18 billion pledged, followed by the United States with $461 million, Australia with $218 million, and the United Kingdom with $202 million. Contributions from the Asia and Pacific region accounted for almost half of the replenishment.

The most recent general capital increase of the AsDB was agreed to in 1994. In April 2009, the Board of Directors (including the United States) approved a resolution providing for a new capital increase allowing for a 200 percent increase in the capital stock of the institution. It is expected that the administration may seek an increase in the U.S. paid-in capital for the institution over the next several years as part of the new general capital increase.

To date, the Asian Development Bank has approved $143.5 billion of operations.

European Bank for Reconstruction and Development

The European Bank for Reconstruction and Development (EBRD) is the newest of the multi-lateral development banks, founded in 1990 to help bring capitalism and market economies to formerly Communist eastern and central European countries and the new states from the former Soviet Union and Yugoslavia. (Mongolia was originally included, too, and

Turkey was added last year.) Unlike the other development banks, it does not have development or poverty alleviation as one of its stated missions, and it usually works with the private sector, state-owned companies or municipal entities, rather than with national governments. As a result, it has until now had little direct role in promoting economic or governance reforms outside of specific sectors. ''We are a project-driven bank,'' one official told staff in August 2009 during an interview in London. Also, uniquely, the EBRD applies a political standard to its clients, namely, that their countries are ''committed to and applying the principles of multiparty democracy, pluralism and market economics.''

EBRD investments, like those of the other development banks, take the form of loans, guarantees, and equity investments. The EBRD's loans are required to meet three criteria-that they have "transition impact;" that they provide additionality, that is, the client must be unable to get reasonable financing elsewhere; and that they be based on "sound banking principles." The EBRD does not have a concessional loan window like the other development banks, it takes commercial risk, and it nearly always gets its money back. In fact, in the three years before the current crisis, the bank turned handsome profits, up to more than two billion euros a year, leading to talk of a dividend for shareholders and raising questions about whether the bank was really necessary in the booming east. (That ended last year when the bank recorded its first annual loss since the Russian financial crisis of 1998.) There is an inherent tension between the additionality and sound banking requirements-if the investment is sound, why couldn't the client get the financing from someone else? Similarly, transition impact is sometimes difficult to define and quantify.

The United States is the largest shareholder in the EBRD. The United Kingdom is the second largest shareholder. As of December 31, 2008, the United States has committed approximately $2.7 billion. The United States has a 10.15 percent voting share.

The most recent general capital increase of the EBRD was agreed to in 1996. The U.S. share was $285 million. Since its founding, the EBRD has approved approximately $59.99 billion in operations.S6602

APPENDIX III. WORLD BANK LENDING AND PARLIAMENTARY APPROVAL

February 2009

Borrowing member countries which require parliamentary approval or ratification of lending instruments (loans, credits, IDA grants) with the Bank and IDA include those requiring approval or ratification of each loan or other agreement, and countries where parliament sets a ceiling within which the executive branch can conclude individual agreements without further approval or ratification.

Table 6. EBRD Operations.[81]
Billions of U.S. Dollars

	2000	2001	2002	2003	2004	2005	2006	2007	2008
EBRD	3.61	4.94	5.267	5.03	5.58	5.78	6.67	7.54	6.87

Sub-Saharan Africa

Angola, Benin, Botswana, Burkina Faso, Burundi, Chad, Comoros, Congo Brazzaville, Cote D'Ivoire, Democratic Republic of the Congo, Ethiopia, Gabon, Ghana, Guinea, Madagascar, Malawi, Mali, Niger, Rwanda, Senegal, Sierra Leone, South Africa, Sudan, Tanzania, Togo, Uganda, Zambia, Zimbabwe*
* in non-accrual, current status unclear. Current status of Liberia also unclear.

East Asia& the Pacific

Cambodia, China, Timor Leste, Republic of Korea, Indonesia,** Mongolia, Palau, Vanuatu
** parliamentary approval of development projects is given through annual budget law.

Eastern Europe& Central Asia

Albania, Armenia, Bosnia& Herzegovina, Bulgaria, Croatia, Georgia, Kazakhstan, Kyrgyz Republic, Macedonia, Moldova, Montenegro, Romania, Russia, Serbia, Tajikistan, Turkey, Ukraine

Latin America& the Caribbean

*Bolivia, Brazil, Colombia, Costa Rica, Dominican Republic, *** El Salvador, Guatemala, Haiti, Honduras, Mexico, Nicaragua, Paraguay, Peru, Trinidad & Tobago, Venezuela*
*** Ecuador currently unclear based on 2008 Constitution.

Middle East& North Africa

Algeria, Djibouti, Arab Republic of Egypt, Lebanon, Tunisia, Republic of Yemen

South Asia

None

Appendix IV. Inter-American Development Bank (IDB)

List of Countries That Require Legislative Authorizationor Ratification of IDB Loan Contracts
August 2009

Countries that Require Legislative Authorization or Ratification of IDB Loan Contracts (for Sovereign or Sovereign Guaranteed Loans)*

Legislative Authorization Required for Signing of Loan Contract	Legislative Ratification of Signed Loan Contract Required for Entry into Effect
Bahamas	Bolivia
Belize (> US$10 million)	Costa Rica
Brazil	Dominican Republic
El Salvador	El Salvador
Guatemala	Haiti
Honduras	Honduras
Venezuela	Nicaragua
	Paraguay

* The summary information included in the above chart was prepared by the Bank based on information provided, as of August 2009, by borrowing member countries concerning their approval of Bank sovereign (or sovereign-guaranteed) loans. The chart does not address the details of any applicable legislation or regulation, and there may be circumstances under which, depending on the details of a specific Bank operation, the rules summarized in the chart may direct a different conclusion. Further, the Bank does not represent itself as having the authority to interpret the laws of its member countries, and authoritative text on the subject of the chart should be provided by those member countries with respect to their own legislation.

Appendix V. Tables

Table 7. U.S. Contribution and Voting Shares in the Multilateral Development Banks.[82.]

	Contribution Share (percentage)	Voting Share (percentage)
World Bank Group		
IBRD	16.8	16.4
IDA	22.1	12.9
IFC	24.1	23.6
MIGA	18.9	15.1
Asian Development Bank		
AsDB	15.6	12.8
AsDF	12.6	12.8
EBRD	10.1	9.8
NADBank	50.0	50.0
Inter-American Development Bank		
IDB	30.3	30.0

Table 8. (Continued)

	Contribution Share (percentage)	Voting Share (percentage)
FSO	50.5	30.0
IIC	25.5	25.1
MIF	39.4	29.1
African Development Bank		
AfDB	6.4	6.4
AfDF	12.7	6.1
IFAD	13.6	13.6

Table 8. Development Bank Management's General Capital Increase (GCI) Requests as of January 13, 2010 (in millions of U.S. dollars)

Multilateral Development Bank	Current Sub-scribed Capital Base (dollars)	Proposed Increase (percent)	Proposed Increase Paid-in Capital (percent)	Implied Annual U.S. Paid-in Contribution over 5 years (dollars)
World Bank Group: IBRD (including SCI)* *	$190,000	30	6	$655
World Bank Group: IFC***	2,400	85	100	482
AfDB	38,000	200	6	270
EBRD	30,000	50	10	150
IDB	101,000	200	4	2,420
AsDB	50,000	200	4	535

* Paid in only. Budget estimates assume five year pay-in period.

** IBRD includes approx. annual cost of a selective capital increase (SCI) to maintain shareholding at $23 million.

***The IFC does not have callable capital.

Source: Treasury Department Staff

Table 9. Projected Net Private Financial Flows to the Emerging Markets and Estimates of MDB Lending, With and Without Implementation of Management's General Capital Increase (GCI) Requests
Net private flows to emerging markets* ($ billion)

	2007	2008	2009(f)	2010(f)
Total	1252	648	348	672
Latin America	229	132	100	151
Emerging Europe	446	270	20	179
Africa/Middle East	155	75	37	69
Emerging Asia	422	171	191	273

* Source: IIF, http://www.iif.com/emr/article+204.php

Table 10. Regional MDB Commitments* ($ billion)

	2007	2008	2009(f)	2010(f)
Total	29.3	31.8	50.2	48.1
IDB with GCI	8.7	11.2	15.1	16.0
EBRD with GCI	8.0	7.4	11.9	14.1
AfDB with GCI	2.6	2.7	10.3	5.3
AsDB with GCI	10.0	10.5	12.9	12.7
Total w/o GCIs	29.3	31.8	50.2	27.5
IDB without GCI	8.7	11.2	15.1	12.0
EBRD without GCI	8.0	7.4	11.9	9.0
AfDB without GCI	2.6	2.7	10.3	2.5
AsDB without GCI	10.0	10.5	12.9	4.0

* Source: MDBs, U.S. Treasury Department estimates

APPENDIX VI. SENATE FOREIGN RELATIONS COMMITTEE HEARINGS CHAIRED BY SENATOR LUGAR

With the intent of strengthening reforms at the multilateral development banks (MDBs), particularly those related to corruption, Senator Lugar chaired six Senate Foreign Relations Committee hearings in the 108th and 109th Congress on May 13, 2004, July 21, 2004, September 28, 2004, April 21, 2005, March 28, 2006, and July 12, 2006. The hearings included representatives from the Treasury Department, the United States Executive Directors to the MDBs, academics, non-governmental organizations and members of civil society. (A summary of recommendations from the hearings is available in Annex I.)

The following witnesses testified at the first hearing on Thursday, May 13, 2004, entitled "Combating Corruption in the Multilateral Development Banks:" Ms. Carole Brookins, U.S. Executive Director, The World Bank; Mr. Hector Morales, Alternate U.S. Executive Director, Inter-American Development Bank; Dr. Jeffrey Winters, Associate Professor, Northwestern University; Mr. Manish Bapna, Executive Director, Bank Information Center; Ms. Nancy Zucker Boswell, Managing Director, Transparency International USA; Professor Jerome I. Levinson, Distinguished Lawyer in Residence, Washington College of Law, American University. Written testimony is available at http://www.foreign.senate.gov/hearings/ 2004/hrg0405 13a.html

At the second hearing on Wednesday, July 21, 2004, named "Combating Multilateral Development Bank Corruption: U.S. Treasury Role and Internal Efforts," the following witnesses testified: The Honorable John B. Taylor, Under Secretary for International Affairs, Department of the Treasury; The Honorable Richard Thornburgh, Of Counsel, Kirkpatrick & Lockhart; Mr. Guido Penzhorn, Advocate and Senior Counsel, Durban Bar (South Africa); and Ms. Kimberly Ann Elliott, Research Fellow, Institute for International Economics. Written testimony is available at http:// www.foreign.senate.gov/hearings/2004/hrg 040721a.html

On Tuesday, September 28, 2004, at the third hearing called "Combating Corruption in the Multilateral Development Banks (III)," Mr. Bruce M. Rich, International Program

Manager, Environmental Defense and Dr. George Ayittey, Distinguished Economist in Residence, Economics Department, American University both testified. Written testimony is available at http:// www.foreign.senate.gov/hearings/2004/hrg040928p.html

The subsequent witnesses testified on Thursday, April 21, 2005, at the fourth hearing entitled "A Review of the Anti-Corruption Strategies of the African Development Bank, Asian Development Bank and European Bank on Reconstruction and Development:" The Honorable Paul Speltz, U.S. Executive Director, Asian Development Bank; The Honorable Mark Sullivan, III, U.S. Executive Director, European Bank for Reconstruction and Development; Mr. Hemantha Withanage, Executive Director Center for Environmental Justice Convenor, Sri Lankan Working Group on Trade and International Financial Institutions; and Mr. Tom Devine, Legal Director, Government Accountability Project. Written testimony is available at http://www.foreign.senate.gov/hearings/2005/hrg 050421 a.html

At the fifth hearing called "Multilateral Development Banks: Promoting Effectiveness and Fighting Corruption" on Tuesday, March 28, 2006, the following witnesses testified:

The Honorable Clay Lowery, Assistant Secretary for International Affairs, Department of the Treasury; The Honorable Cynthia Shepard Perry, U.S. Executive Director of the African Development Bank; Dr. William Easterly, Professor of Economics, Co-Director of the Development Research Institute, New York University; Dr. Ruth Levine, Acting President, Director of Programs and Senior Fellow, Center for Global Development; and Dr. Adam Lerrick, The Friends of Allan H. Meltzer Chair in Economics, Director of the Gailliot Center for Public Policy, Tepper School of Business, Carnegie Mellon University. Written testimony is available at http://www.foreign.senate.gov/hearings/2006/hrg060328a. html

At the sixth hearing named "Multilateral Development Banks: Development Effectiveness of Infrastructure Projects" on Wednesday, July 12, 2006, the following witnesses testified: The Honorable Clay Lowery, Assistant Secretary for International Affairs, Department of the Treasury; The Honorable Jaime Quijandra, Executive Director for Argentina, Bolivia, Chile, Paraguay, Peru and Uruguay, The World Bank; The Honorable Carlos Herrera Descalzi, Former Minister of Energy and Mines, Vice-Dean, National Engineers Association of Peru; Dr. Korinna Horta, Senior Economist, Environmental Defense; and Mr. Manish Bapna, Executive Director, Bank Information Center. Written testimony is available at http://www.foreign.senate.gov/hearings/2006/hrg060712a.html

APPENDIX VII. ACRONYMS AND ABBREVIATIONS

AfDF	African Development Fund
AfDB	African Development Bank
AFT	Transantiago Financial Administrator
AIDS	Acquired Immune Deficiency Syndrome
APs	Affected Persons
AsDB	Asian Development Bank
AsDF	Asian Development Fund
BIC	Bank Information Center
CIS	Commonwealth of Independent States

CPIA	Country Policy and Institutional Assessment
CPPR	Country Portfolio Performance Ratio
CRP	Compliance Review Board
CRR	Capital Resources Review
DIR	Detailed Implementation Review
EBRD	European Bank for Reconstruction and Development
ECF	Extended Credit Facility
EFF	Extended Fund Facility
EITI	Extractive Industry Transparency Initiative
ESF	Exogenous Shocks Facility
EU	European Union
EU-8	Poland, Czech Republic, Slovakia, Hungary, Estonia, Latvia, Lithuania, Slovenia
FDI	Foreign Direct Investment
FSO	Fund for Special Operations
G20	Group of 20 (Argentina, Australia, Brazil, Canada, China, France, Germany, India, Indonesia, Italy, Japan, Mexico, Russia, Saudi Arabia, South Africa, Republic of Korea, Turkey, United Kingdom, United States, and the European Union)
GAO	Government Accountability Office
GCI	General Capital Increase
GDP	Gross Domestic Product
GOI	Government of India
GOL	Government of Lebanon
GRA	General Resources Account
HIV	Human Immunodeficiency Virus
H.R.	House Resolution
IADB	Inter-American Development Bank
IBRD	International Bank for Reconstruction and Development
IDA	International Development Association
IDB	Inter-American Development Bank
IEO	Independent Evaluation Office
IFAD	International Fund for Agricultural Development
IFC	International Finance Corporation
IFI	International Financial Institution
IIC	Inter-American Investment Corporation
IMF	International Monetary Fund
LHWP	Lesotho Highlands Water Project
LNG	Liquefied Natural Gas
LTTE	Liberation Tigers of Tamil Eleem
MDB	Multilateral Development Bank
MDRI	Multilateral Debt Relief Initiative
MIGA	Multilateral Investment Guarantee Agency
MIF	Multilateral Investment Fund
MTS	Mobile TeleSystems
NADBank	North American Development Bank

OC	Ordinary Capital
OED	Operations Evaluation Department
ROYG	Republic of Yemen Government
PRGF	Poverty Reduction and Growth Facility
RCF	Rapid Credit Facility
SBA	Standby Arrangements
SCF	Standby Credit Facility
SDR	Special Drawing Rights
SEI	Sustainable Energy Initiative
SFRC	Senate Foreign Relations Committee
SPF	Special Project Facilitator
UN	United Nations
US	United States
USAID	United States Agency on International Development
USED	United States Executive Director
WGMA	Working Group on Multilateral Assistance

REFERENCES

Collier, Paul. (2009). *Wars, Guns and Votes*. New York, New York: Harper Collins Press.

Crocket, Andrew, et al. (2007). *"Committee to Study Sustainable Long- Term Financing of the IMF."* January, http:// www.imf.org/External/np/oth/2007/013107.pdf.

Fishman, Raymond, & Edward Miguel. (2008). *Economic Gangsters*. Princeton, New Jersey: Princeton University Press.

Government Accountability Office (GAO). (2008). *"International Monetary Fund Lending Programs Allow for Negotiations and Are Consistent with Economic Literature."* November. http:// www.gao.gov/new.items/d1044.pdf.

Government Accountability Office (GAO). (2009). *"The United States Has Not Fully Funded Its Share of Debt Relief, and the Impact of Debt Relief on Countries' Poverty-Reducing Spending Is Unknown."* January. http://www.gao.gov/new.items/d09162. pdf

Malan, Pedro, et al. (2007). *"Report of the External View Committee on Bank-Fund Collaboration."* February https://www.imf.org/ external/np/pp/eng/2007/022307. pdf

Manuel, Trevor. (2009). *"Committee on IMF Governance Reform."* March: http://www.imf.org/external/np/omd/2009/govref/ 032409 .pdf

Meltzer, Allan H. *"International Financial Institution Advisory Commission."* March 2000. http://www.house.gov/jec/imf/melt zer.pdf

Meltzer, Allan H. (2003). *"What Future for the IMF and the World Bank?"* June. http://www.house.gov/jec/imf/07-18-03.pdf

Thornburgh, Dick. et al. (2002). *"Report Concerning the Debarment Process of the World Bank."* August. http://siteresources. / PROCUREMENT / Resources/thorn burgh report. pdf

Thornburgh, Dick. et al. *"Report Concerning the Anti-Corruption Framework of the Inter-American Development Bank."* November 2008. http://idbdocs.iadb.org/wsdocs/ getdocument.aspx? doc num=1824265

The International Financial Institutions: A Call for Change — 103

Volcker, Paul A., et al. (2007). *"Independent Panel Review of the World Bank Group Department of Institutional* Integrity." September. http://siteresources. worldbank.org/NEWS/Resources/Vol-cker_Report_Sept._12,_for_website _FINAL.pdf

Weaver, Catherine. (2008). *Hypocrisy Trap: The World Bank and the Poverty of Reform.* Princeton, New Jersey: Princeton University Press.

Zedillo, Ernesto. (2009). *"Repowering the World Bank for the 21st Century: Report of the High-Level Commission on Modernization of World Bank Group Governance."* October. http:// siteresources.worldbank.org/NEWS/Resources/WBGovernance COM MISSIONREPORT.pdf

End Notes

[1] The International Monetary Fund, the World Bank, the African Development Bank, the Asian Development Bank, the European Bank for Reconstruction and Development, and the Inter-American Development Bank.

[2] http://www.whitehouse.gov/the_press_office/Statement-from-the-President-upon-igning-HR-2346

[3] http://www.imf.org/external/np/sec/pr/2009/pr0985.htm

[4] "The Global Financial Crisis: Analysis and Policy Implications," Dick K. Nanto, Coordinator, Specialist in Industry and Trade, Congressional Research Service, September 18, 2009 (RL34742)

[5] Communique´ Meeting of Finance Ministers and Central Bank Governors, United Kingdom, November 7, 2009 http://www.g20.org/Documents/2009_communique_standrews.pdf

[6] G-20 Leaders' Statement, The Pittsburgh Summit, September 24-25, 2009 http:// www.g20.org/Documents/pittsburgh_summit_leaders_statement_250909.pdf

[7] Communique´ Meeting of Finance Ministers and Central Bank Governors, United Kingdom, November 7, 2009 http://www.g20.org/Documents/2009_communique_standrews.pdf

[8] The G-20 includes: Argentina, Australia, Brazil, Canada, China, France, Germany, India, Indonesia, Italy, Japan, Mexico, Russia, Saudi Arabia, South Africa, Republic of Korea, Turkey, the United Kingdom and the United States.

[9] G-20 Leaders' Statement, The Pittsburgh Summit, September 24-25, 2009 http:// www.g20.org/Documents/pittsburgh_summit_leaders_statement_250909.pdf

[10] "Multilateral Development Banks: Promoting Effectiveness and Fighting Corruption," Senate Foreign Relations Committee hearing, Opening Statement by Senator Lugar, Tuesday, March 28, 2006, http://lugar.senate.gov/press/record.cfm?id=253172

[11] These points were enumerated in the Findings section of S. 1129 the Multilateral Development Bank Reform Act of 2005. The full text of S. 1129 may be found at: http://frwebgate.access_cong_bills&docid=f:s1129rs.txt.pdf

[12] The letter is available at http://lugar.senate.gov/sfrc/pdf/GAO_world_bank.pdf

[13] http://www.treas.gov/offices/international-affairs/intl/fy2010/budget-FY2010.pdf "The U.S. and the G-20: Remaking the International Economic Architecture," Senate Foreign Relations Committee hearing, Response from Secretary Geithner to Senator Casey's Question for the Record, November 17, 2009.

[14] "The U.S. and the G-20: Remaking the International Economic Architecture" Senate Foreign Relations Committee hearing, Response from Secretary Geithner to Senator Casey's Question for the Record, November 17, 2009.

[15] "Multilateral Development Banks: U.S. Contributions FY1998-2009," Jonathan E. Sanford, Specialist in International Trade and Finance, Congressional Research Service, January 27, 2009 (RS20792).

[16] "Multilateral Development Banks: U.S. Contributions FY1998-2009" Jonathan E. Sanford, Specialist in International Trade and Finance, Congressional Research Service, January 27, 2009 (RS20792).

[17] "The U.S. and the G-20: Remaking the International Economic Architecture," Senate Foreign Relations Committee hearing, Opening Statement by Senator Lugar, November 17, 2009.

[18] "Straus-Kahn calls for further IMF resource increase," *Reuters,* October 2, 2009, http:// uk.reuters.com/article/idUSTRE5912 DK20091002

[18] "Straus-Kahn calls for further IMF resource increase,'' *Reuters,* October 2, 2009, http://uk.reuters.com/article/idUSTRE5912DK20091002

[19] http://online.wsj.com/article/BT-CO-20091005-706072.html

[20] "AfDB Will Need a Capital Increase by 2011 to Address the Financial Crisis and its Development Mandate, says AfDB President," African Development Bank Group, December 3, 2009, http://www.afdb.org/en/news-events/article/afdb-will-need-a-capital-increase-by-2011-to-address- the-financial-crisis-and-its-development-mandate-says-afdb-president-4386/

[21] Joe Parkinson, "EBRD to Seek Funding Increase," *The Wall Street Journal,* September 30, 2009, http://online.wsj.com/article/SB125425896193950481.html

[22] "Ninth Capital Increase," Inter-American Development Bank, http://www.iadb.org/ CapitalIncrease/index.cfm

[23] Table 8.—Development Bank Management General Capital Increase (GCI) Requests as of January 13, 2010.

[24] "The U.S. and the G-20: Remaking the International Economic Architecture," Senate Foreign Relations Committee hearing, Response from Secretary Geithner to Senator Lugar's Question for the Record, November 17, 2009.'

[25] Excerpt from President Obama's signing statement (http://www.whitehouse.gov/ the _press _office/Statement-from-the-President-upon-signing-HR-2346):—"It [the Act] also expands the resources available to the International Monetary Fund (IMF) by allowing it to boost its lending ability. Many developing countries are experiencing severe economic decline and a massive withdrawal of capital, and the IMF needs to make sure it has the resources necessary to effectively respond to the current financial crisis. However, provisions of this bill within sections 1110 to 1112 of title XI, and sections 1403 and 1404 of title XIV, would interfere with my constitutional authority to conduct foreign relations by directing the Executive to take certain positions in negotiations or discussions with international organizations and foreign governments, or by requiring consultation with the Congress prior to such negotiations or discussions. I will not treat these provisions as limiting my ability to engage in foreign diplomacy or negotiations."

[26] "The U.S. and the G-20: Remaking the International Economic Architecture," Senate Foreign Relations Committee hearing, Response from Secretary Geithner to Senator Lugar's Question for the Record, November 17, 2009.

[27] "Building on International Debt Relief Initiatives" Senate Foreign Relations Committee hearing, Opening Statement by Senator Lugar, Thursday, April 24, 2008, http://lugar.senate.gov/ press/record.cfm?id=296717; "Multilateral Development Banks: Promoting Effectiveness and Fighting Corruption," Senate Foreign Relations Committee hearing, Opening Statement by Senator Lugar, Tuesday, March 28, 2006, http://foreign.senate.gov/testimony/2006/Lugar Statement060328.pdf

[28] "Review of the Anti-Corruption Strategies of the Regional Development Banks," Senate Foreign Relations Committee hearing, Opening Statement by Senator Lugar, Thursday, April 21, 2005, http://foreign.senate.gov/testimony/2005/LugarStatement050421.pdf; "Multilateral Development Banks: Promoting Effectiveness and Fighting Corruption," Senate Foreign Relations Committee hearing, Opening Statement by Senator Lugar, Tuesday, March 28, 2006, http://foreign.senate.gov/testimony/2006/Lugar Statement060328.pdf

[29] Pedro Malan, et al. "Report of the External View Committee on Bank-Fund Collaboration," February 2007 https://www.imf.org/external/np/pp/eng/2007/022307.pdf

[30] "IMF implements major lending policy improvements," International Monetary Fund, March 24, 2009, http://www.imf.org/external/np/pdr/fac/2009/032409.htm

[31] "AfDB Approves US$ 1.5 Billion Budget Support for Botswana to Help Country Cope with the Financial Crisis," African Development Bank Group, February 6, 2009, http://www.afdb.org/ en/news-events/article/afdb-approves-us-1-5-billion-budget-support-for-botswana-to-help-country- cope-with-the-financial-crisis-4724/

[32] http://web.worldbank.org/WBSITE/EXTERNAL/EXTINSPECTIONPANEL/0,,menuPK:6412 9249~pagePK:64132081~piPK:64132052~theSitePK:380794,00.html

[33] Comisión Investigadora respecto al Cre´dito BID-Transantiago, p. 86. http: //www. camara. cl/pdf. aspx? prmID = 95&prmTIPO = INVESTIGAFIN http://www.camara. cl/pdf.aspx? prm ID=95 & prm TIPO= INVESTIGAFIN

[34] http://siteresources.worldbank.org/NEWS/Resources/goi_resp.pdf

[35] Indonesia: A Global Studies Handbook, Florence Lamoreux, (Santa Barbara: ABC-CLIO) 2003, p. 62

[36] *Ibi.d*

[37] "Indonesia: History of a Bankruptcy Orchestrated by IMF and the World Bank," Eric Toussaint and Damien Millet, Committee for the Abolition of Third World Debt, July 10, 2005.

[38] *Ibid.*

[39] Indonesia: A Global Studies Handbook, Lamoreux, pp. 63-64.

[40] The International Monetary Fund Under Constraint: Legitimacy of its Crisis Management, Eva Riesenhuber, The Hague: Kluwer Law International, 2001, p. 140.

[41] The Globalizers: The IMF, the World Bank and Their Borrowers, Ngaire Woods, (New York: Cornell University Press, 2006), p. 75.

[42] *Ibid.*

[43] The International Monetary Fund Under Constraint: Legitimacy of its Crisis Management, Riesenhuber, p. 141.

[44] *Ibid.*

[45] IMF-Supported Programs in Indonesia, Korea and Thailand: A Preliminary Assessment, Timothy Lane, Atish Ghosh, Javier Hamann, Steven Phillips, Marianne Schulze-Ghattas and Tsidi Tsikata, (Washington, D.C., IMF. 1999).

[46] Indonesia's Battle of Will with the IMF." Smitha Francis, International Development Economics Associates, February 25, 2003.

[47] "Economic Recovery and Reform" John Bresnan, in John Bresnan, ed., "Indonesia: The Great Transition," Lanham, MD, Rowman & Littlefield Publishers, Inc., 2005, p. 191.

[48] Excerpted from "Following the Money in Yemen and Lebanon: Maximizing the Effectiveness of U.S. Security Assistance and International Financial Institution Lending," January 2010, Senate Foreign Relations Committeehttp://foreign.senate.gov/imo/media

[49] Excerpt from "Sri Lanka: Recharting U.S. Strategy After the War" December 2009, Senate Foreign Relations Committee.

[50] Document of the International Monetary Fund, Buff Document No. 91/186—October 3, 1991, "Concluding Remarks by the Acting Chairman Military Expenditure and the Role of the Fund," Executive Board Meeting 91/138 October 2, 1991.

[51] Excerpted from "Following the Money in Yemen and Lebanon: Maximizing the Effectiveness of U.S. Security Assistance and International Financial Institution Lending," January 2010, Senate Foreign Relations Committeehttp://foreign.senate.gov/imo/media

[52] "About the IMF," International Monetary Fund, http://www.imf.org/external/about.htm

[53] "The International Monetary Fund: Organization, Functions, and Role in the International Economy," Jonathan E. Sanford and Martin A. Weiss, Congressional Research Service, April 22, 2004.

[54] "IMF Lending." http://www.imf.org/external/np/exr/facts/howlend.htm

[55] "IMF Support for Low-Income Countries." International Monetary Fund, http://www.imf.org/External/np/exr/facts/poor.htm

[56] The SDR is an international reserve asset, created by the IMF in 1969 to supplement the existing official reserves of member countries. SDR also serves as the unit of account of the IMF and some other international organizations.

[57] "IMF Members' Quotas and Voting Power, and IMF Board of Governors," International Monetary Fund, http://www.imf.org/external/np/sec/memdir/members.htm

[58] "Bolstering the IMF's Lending Capacity," International Monetary Fund, http://www.imf.org/external/np/exr/faq/contribution.htm

[59] "Total IMF Credit Outstanding for all Members from 1984-2009," http://www.imf.org/external/np/fin/tad/ extcred 1 .aspx

[60] "About Us," http://web

[61] "Who We Are and What We Do," http://web EXTABOUTUS

[62] "The World Bank's International Development Association (IDA)," Martin A. Weiss, Analyst in International Trade and Finance, Congressional Research Service, April 1, 2008.

[63] Callable capital is a contingent liability, payable only if a multilateral development bank (MDB) lacks sufficient funds to repay its own creditors. None of the MDBs has ever attempted to collect a portion of their callable capital.

[64] "The World Bank Annual Report 2008," The World Bank, http://siteresources.worldbank.org/EXTANNREP 2K8/Resources/YR00 _ Year _ in _ Review _English.pdf

[65] *Ibid.*

[66] "The World Bank's International Development Association (IDA)." Martin A. Weiss, Analyst in International Trade and Finance, Congressional Research Service, April 1, 2008.

[67] "Contributions to the Fifteenth Replenishment," The World Bank, http:// siteresources.worldbank.org/IDA/Resources/Table1IDA15.pdf

[68] "The World Bank Annual Report 2008,"'The World Bank, http://siteresources.worldbank.org/ EXTANNR EP2K8/Resources/YR00 _Year _in _Review _English. pdf.

[69] "What We Do," Inter-American Development Bank, http://www.iadb.org/aboutus/ whatWeDo.cfm?lang=en

[70] "Annual Report 2008," Inter-American Development Bank, http://idbdocs.iadb.org/wsdocs/ getdocument.aspx? docnum=1924122

[71] "Report on the Eighth General Increase in the Resources of the Inter-American Development Bank," Inter-American Development Bank, http://idbdocs.iadb.org/wsdocs/ getdocument.aspx?docnum=2080953

[72] "IDB Governors set roadmap to strengthen Bank, increase resources to fight crisis," IDB News Release, July 2, 2009, http://www.iadb.org/news/detail.cfm?language

[73] "IDB Annual Report," Inter-American Development Bank, www.iadb.org/ar/2008

[74] "About Us," African Development Bank Group, http://www.afdb.org/en/about-u

[75] "The African Development Bank Group," Martin A. Weiss, Analyst in International Trade and Finance, Congressional Research Service, January 30, 2009.

[76] "The African Development Bank 2008 Annual Report," African Development Bank Group, http://www.afdb.org/en/about-us/financial-information/annual-report

[77] "The African Development Bank Group," Martin A. Weiss, Analyst in International Trade and Finance, Congressional Research Service, January 30, 2009.

[78] "The African Development Bank 2008 Annual Report," African Development Bank Group, http:// www.afdb.org/en/about-us/financial-information/annual-report

[79] "Our Vision," Asian Development Bank, http://www.adb.org/About

[80]"Asian Development Bank Annual Report 2008," Asian Development Bank, http://www.adb.org/Documents/Reports/Annual_Report/2008

[81]EBRD Annual Report and Financial Statements," European Bank for Reconstruction and Development, 2008, http://www.ebrd.com/pubs/general/ar08.htm

[82]"Multilateral Development Banks: U.S. Contributions FY1998-2009," Jonathan E. Sanford, Specialist in International Trade and Finance. Congressional Research Service, January 27, 2009 (RS20792).

In: Multilateral Development Banks and International Finance   ISBN: 978-1-61728-883-8
Editor: Leah M. Groffe   © 2010 Nova Science Publishers, Inc.

Chapter 5

THE WORLD BANK'S INTERNATIONAL DEVELOPMENT ASSOCIATION (IDA)[*]

Martin A. Weiss

SUMMARY

The World Bank is a Multilateral Development Bank (MDB) that makes loans and grants to low and middle-income countries to reduce poverty and promote economic development. Both the World Bank and the International Monetary Fund (IMF) were founded at the Bretton Woods Conference in 1944. Two of the World Bank facilities, the International Bank for Reconstruction and Development (IBRD) and International Development Association (IDA) lend directly to governments to finance projects and programs.

IDA was established in 1960, 16 years after the creation of the World Bank to address concern that the poorest countries could not afford to borrow at the near- market rate terms offered by the IBRD. Consequently, IDA was established as a revolving fund, providing concessional loans to the poorest countries subsidized by donor contributions and transfers from the IBRD. IDA assistance is highly discounted, it is increasingly provided as grants, and only available to low-income member countries. Since IDA provides loans and grants to the poorest countries at subsidized rates, its resources must be periodically replenished. Donor nations have replenished IDA 14 times since its founding.

On March 5, 2007, donor nations began to discuss a possible fifteenth replenishment of funds for IDA. This is the first replenishment since the G8 summit at the Gleneagles Resort in Scotland in 2005 where world leaders proposed the creation of the Multilateral Debt Relief Initiative (MDRI). The MDRI cancels the remaining debt of the world's poorest countries and pledges to double the amount of aid to Sub-Saharan Africa between 2004 and 2010, primarily in the form of grant- based assistance.

---

[*] This is an edited, reformatted and augmented version of a CRS Report for Congress publication, Report #RL33969, dated April 1, 2008.

Donor governments selected three themes for IDA-15: (1) IDA's role in the international foreign aid system, (2) the role of the World Bank in post-conflict reconstruction and fragile states, and (3) the need to improve the effectiveness of IDA assistance. This chapter provides brief background material on the World Bank's IDA, the U.S. role at the institution, and information on the status of the current IDA-14 replenishment. It then examines the negotiations for IDA-15, and analyzes the three core themes identified for IDA-15.

INTRODUCTION

On March 5, 2007, donor nations began to discuss a fifteenth replenishment of funds for the World Bank's (the Bank) concessional lending facility, the International Development Association (IDA). This is the first replenishment since the 2005 G8 summit at the Gleneagles Resort in Scotland, where world leaders proposed the creation of the Multilateral Debt Relief Initiative (MDRI). The MDRI cancels the remaining debt of the world's poorest countries, and pledges to double the amount of aid to sub-Saharan Africa between 2004 and 2010, primarily in the form of grant- based assistance.[1]

It is also the first replenishment since the 2005 Paris Declaration on Aid Harmonization, in which IDA and over 100 other signatories agreed to increase coordination among donors in an effort to raise aid effectiveness. The declaration was prompted by concerns that aid is ineffective under the current structure. The lack of coordination of donors on the one hand, and the increasing restrictions on projects themselves through donor earmarks and time limits on the other, have raised the cost and difficulty for implementing foreign aid. According to one foreign aid expert, "managing aid flows from many different donors is a huge challenge for recipient countries, since different donors usually insist on using their own unique processes for initiating, implementing, and monitoring projects. Recipients can be overwhelmed by requirements for multiple project audits, environmental assessments, procurement reports, financial statements, and project updates."[2] Thus, the role of IDA in the international aid architecture has emerged as the dominant theme of the IDA-15 negotiations.

Higher levels of debt relief will lead to lower levels of IDA assistance unless donors increase their contributions significantly over the next several years, according to Bank economists and outside experts. Some argue that by forgiving the repayment of debt owed to IDA, the Bank has substantially reduced the amount of money it has to fund new operations. The Bank asserts that without additional compensation from donors and an increase in regular contributions, IDA's future commitments would remain flat in nominal terms, and decrease by 2% per year in real terms. A concerted effort toward aid coordination would likely result in higher levels of IDA funding.

Analysts in the United States and in other donor countries actively debate the pros and cons of providing foreign assistance through multilateral organizations rather than solely on a bilateral basis. In addition to the aid fragmentation problem discussed earlier, it is believed by many that multilateral aid is more effective since it is likely to be better insulated from political pressure than bilateral assistance. In the World Bank's case, since the Bank's charter disallows its involvement in the domestic politics of any of its member nations, many analysts believe that the Bank has a greater degree of credibility among borrower nations and is thus better able to secure often difficult and economically painful reforms.[3] Furthermore, some analysts argue that a major benefit of the World Bank's multilateral assistance is that the Bank is not directly subject to the often shifting priorities of individual donor nations and is thus able to focus on long-term multi-sectoral development assistance. For example, some point out that the current international focus on combating HIV/AIDS and other infectious diseases may have implications for cost of service of other health-care programs, drugs, and availability of resources, in addition to a possible brain-drain as doctors and medical professionals switch focus to work for programs with a higher profile and greater availability of funding. In these cases, the World Bank often plays an important role by focusing on a country's overall development needs, through their Country Assistance Strategies, and continuing to provide assistance to all sectors of a country's economy.

On the other hand, some analysts raise concerns that the United States loses too much control over the provision of its aid with a multilateral approach. First, they argue, it is very difficult for donors to earmark funds when they are contributed multilaterally. If other donors are not in broad support of the U.S. aid agenda, the United States might be able to achieve its foreign policy objectives more directly by providing bilateral aid through the U.S. Agency for International Development (USAID) or another U.S. agency. Second, since the United States does not have veto power on World Bank lending, the Bank sometimes provides assistance to countries despite strong U.S. opposition. For example, the World Bank has several loan projects in Iran, a country that the United States has designated as a state-sponsor of international terrorism. Although Congress requires the United States to oppose any World Bank loan to Iran (or any other country so-designated by the State Department), since the United States does not have a veto, several projects to Iran have gone through over the past few years. Most recently, the World Bank approved a $224 million water supply and sanitation project in May 2005. Currently, the World Bank has ten active projects in Iran worth $1.36 billion.[4]

According to some Members of Congress, a purely bilateral approach might ensure that no U.S. funds are used to support aid programs to countries that run counter to U.S. foreign policy. Others argue that for some countries, it may in the interest of the United States for certain types of programs to be funded by the World Bank (humanitarian, environmental, for example), since certain countries might not be willing to accept aid if it were offered by the United States for domestic political reasons.

BACKGROUND

The World Bank is a Multilateral Development Bank (MDB) that makes loans and grants to low and middle-income countries to promote poverty alleviation and economic development.[5] Both the World Bank and the IMF were founded at the Bretton Woods Conference in 1944. Two of the World Bank facilities, the International Bank for Reconstruction and Development (IBRD) and International Development Association (IDA) lend directly to governments to finance projects and programs.

The IBRD provides middle-income developing countries with loans at near- market rates using funds raised by the World Bank on the international capital markets. While many of these countries can borrow on the international capital markets, and are increasingly doing so, some seek loans from the World Bank to gain access to World Bank technical assistance and advisory services, as well as the prestige and perceived legitimacy that come with World Bank-backed projects.

IDA was established in 1960, 16 years after the creation of the World Bank due to concerns that low-income countries could not afford to borrow at the near-market rate terms offered by the World Bank.[6] Consequently, IDA was established as a revolving fund, providing concessional loans to the poorest countries and subsidized by both donor contributions and transfers from the IBRD. IDA assistance is highly discounted and is increasingly provided as grants. Both IDA and IBRD also make non-project loans to promote economic policy and institutional reform, and share the same staff. Both are headquartered in Washington, DC.[7]

Initial IDA funding in 1960 was $1.1 billion: $900 million from donor contributions and $210 million from IBRD net income.[8] According to the Bank, between IDA-1 (1960-1962) and IDA-14 (2006-2008) total resources for IDA have increased on average 9.5% per year (in nominal terms). Over the three-year IDA-14 period, IDA will provide $33 billion in concessional assistance. In real terms, however, since IDA-6 (1981-1984) available resources for IDA have been flat (Figure 1).

The Donor Replenishment Process

Donor contributions account for over 70% of all resources available for IDA (providing about $138 billion). The remainder is funded by internal IDA resources (primarily principal repayments from IDA borrowers) and transfers from IBRD net income. Internal resources have accounted for about $46 billion of IDA's funding, while transfers from the IBRD's net income and budget surplus have provided $11.7 billion to IDA. As of the end of the World Bank's FY2006, IDA's total assets were $102.9 billion. This is a $32.1 billion decrease from FY2005's available resources of $130.4 billion due to debt write-off provided by the MDRI.

Every three years, IDA donors meet to negotiate the terms of a new round of IDA. Since 1960, there have been 14 such replenishments. Negotiations for the 15th round began March 5, 2007. At the replenishment, donors revisit the overall amount of IDA financing for the round. In addition, the replenishment is the primary opportunity for donor nations to influence World Bank policy making.[9] For the United States, IDA contributions are typically the largest component of the annual U.S. contributions to the International Financial Institutions (IFIs).

IDA replenishments comprise two distinct phases: negotiating the replenishment round and annual contributions. First, the donor nations negotiate the overall amount of a three-year replenishment, individual donor contributions, and general policy considerations for the round. Following this, each member country seeks annual contributions, typically through its legislative process, to meet their IDA commitments. For the United States, participation in any given IDA replenishment requires congressional authorization of the total IDA package. Following this authorization, the President seeks annual appropriations to the U.S. share of each round.

This bifurcated process, where the Executive Branch commits to a overall replenishment amount prior to annual contributions are appropriated has led to an arrearage problem since the United States is obligated to contribute the amount agreed to at the replenishment. Congress authorizes U.S. participation in the replenishment agreement — including the terms of that agreement — when it authorizes funding for U.S. contributions to the plan. The Constitution does not require, however, that Congress appropriate the sums necessary to meet the terms of international agreement negotiated by the Executive Branch and authorized by Congress.

U.S. arrears to IDA are $377.9 million. These arrears have had a bandwagon effect — unpaid U.S. contributions have triggered a pro-rata withholding of contributions during IDA-12 and IDA-13 by three other IDA donors, totaling about $72 million. Notwithstanding U.S. arrears, the U.S. remains the largest contributor to IDA (and the IBRD) and has a commensurate share of influence in World Bank operations. An appendix provides more information about U.S. influence at the World Bank.

IDA Assistance

IDA assistance is categorized as Official Development Assistance (ODA)[10] by the Organization for Economic Development (OECD) and is tracked in the OECD's Development Assistance Committee (DAC) database. Donor nations provide a wide variety of foreign aid, some provided bilaterally, other channeled through multilateral organizations. According to the OECD, bilateral assistance accounts for 75% of all international foreign aid. However, they consider ODA bilateral if a donor channels assistance to a multilateral agency but specifies the recipient country. If all aid that is channeled through international organizations is categorized as multilateral aid, the division between bilateral and multilateral assistance would be 50%-50%.[11]

From 1960 through the 1980s, IDA was the largest individual provider of multilateral assistance. With the flattening of IDA assistance over the past twenty years, other multilateral organizations have surpassed IDA as a provider of multilateral aid. IDA's share of multilateral ODA declined from 42% in the 1970s to an average of 20% in the 2001-2005 period.[12] The primary cause of this decline is the increasing fragmentation of donor flows among a multitude of agencies, such as the United Nations, European Commission, World Health Organization (part of the United Nations), and the IMF and World Bank, among many others.

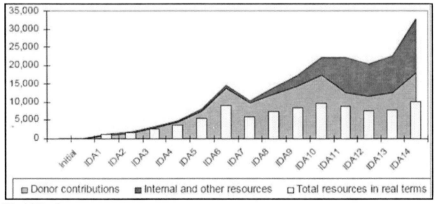

Source: World Bank

Figure 1. Growth of IDA Since Inception, in Nominal and Real Terms ($ in millions)

While IDA assistance has decreased as a percentage of overall multilateral aid, for the poorest countries (those eligible to receive IDA assistance), IDA remains the largest provider of multilateral ODA. For core development programs (excluding debt relief, administrative costs of donors, emergency assistance, and other special purpose grants), IDA's cumulative net ODA for 2001 to 2005 exceeded $33 billion (about 20% of total core-development ODA for IDA-eligible countries). In the same time period, IDA contributed more than 20% of ODA in 17 countries; between 10% and 20% in 34 countries; between 5% and 10% in 12 countries; and less than 5% in 18 countries.

There are 82 low-income countries currently eligible for IDA assistance, including 39 in Sub-Saharan Africa. IDA loans are typically interest-free, and have a 10-year grace period with repayments stretched over 3 5-40 years. (There is a small service charge, however, currently 0.75% of funds paid out.) Increasingly, IDA is providing a growing amount of its assistance in the form of grants. IDA also supports some countries, including several small island economies, which are above the per-capita income cutoff but lack the creditworthiness needed to borrow from IBRD. Some countries, such as India, Indonesia and Pakistan, are IDA-eligible based on per capita income levels, but are also creditworthy for some IBRD borrowing. These are referred to as "blend" countries and receive loans from both agencies.

In the World Bank's FY2006 (which ended June 30, 2006), IDA made commitments to its members totaling $9.5 billion. Half of these commitments were in Sub Saharan Africa. South and East Asia received 38% of new commitments with the remainder scattered throughout South America and Eastern Europe. In 2006, Pakistan was the largest IDA borrower, receiving $1.18 billion in new assistance. Vietnam, Tanzania, and Ethiopia were other large borrowers (**Figure 2**).

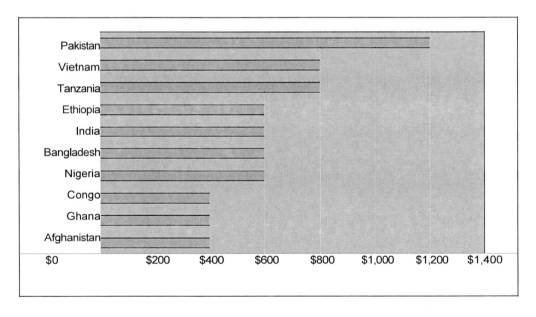

Source: World Bank

Figure 2. FY2006 Top Ten IDA Borrowers ($ in millions)

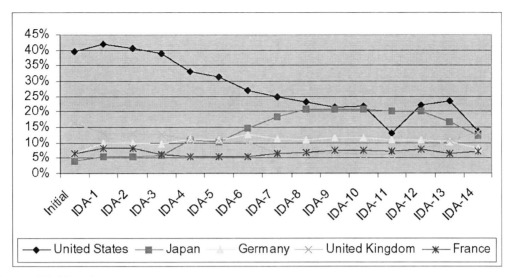

Source: World Bank

Figure 3. Donor Contributions to IDA

At IDA's founding, the United States contributed the largest percentage of resources to IDA: 39.65%. After peaking in IDA-1 at 41.89%, the U.S. percentage of contributions to each round of IDA has steadily declined. While the U.S. remains the largest individual contributor to IDA, its share in IDA- 14 dropped to 13.78% after maintaining above a 20% share for much of the past three decades (Figure 3). The decrease in U.S. percentage is largely attributed to higher levels of foreign donor contributions and an increase in the number of IDA donor nations.

The five largest contributors to IDA-14, the United States, Japan, Germany, the United Kingdom, and France, are contributing between 7.11% and 13.78% of the total. The decline in U.S. percentage contributions does not affect the U.S. voting share, since the voting weights used for IDA loans are the same as for overall contributions to the World Bank. Since European member countries combined hold a much larger percentage of World Bank shares than the United States, some analysts argue that Europe could exert more force in IDA lending decisions and/or future replenishment negotiations if they negotiate together.[13]

IDA-14

On April 18, 2005, the Board of Governors of IDA approved the fourteenth replenishment of IDA's resources.[14] At the conclusion of the IDA-14 negotiations, IDA donors announced that at least $34 billion in resources would be made available to the 81 IDA-eligible countries during the three years of IDA-14 (2005-2008). Of the $34 billion, $18 billion would be in new donations from the 40 contributor countries. The remaining $16 billion would come from reflows (repayments on former IDA loans) and transfers from the IBRD and the IFC. The $34 billion in resources made available by IDA-14 is a $11.6 billion increase from the total IDA-13 level of $22.8 billion. It includes an almost 40% increase in donor contributions from $12.7 billion in IDA-13 to $20.7 billion in IDA-14.

Table 1. IDA-14 Appropriations (in $ Millions)

FY2006		FY2007		FY2008		Total Arrears (Includes arrears from IDA-13)
Request	Approp.	Request	Approp.	Request	Approp.	
950.0	909.15*	950.0	940.5	1,060.0	$950.0	377.9

* In FY2006, $940.5 million was appropriated, however, the enacted Continuing Resolution (P.L. 110-5) rescinded $31.35 million of this amount since Treasury was unable to certify that the World Bank complied with certain congressionally mandated transparency initiatives.

The Bush Administration pledged $2.85 billion to IDA-14 to be split into three payments of $950 million for fiscal years 2006, 2007, and 2008. The FY2006 appropriations bill included full authorization for the United States to participate in IDA-14. For the United States, this represents no real increase from the amount budgeted and requested for IDA- 13. For that replenishment, the Administration requested $2.55 billion annually over three years ($850 million per year, FY2003- FY2005) and $300 million in incentive agreements if the World Bank met certain Treasury-specified performance targets ($100 million in FY2004 and $200 million in FY2005). Since the total size of donor contributions to IDA has increased by 40% while the U.S. contribution has remained constant, the U.S. share of IDA decreases to 13% in IDA-14 from 21% in IDA-13. Table 1 includes U.S. budget requests and appropriations for IDA-14 and total arrears.

U.S. Policy

The United States Government pursued many priorities at the IDA-14 negotiations. According to the Administration, the major U.S. objectives at IDA-14 were: implementing a results measurement framework for performance-based allocation, increasing the percentage of IDA assistance provided as grants, and increasing World Bank transparency.[15]

Measuring Results and Performance-Based Allocation

In recent years, many observers — both critics and supporters of the MDBs — have cited a need to better measure the performance of World Bank projects. A criticism, often voiced by the U.S. Administration, is that it is unclear what MDB assistance has accomplished due to vague objectives and too much emphasis on outputs (volume of aid) rather than country outcomes.

The focus on performance requirements and measurable results follows from analysis undertaken by World Bank economists that suggested that foreign aid, such as that provided by the World Bank, is most effective for countries that have good policies. According to the report, "aid has a positive impact on growth in developing countries with good fiscal, monetary, and trade policies. In the presence of poor policies, on the other hand, *aid has no positive effect on growth* (emphasis added)."[16]

The notion that effective aid is conditional on underlying economic policy performance has become central to the Bush Administration's foreign aid strategy and policy toward the World Bank. The Bush Administration has made measuring results and performance-based allocation central to U.S. foreign assistance and has made the practice of these ideas central to the operations of a new foreign aid initiative, the Millennium Challenge Account (MCA).[17] Reportedly, this plan was based heavily on World Bank research.[18]

Most analysts agree that improvements in health and education levels, good governance, reduced corruption, increased opportunities for private enterprise, and improvements in the trade capacity and investment climate are necessary in order to raise quality of life and the standard of living in developing countries. Some argue, however, that the obstacles that block progress in these areas are substantial and much effort and time may be needed to realize gains. Furthermore the Administration's emphasis on growth may beg the question of income distribution. It is unclear how the Administration's emphasis on growth fits with the assertion by the MDBs and their executive boards that poverty alleviation should be the MDBs' principal goals.

Introducing stronger performance requirements thus became one of the Administration's most sought after goals at IDA. Building on the new results measurement system, the U.S. Administration would like to channel more IDA resources to the strongest performing countries. This would mirror new domestic U.S. foreign assistance programs such as the Millennium Challenge Corporation (MCC), that were designed with performance-based allocation strictly in mind.

The IDA-14 performance measurement system is two-fold, assessing both (1) progress on aggregate country outcomes, and (2) IDA's contribution to country outcomes. To assess country performance, the World Bank monitors a set of 14 country indicators for all IDA countries. To analyze IDA performance, the World Bank created output indicators measuring IDA's contribution in the health, education, water supply and transportation sectors. Regarding performance-based allocation, IDA-14 allocations are determined using a formula that includes the IDA Country Performance Rating,[19] Gross National Income (GNI) per capita, and population. The IDA Performance Rating is the dominant factor, and higher performance can increase IDA allocations exponentially.

Grants

The United States has advocated for several years the use of grants rather than loans at the MDBs concessional lending facilities. This view is a response to the debt situation of many of the poorest countries, principally in sub- Saharan Africa.[20] Bilateral and multilateral debt of the poorest countries increased heavily between the 1970s and the present. It has become increasingly clear that the poorest countries are unable to service their old loans let alone new debt. Thus President Bush introduced a proposal in 2001 that the World Bank shift its assistance to the poorest countries away from loans to grants.[21] For IDA-14, deputies agreed on 30% of total IDA assistance in the form of grants, an 8% increase from IDA-13.

According to Bobby Pittman, U.S. Treasury Deputy Assistant Secretary for Multilateral Development Banks, "grants can be useful for ending the lend-and-forgive cycle."[22] Other donor countries agree with the concept of grants, yet assert that without commensurate increases in IDA funding, the bank's financial strength may suffer. They also note that most IDA loans are repaid in full and on time and only a minority of borrowers have needed debt cancellation. Some analysts argue that an unstated component of the long-term U.S. Administration policy-shift towards increased MDB grants may be a shrinking of the institution. Barring additional donor funds, the capacity to provide future assistance will decline because of fewer loan repayments. Money from loan repayments accounts for about

40% of the resources available for IDA to fund new aid. Without these funds, new IDA aid would have to shrink. Critics of grants also note that the World Bank's IDA loans are already provided on highly concessional terms, with little or no interest.

Transparency

Increasing transparency and public disclosure of World Bank documents and policies has also been a longstanding U.S. priority at the World Bank. Section 581 of the *FY2004 Consolidated Appropriations Act* (PL 108-199) directed the Treasury Department to pursue policy goals related to transparency and accountability across the MDBs.

These priorities influenced U.S. objectives at IDA-14. A major component of the IDA-14 agreement is the World Bank's commitment to full disclosure of the numerical ratings for the Country Policy and Institutional Assessments (CPIA), which Bank began releasing in 2005. The CPIAs are the main component for determining IDA lending allocations. Although the World Bank began disclosing the CPIA ratings in 2000, non-governmental organizations (NGOs) argued that they were released in an aggregated format that did not reveal anything about how country rating differed between countries and how the ratings were calculated.[23]

In addition to releasing the CPIA indicators and their supporting data, the IDA-14 Agreement called on the World Bank Executive Board to implement other important transparency reforms. Specifically, the Agreement directed the Board to: (1) disclose Board minutes; (2) strengthen procedures for documenting public consultation processes; (3) make interim results of projects during their execution publicly available; and (4) require an independent audit or assessment of internal management controls and procedures for meeting operational objectives. While Board minutes are still classified, donor countries have noted progress on the other IDA-14 objectives. On November 20-21, 2006, IDA Deputies and representatives from IDA borrower countries met in Washington, DC to review progress on implementing the IDA-14 recommendations. Participants were satisfied with the level of IDA commitments and progress made on reforms to date.

Lastly, during the FY2006 appropriations process, Congress added a provision (Section 599D) that 20% of the funds appropriated to IDA be withheld from disbursement until the Secretary of the Treasury certifies to Congress that several anti-corruption measures (primarily relating to World Bank procurement guidelines) are met. Treasury was unable to certify that the World Bank had met all of the required anti-corruption provisions by the completion of the FY2007 spending measure. Consequently, the Continuing Resolution (CR) for FY2007 appropriations (PL110-5, as amended) rescinded $31.35 million from the FY2006 appropriations. .

IDA-15

At the end of the IDA-14 discussions, donor countries agreed that the scope of policy issues addressed during the replenishment rounds had proliferated beyond reason. They concluded that significant progress on any one area may be constrained unless donor countries limited their priorities for each round. Consequently, IDA 14 participants agreed that for future rounds they would concentrate on fewer areas for reform and seek greater specificity in the main issues for discussion within each area.

At the March 5-6, 2007 kick-off meeting for the IDA-15 round, IDA Deputies selected three themes for IDA-15: (1) IDA's role in the international aid architecture, (2) the role of the World Bank in post-conflict reconstruction and fragile states, and (3) improving the effectiveness of IDA assistance. Negotiations for IDA-15 concluded on December 14, 2007. At the meeting, donors agreed to provide $41.6 billion, an increase of US$ 9.5 billion over the previous replenishment (IDA14) ($32.1 billion). The United Kingdom pledged donations of $4.3 billion over three years, making it the largest single donor to IDA-15. The United States increased its pledge by 30% to $3.7 billion, and will see its share rise from 13.8 to 14.7%. This will be the first time in IDA's history that the United States is not the largest shareholder.[24] Several countries are contributing to IDA for the first time: China, Cyprus, Egypt and Estonia, Latvia, and Lithuania.[25]

IDA's Role in the International Aid System

During the run-up to the IDA-15 negotiations, IDA's role in the international aid system emerged as the most pressing issue for IDA deputies. As noted earlier in this chapter, the proliferation of providers of foreign assistance and its increasing fragmentation among narrowly defined projects has emerged as a concern among foreign aid professionals.

Responding to these concerns, analysts have suggested that the trend of decreasing multilateral assistance be reversed and that a greater percentage of foreign assistance be channeled through IDA or other multilateral providers. According to one Brookings Institution analyst, "bilateral donors should put the politics aside and get serious on aid scale-up and harmonization through IDA."[26] Possible questions identified by the World Bank that IDA-15 deputies may discuss during the IDA-15 negotiations include (1) IDA's role in the global aid architecture; (2) concerns regarding vertical or global aid funds (aid programs that focus on specific policy issues rather than country-based assistance); (3) IDA's role at the regional level and the best division of labor between IDA and the regional development banks; (4) implications for IDA of the 2005 Paris Declaration agenda on aid harmonization; (5) IDA's role be in building country institutional capacity to promote good governance, especially at the local level in countries that have weak or non-participatory central governments; and (6) IDA efforts to improve global aid harmonization.

IDA and Fragile States

With the collapse of the Soviet Union and the rise of civil conflict in many countries throughout (primarily) Africa and South Asia, the World Bank has significantly enhanced its involvement in post-conflict countries and other so-called fragile states. In 2002, the World Bank launched the LICUS (Low Income Countries Under Stress) initiative to provide special assistance for high-risk countries, defined as scoring a 3.0 or less on the World Bank's CPIA rating. In January 2006, the Bank adopted the term "Fragile States" to refer to LICUS countries and the program.

As of 2008, there are around 25 countries classified as fragile states by the Bank. The goal of the LICUS/Fragile States program is to provide additional and coordinated assistance targeted to the needs of fragile states, which are characterized by weak policies, institutions, and governance. Thus, many analysts argue that World Bank assistance in fragile states requires additional focus on state-building and peace-building objectives in addition to the Bank's traditional emphasis on economic growth and poverty alleviation.

During IDA-15, member countries and IDA officials are expected to further refine the IDA strategy for fragile states. This may involve better integrating fragile states issues in IDA's work — for example, staff incentives, increased analytic work of fragile state needs, increased coordination with bilateral donors, and the creation of results measurement systems designed specifically for fragile states. The Bank may also revise the types of financial assistance that it currently provides to fragile states. For many fragile states and other post-conflict countries, the World Bank is unable to lend because the fragile state either does not have a functioning government or is in arrears to the World Bank. In these cases where the World Bank cannot lend directly, trust funds have been established to channel donor funds earmarked for a specific country or project. IDA officials have recognized this challenge and are looking to establish a framework for arrears clearance in IDA-15.

IDA and Development Effectiveness

Building on efforts undertaken in IDA-14, increasing the effectiveness of IDA assistance is the third focus of IDA-15. The challenges facing IDA, as well as the rest of the aid system, are formidable. According to one study of World Bank evaluation, "Despite the billions of dollars spent on development assistance each year, there is still very little known about the actual impact of projects on the poor."[27] A 2006 report from the World Bank's Independent Evaluation Group (IEG), found that while the Bank has instituted numerous policies and procedures to "manage better for results," these efforts have not translated into improved Bank processes at the operational project level.[28] According to the report, Bank managers and staff continue to struggle to link operations to clearly defined goals. Moreover, the report found that performance indicators are inadequate; staff are unclear how to use performance information in their day to day work; and that the World Bank culture acts as a disincentive to managing for results by focusing on the amount of projects and money lent rather than the quality of individual projects.

Members of Congress have exhibited significant interest in improving the effectiveness of IDA assistance. A Senate hearing in spring 2006 focused on improving the effectiveness of World Bank lending and several proposals were discussed which may resurface during IDA-15. For example, several development experts discussed at the hearing the need for better results measurement and proposed creating a fully independent evaluation group for the World Bank.

While the Bank renamed its internal evaluation group from the Operations Evaluation Department (OED) to the Independent Evaluation Group in 2005, it is not truly independent since OED staff are World Bank employees and frequently rotate between OED and other Bank offices. However, the IEG reports directly to the Executive Board, not the Bank President. According to one hearing participant:

> The World Bank makes some attempt to achieve independence for its Operations
> Evaluation Department (OED), which reports directly to the Board of the World Bank, not to

the President. However, staff move back and forth between OED and the rest of the Bank — a negative evaluation could hurt staff's career prospects. The OED evaluation is subjective. Unclear methods lead to evaluation disconnects ... It has to be asked how the largely positive findings of the evaluations can be reconciled with the poor development outcomes observed over the same period (1985-1995).[29]

Another testified that,

"Independence" at the Bank is purely cosmetic, for a temporary change of desk and a new nameplate do not alter the signature on the paycheck nor the rewards of the Bank's personnel system. The Independent Evaluation Group is a department of the Bank like any other, save the ceremony of reporting to an Executive Board that is passive at best. For everyone save the titular Director General, a revolving door leads back to standard line jobs and advancement at the Bank. Because results are published, there is strong pressure to display success. Outside verification is precluded because there is no public access to the underlying data. This hardly fosters disinterested and rigorous judgments, even though the Bank boasts that staff cannot review projects that they themselves designed.[30]

In response to these concerns, experts at the hearings proposed creating an outside independent evaluation group that would be able to perform rigorous and independent impact evaluation of what does and what does not work in World Bank programs.[31] Members of Congress have expressed significant interest in this proposal, directing the Executive Branch to pursue further reforms of the World Bank evaluation system in the FY2006 appropriations measure (PL 109-102). Congress required the Secretary of the Treasury to seek at the World Bank (and the other MDBs) a "functionally independent Investigations Office, Auditor General Office and Evaluation Office that are free from interference in determining the scope of investigations (including forensic audits), internal auditing (including assessments of management controls for meeting operational objectives and complying with bank policies), performing work and communicating results, and that regularly report to such bank's board of directors," as well as other transparency and effectiveness related reforms.

APPENDIX I: THE UNITED STATES AND THE WORLD BANK

Over the life of the Bank, the United States has contributed the largest amount of resources ($26.49 billion total committed, 16.84% of total committed shares). As the largest contributor, the United States enjoys a single seat on the World Bank's Board of Executive Directors and carries 16.3 8% of the total votes in World Bank decision making. Congressional authorization is required by law before the United States may agree to participate in any World Bank funding agreements, such as the tri-annual IDA replenishment agreements. While Congress does not have a representative at the negotiations, the Executive Branch is required to consult with Members of Congress, before and during the replenishment process.

The U.S. Executive Director (ED) is the primary U.S. representative to the Bank and sits on the Executive Board, which is comprised of 24 members representing all of the Bank's 185 members. The ED handles the day-to-day operations of the Fund. The majority of Bank decisions require a 50% majority vote. Some special matters (changes in the Articles of Agreement or approval of funding increases, for example) require an 85% affirmative vote. Since the U.S. vote exceeds 15%, no funding increases, amendments or other major actions can go into effect without U.S. consent. By tradition, the president of the World Bank is an American citizen. The position is currently held by Robert Zoellick, who began his term July 1, 2007.

While the Executive Branch manages the day-to-day U.S. relationship at the World Bank, Congress decides the overall terms of U.S. involvement in the Bank by setting the level of U.S. contributions, and through legislation, directing how the U.S. shall vote at the Bank. There are three primary ways that Congress can seek to influence or govern U.S. policies towards MDB policy: through conditions attached to new funding agreements; through periodic Sense of Congress resolutions or legislation suggesting specific goals and priorities the United States ought to emphasize at the MDBs or directing how the U.S. should vote on certain countries or types of projects; and through oversight hearings.

End Notes

[1] CRS Report RS22534, *The Multilateral Debt Relief Initiative*, by Martin A. Weiss.

[2] Steven Radelet, "A Primer on Foreign Aid," Center for Global Development Working Paper No. 92, July 2006. p.15.

[3] Andrew Powell and Matteo Bobba, "Multilateral Intermediation of Foreign Aid: What is the Trade-off for Donors?," Inter-American Development Bank Research Department Working Paper #594, November 2006.

[4] More information on the World Bank's projects in Iran is available at the World Bank's Iran Country webpage: [http://web.worldbank.org/WBSITE/EXTERNAL/COUNTRIES/ MENAEXT/IRANEXTN/0,,menuPK:3 1 2962~pagePK: 1411 59~piPK: 14111 0~theSitePK: 312943,00.html].

[5] The United States is a member of five multilateral development banks (MDBs): the World Bank, Inter-American Development Bank (IDB), Asian Development Bank (ADB), African Development Bank (AFDB), and European Bank for Reconstruction and Development (EBRD). It also belongs to two related institutions: the North American Development Bank (NADB) and the International Fund for Agricultural Development (IFAD). The U.S. Department of the Treasury provides additional information on its participation in these organizations in its annual *Justifications for Appropriations Report*. The most recent, for the FY2008 request, is available at [http://www.treasury.gov/offices/international-affairs/ intl/fy2008/fy2008-budget.pdf].

[6] For the World Bank FY2007, low-income countries are those with a per capita income of less than $1,025.

[7] Three other World Bank affiliated organizations are dedicated to the private sector. The International Finance Corporation (IFC) promotes private sector development in poor and developing countries by making loans and investments in small and medium-sized companies. In many poor countries, the banking sector is weak and there is little or no access to equity financing. Complementing IFC investments, the Multilateral Investment Guarantee Agency (MIGA) provides private investors coverage against non-commercial risk in developing countries. Coverage is provided against a broad range of risks including expropriation, war and civil disturbance, and/or breach of contract. Lastly, the International Center for the Settlement of Investment Disputes (ICSID) provides dispute resolution for investment disputes between governments and foreign investors. More information is available from the World Bank's Website: [http://www.worldbank.org].

[8] This section draws from Aid Architecture: An Overview of the Main Trends in Official Development Assistance, International Development Association, February 2007. p. 30. Hereafter *Aid Architecture*.

[9] "The establishment of IDA meant the recognition that there was a legitimate need for concessional assistance and that the Bank could provide this assistance without compromising its strict standards for lending. However, IDA, with its periodic replenishments by member governments, meant that the Bank had to pay increasing attention to the views and priorities of the parliamentary bodies that provided the replenishment funds. Whereas the Bank had previously to consider only the productive and economic aspects of lending, now the internal politics of the shareholding governments began to play a larger role in the Bank's activities." World Bank, profile of its third President, Eugene R. Black , cited in *Aid Architecture*.

[10] ODA is defined by the OECD "those flows to developing countries and multilateral institutions provided by official agencies, including state and local governments, or by their executive agencies, each transaction of which meets the following tests: i) it is administered with the promotion of the economic development and

The World Bank's International Development Association (IDA) 121

welfare of developing countries as its main objective; and ii) it is concessional in character and conveys a grant element of at least 25 per cent." For more information, see CRS Report RS22032, *Foreign Aid: Understanding Data Used to Compare Donors*, by Larry Q. Nowels.

[11] For more information on U.S. bilateral and multilateral foreign aid, see CRS Report RL3349 1, *Restructuring U.S. Foreign Aid: The Role of the Director of Foreign Assistance in Transformational Development*, by Connie Veillette, and CRS Report 98-916, *Foreign Aid: An Introductory Overview of U.S. Programs and Policy*, by Curt Tarnoff and Larry Q. Nowels.

[12] Aid Architecture, pg. 4.

[13] By tradition, the president of the World Bank is appointed by the United States while the managing director of the International Monetary Fund is a European national. For more information on the selection processes for these organizations see CRS Report RS22029, *The World Bank: Changing Leadership and Issues for the United States and Congress*, by Martin A. Weiss, and CRS Report RS21810, *International Monetary Fund: Selecting a New Managing Director (2004)*, by Martin A. Weiss and Jonathan E. Sanford.

[14] The World Bank, "Additions to IDA Resources: Fourteenth Replenishment," available at [http://siteresources.worldbank.org/IDA/Resources/14th_Replenishment_Final.pdf].

[15] See Secretary of the Treasury John Snow, *Remarks: IDA-14 Replenishment Meeting*, February 22, 2005, available at [http://www.treas.gov/press/releases/js2270.htm].

[16] Craig Burnside and David Dollar, "Aid, Policies and Growth," *American Economic Review*, September 2000.

[17] See CRS Report RL32427, *Millennium Challenge Account*, by Curt Tarnoff.

[18] Daphne Eviatar, "Do Aid Studies Govern Policies or Reflect Them?," *The New York Times*, July 27, 2003.

[19] The IDA country performance rating is determined by two World Bank ratings: the Country Policy and Institutional Assessment (CPIA) and the Portfolio Performance Rating (ARPP). The CPIA constitutes 80% of IDA's country performance rating, and is a combined index of 16 pieces of information evaluating economic management, structural policies, policies for social inclusion/equity, and governance. The CPIA system was a U.S. initiative and was put in place during the IDA negotiations in 1998. The ARPP assesses each country's performance on implementing prior programs, and accounts for 20% of the performance rating. The CPIA/ARPP number is multiplied by a country measure of good governance to determine the IDA Country Performance Rating.

[20] See CRS Report RS22534, *The Multilateral Debt Relief Initiative*, and CRS Report RL33073, *Debt Relief for Heavily Indebted Poor Countries*, both by Martin A. Weiss.

[21] "I propose that up to 50 percent of the funds provided by the development banks to the poorest countries be provided as grants for education, health, nutrition, water supply, sanitation and other human needs" President George Bush, speech to the World Bank, July 17, 2001. Available at [http://www.whitehouse.gov/news/releases/2001/07/ 20010717-1 .html]. See also CRS Report RL31136, *World Bank: IDA Loans or IDA Grants?*, by Jonathan E. Sanford.

[22] Paul Blustein, "World Bank Plans to Shift to Grant Aid," *The Washington Post*, January 14, 2005.

[23] Jeff Powell, "The World Bank policy scorecard: The new conditionality?" The Bretton Woods Project, November 22, 2004. Document is available at [http://www.brettonwoodsproject.org/doc/knowledge/cpia.PDF].

[24] The diminished share, however, will not impact the weight of U.S. voting at the World Bank.

[25] The full IDA- 15 report is available at: [http://siteresources.worldbank.org/IDA/Resources/Seminar%20PDFs/73449-1172525976405/ FinalreportMarch2008.pdf].

[26] Amanda Glassman, "Time to be serious on aid harmonization through the IDA," *Financial Times*, March 7, 2007.

[27] Judy L. Baker, Evaluating the Impact of Development Projects on Poverty: A Handbook for Practitioners, The World Bank, 2000.

[28] 2006 Annual Report on Operations Evaluation, The World Bank, 2006.

[29] William Easterly, "Accountability for Multilateral Development Banks" Statement Presented to the Committee on Foreign Relations of the United States Senate, March 28, 2006.

[30] Adam Lerrick, "Is the World Bank's Word Good Enough?", Statement Presented to the Committee on Foreign Relations of the United States Senate, March 28, 2006.

[31] For example, see "When Will We Ever Learn? Improving Lives Through Impact Evaluation, the Report of the Evaluation Gap Working Group," Center for Global Development, May 2006.

In: Multilateral Development Banks and International Finance ISBN: 978-1-61728-883-8
Editor: Leah M. Groffe © 2010 Nova Science Publishers, Inc.

Chapter 6

THE MULTILATERAL DEBT RELIEF INITIATIVE[*]

Martin A. Weiss

SUMMARY

In June 2005, G8 finance ministers proposed the new Multilateral Debt Relief Initiative (MDRI). The MDRI proposes to cancel debts of some of the world's poorest countries owed to the International Monetary Fund, World Bank, and African Development Bank. This chapter discusses MDRI's implementation and raises some issues regarding debt relief's effectiveness as a form of foreign assistance for possible congressional consideration.

The Multilateral Debt Relief Initiative (MDRI) is the most recent effort by the International Monetary Fund (IMF), World Bank, and African Development Bank (AfDB) to provide poor country debt relief. Proposed by G8 finance ministers in June 2005, the MDRI provides 100% debt relief to select countries that are already participating in the joint-IMF/World Bank Heavily Indebted Poor Countries (HIPC) program.[1] The goal of the MDRI program is to free up additional resources for the poorest countries in order to help them reach the United Nations' Millennium Development Goals (MDGs), which are focused, among other things, on reducing world poverty by half by 2015.[2]

There are several key features of the MDRI:

All pre-existing IMF, World Bank, and AfDB debt will be cancelled for any country that completes the HIPC program. (The Asian Development Bank, Inter-American Development Bank, and other development banks are not participating in the Initiative.)[3]

The MDRI Agreement provides no additional net assistance. HIPC countries that receive debt reduction will have their total assistance flows from the agency canceling their debt reduced by the amount of debt forgiven.

---

[*] This is an edited, reformatted and augmented version of a CRS Report for Congress publication, Report #RS22534, dated April 1, 2008.

The IMF will internally fund its debt relief while the World Bank and AfDB will be compensated by G8 donors. IMF debt relief will be funded with the money obtained from the sale of some IMF gold in the late 1990s.

The MDRI raises several questions for policy makers: What is the effect of debt on the poorest countries? What impact can the MDRI be expected to have on poverty reduction? What policies could make debt relief more effective?

Looking at several studies of the effectiveness of the HIPC program from 1996-2006, it appears that although debt relief can slightly increase the amount of financial resources available to poor countries, the debt burden is not the main impediment to poverty reduction and economic growth in the poorest countries. Weak macroeconomic institutions and difficulty absorbing foreign assistance, as well as political challenges, appear more likely hurdles. Alleviating the debt burden in the absence of other strategic reforms is unlikely to substantially contribute to improved conditions in the poorest countries. If combined with other efforts, however, debt relief can have a complementary effect on domestic government finances and can help promote further reform.

Past Debt Relief Efforts

The MDRI builds on several bilateral and multilateral debt relief initiatives conducted over the past twenty years. In the 1980s and early 1990s, as the debts of the poorest countries increased rapidly compared to other low-income countries, the G7 and other creditor countries implemented several plans aimed at reducing the countries' debt payment burden.

Bilateral Debt Relief

In 1988, in response to a G7 initiative, a group of major creditor nations, known as the Paris Club, agreed for the first time to cancel debts owed to them by up to one-third instead of refinancing them on easier terms as they had done previously.[4] Over the next decade, the Paris Club gradually increased the amount of debt that it would be willing to write off by up to 90% in 1999. The United States did not participate in the initial debt forgiveness plans, but in 1991, at the initiative of Congress, independently forgave almost all of the debt owed to it by the poorest nations. Since 1991, the United States has forgiven $23.9 billion in foreign debt.[5]

HIPC Debt Relief

The IMF and World Bank introduced debt relief in 1996 through the Heavily Indebted Poor Country (HIPC) Initiative. When conceived, the intention of the program was to reduce poor countries' debts to a so-called "sustainable" level. Sustainability was defined as multilateral debts not exceeding a maximum debt-to-exports ratio of 250%. In 1999, the program was redesigned in response to criticism that the debt-to-export ratio was too large, disqualifying many countries from debt relief. The target debt service-to-exports ratio was reduced to 150%, and the time period for eligibility was shortened. The HIPC program was also modified to require increased poverty reduction efforts. Any money freed up by debt relief must now be used explicitly on poverty reduction efforts.

Table 1. Countries Eligible for HIPC Debt Relief (As of 04/2008)

Completion Point (22 countries)		Decision Point (11 countries)	Pre-Decision Point (8 countries)
Benin	Mali	Afghanistan	Comoros
Bolivia	Mauritania	Burundi	Cote d'Ivoire
Burkina	Mozambique	Central African	Eritrea
Faso	Nicaragua	Republic	Krgyz Republic
Cameroon	Niger Rwanda	Chad	Nepal
Ethiopia	Sao Tome &	Republic of Congo	Somalia
Ghana	Principe	Democratic Rep. of	Sudan
Guyana	Senegal Sierra	Congo	Togo
Honduras	Leone	The Gambia	
Madagascar	Tanzania	Guinea	
Malawi	Uganda	Guinea-Bissau	
	Zambia	Haiti	
		Liberia	

Source: World Bank

HIPC debt relief is provided in stages, based on each country's performance against a defined set of economic targets and requirements. HIPC-eligible countries must successfully implement IMF-proscribed reforms for three years before reaching the "decision point" and receiving intermediate debt relief. Following a further track record of good economic policy, a country reaches "completion point" where the remaining debt relief is granted. Table 1 shows the current status of countries in HIPC initiative.

MDRI Debt Relief

The eventual MDRI agreement was a compromise agreement between the United States and the Europeans. U.S. officials had reportedly argued that the cost of multilateral debt relief could be borne by the institutions and did not require donors' contributing any new assistance. Other creditors believed the institutions should be compensated for their debt forgiveness to avoid diverting potential resources that could be lent to the poorest countries. Any debt relief, they argued, should be additional to existing multilateral assistance. The compromise plan entailed the multilateral development banks receiving new money from creditor nations to offset their debt reductions while the IMF would absorb the cost of debt relief using internal resources.[6]

MDRI Implementation

The IMF was the first of the participating institutions to implement its MDRI debt relief. Under MDRI, the IMF is cancelling all HIPC debt incurred by year-end 2004. In addition to the eligible HIPC countries, the IMF expanded MDRI to all IMF members with per capita incomes of $380 or less. Two non-HIPC countries — Cambodia and Tajikistan — have qualified for MDRI debt relief. To date, the IMF has provided MDRI debt relief to 21 countries, totaling $3.67 billion. The IMF expects that total MDRI debt relief will be around $5 billion if all eligible countries complete the program.

Unlike the IMF, both the World Bank and the Asian Development Bank are only providing MDRI relief to HIPC completion point countries. Only debts accrued prior to year-end 2003 are eligible for World Bank/AfDB MDRI debt relief. If fully implemented, the World Bank will provide about $37 billion in debt relief. African Development Bank debt relief would be $8.5 billion.

Policy Issues

There are numerous reasons why policy-makers support poor country debt relief. Debt relief emerged as a foreign policy issue mainly through moral arguments against requiring the poorest countries to repay their debts. At a United Nations conference on Africa in 2004, Columbia University professor and United Nations advisor Jeffrey Sachs remarked: "No civilized nation should try to collect the debts of people who are dying of hunger and disease and poverty."[7]

Others, including the Bush Administration, presented what they viewed as a pragmatic argument for debt relief. They argued that debt was "locking these poorest countries into poverty and preventing them from using their own resources [for development]."[8] By providing debt relief, they argued, resources that would have been allocated for debt repayments would now be redirected toward new investment and/or domestic social services. At a press release announcing the MDRI deal, former World Bank president Paul Wolfowitz announced that, "across Africa and around the world, leaders in 38 countries will no longer have to choose between spending to benefit their people and repaying impossible debts."[9]

Recent studies cast doubt, however, on debt relief's contribution to larger development and poverty reduction goals. These studies argue that poor underlying economic and political conditions are the main reason for the HIPCs' poor performance. In light of this research, Congress may wish to explore in more depth what effect debt has on poor countries' economies and under what conditions debt relief can help promote economic growth and poverty reduction.

How Debt Affects the HIPC Countries

Historically, policymakers and academics viewed high levels of debt as a constraint on economic growth. It was argued that as long as investors expected a country's debt level to impair its ability to repay its loans — its "debt overhang" — investors would abstain from entering a country out of a concern that the government may resort to distortionary or inflationary measures, such as expanding the money supply or raising taxes on their profits, to finance debt payments. Even if the debt is not being serviced, the theory suggests that it is still an impediment to economic growth because of the effect the large debt stock has of dissuading private investors. In a debt overhang situation, the appropriate policy response is to forgive the debt, either entirely or to some "sustainable" level so that investor confidence will be restored.[10] Debt overhang theory was instrumental in driving the development of the HIPC program. Over time however, it became apparent that the theory was not especially well suited for the poorest countries, which relied on foreign assistance, rather than private investment, as their key source of foreign capital.

According to the World Bank's 2006 evaluation of the HIPC program, debt relief alone is not sufficient for debt sustainability in the poorest countries. Under HIPC, 18 countries had their debt levels reduced to half their initial levels, cancelling $19 billion of external debt. However, in 11 out of the 13 countries (with data available), the debt situation has worsened. In 8 countries, debt levels once again exceed HIPC thresholds.[11]

Several reasons may explain this situation. First, the concepts of "sustainable debt" and "debt overhang" may be inappropriate for the HIPC countries. Earlier debt overhang models were designed with middle-income countries in mind, which were suffering under heavy non-concessional private debt. For example, when financial crises hit Latin American countries in the 1980s, their debts were resolved under the "Brady Plan" (negotiated by former Secretary of the Treasury Nicholas Brady). The forgiveness of debt amounted to $60 billion, after which, private capital surged into the Brady countries. These countries received $210 billion dollars in net capital flows in the five years following their debt write-off.[12]

In the case of the HIPC countries, investors were more likely to stay away for other reasons, such as political and economic instability, rather than any concerns about indebtedness per se. Moreover, unlike other debtor nations, bilateral and multilateral HIPC debt is highly concessional (i.e., inexpensive) compared to private sector debt. Foreign aid providers have not stopped their aid just because they are not being repaid 100% on their bilateral debt. Moreover, the inflow of foreign aid funds is typically more than sufficient to cover debt payments, so the cost of debt service is effectively borne by the donor countries rather than by the debtors.

Secondly, there are additional factors, unique to the poorest countries, that may promote increased indebtedness. Since their debt is highly concessional, there may be a perverse incentive for countries not to grow in order to remain eligible for multilateral assistance. Preliminary evidence looking at 94 countries (33 of which are low income) over 1988-2000 found evidence of this effect. A significant number of countries appeared to stagnate around the income level that defined eligibility for concessional assistance. Above the cutoff level, countries would no longer be able to receive concessional aid. By diverting their assistance away from investment toward consumption they were able to hover just below the eligibility cutoff.[13]

Issues for Congress

High levels of debt, especially in the case of the poorest and most indebted countries, are largely a symptom of deeper, more fundamental economic and societal difficulties. Removing pre-existing debt is not seen as improving growth or reducing poverty by itself. This raises two key questions that the second session of the 110th Congress may wish to consider: (1) what impact can the MDRI be expected to have on poverty reduction; and (2) what policies could make poor country debt relief more effective in reducing poverty and/or promoting economic growth?

The impact of MDRI debt relief will likely be modest at best. First, by definition, MDRI debt relief does not increase the overall resources available to poor countries. Any debt relief that a country receives results in a net decrease in future multilateral aid resources allocated. Second, the amount of debt relief provided by MDRI is small. In the case of the 15 African HIPCs, on average, they paid $19 million in debt service to the World Bank in 2004. That same year, they received $197 million in new World Bank aid and $946 million in total aid.[14] Any debt relief, even if it were in addition to existing foreign aid, would provide only a minuscule increase in domestic resources. Thus it appears that debt relief can have its largest impact if it is situated as part of a broader package of reforms that include, among other things, increased debt management capacity, and targeted growth enhancing changes in national policy.[15]

End Notes

[1] See CRS Report RL33073, *Debt Relief for the Heavily Indebted Poor Countries: Issues and Options for Congress*, by Martin A. Weiss.

[2] *The Millennium Development Goals Report 2006*, United Nations, New York, 2006.

[3] In November 2006, the Inter-American Development Bank separately announced that it agreed to provide 100% debt relief to five Latin American HIPCs: Bolivia, Guyana, Haiti, Honduras, and Nicaragua. Bachelet, Pablo. "IDB OK's massive debt relief package for five nations," *Miami Herald*. November 18, 2006.

[4] See CRS Report RS2 1482, *The Paris Club and International Debt Relief*, by Martin A. Weiss.

[5] U.S. Treasury Department and the Office of Management and Budget. U.S. Government Foreign Credit Exposure as of December 31, 2005, Part I, p. 19

[6] Eric Helleiner and Geoffrey Cameron, "Another World Order? The Bush Administration and the HIPC Debt Cancellation," *New Political Economy*, Vol. 11, No. 1, March 2006.

[7] Quoted in "Is There a Way Out of the Debt Trap?" *International Food Policy Research Institute Forum*, December 2004.

[8] Quoted in Paul Blustein, "Debt Cut Is Set for Poorest Nations — Deal Would Cancel $40 Billion in Loans," *The Washington Post*, June 12, 2005.

[9] International Monetary Fund& World Bank Development Committee Press Briefing, September 25, 2005.

[10] Paul Krugman, "Financing vs. Forgiving a Debt Overhang." *Journal of Development Economics*, vol. 29, 1988, pp. 253-268; and Jeffrey Sachs, "The Debt Overhang of Developing Countries," in Guillermo A. Calvo and others, eds., *Debt Stabilization and Development, Essays in Memory of Carlos Dias Alejandro*, Oxford, U.K.: Basil Blackwell, 1989.

[11] *Debt Relief for the Poorest: An Evaluation Update of the HIPC Initiative*, The World Bank Independent Evaluation Group, 2006.

[12] Serkan Arslanalp and Peter Blair Henry, "Helping the Poor to Help Themselves: Debt Relief or Aid?" in *Sovereign Debt at the Crossroads*, edited by Chris Jochnick and Fraser A. Preston. Oxford University Press, 2006.

[13] Junko Koeda, "A Debt Overhang Model for Low Income Countries: Implications for Debt Relief," *International Monetary Fund Working Paper WP/06/224*, October, 2006.

[14] Todd Moss, "Will Debt Relief Make a Difference? Impact and Expectations of the Multilateral Debt Relief Initiative," *Center for Global Development Working Paper Number 88*, May 2006.

[15] CRS Report RL3 0449, Debt *and Development in Poor Countries: Rethinking Policy Responses*, by J.F. Hornbeck.

In: Multilateral Development Banks and International Finance   ISBN: 978-1-61728-883-8
Editor: Leah M. Groffe   © 2010 Nova Science Publishers, Inc.

Chapter 7

DEVELOPING COUNTRIES: THE UNITED STATES HAS NOT FULLY FUNDED ITS SHARE OF DEBT RELIEF, AND THE IMPACT OF DEBT RELIEF ON COUNTRIES' POVERTY-REDUCING SPENDING IS UNKNOWN[*]

United States Government Accountability Office

WHY GAO DID THIS STUDY

In 1996, the Heavily Indebted Poor Countries (HIPC) Initiative was created to provide debt relief to poor countries that had reached unsustainable levels of debt. In 2005, the Multilateral Debt Relief Initiative (MDRI) expanded upon the HIPC Initiative by eliminating additional debt owed to four international financial institutions (IFI): the International Monetary Fund (IMF), World Bank's International Development Association (IDA), African Development Fund (ADF), and Inter-American Development Bank (IaDB). These four IFIs are projected to provide $58 billion in total debt relief to 41 countries. GAO (1) analyzed the U.S. financing approach for debt relief efforts; (2) reviewed the extent to which MDRI might affect resources available to countries for poverty-reducing activities; and (3) assessed revisions to the analyses conducted by the World Bank and IMF to review and promote future debt sustainability. GAO analyzed Treasury, IFI, and country documents and data, and interviewed officials at Treasury and the four IFIs.

WHAT GAO RECOMMENDS

To address limitations in the U.S. approach for financing MDRI, GAO recommends that the Secretary of the Treasury consider the use of different funding options, such as requesting

---

[*] This is an edited, reformatted and augmented version of a U. S. Government Accountability Office publication, Report #GAO-19-162, dated January 2009.

separate appropriations from Congress. Treasury responded that it is open to considering alternative MDRI funding approaches in the future.

To view the full product, including the scope and methodology, click on GAO-09-162.

For more information, contact Thomas Melito at (202) 512-9601 or MelitoT@gao.gov.

WHAT GAO FOUND

Treasury's approach to financing MDRI, known as early encashment, does not fully fund current and future U.S. commitments. The approach does not fully fund the current U.S. MDRI commitment because the United States is in arrears on its IDA replenishment. These arrears are due to requirements under U.S. law for withholdings and across-the-board rescissions. Under early encashment, the World Bank requires that the U.S. commitment to the IDA replenishment be paid in full before early encashment income can be used to fund MDRI. The World Bank deducts the U.S. arrears to IDA from any early encashment income before applying this income toward the U.S. MDRI commitment, resulting in a current MDRI shortfall of $149 million. Treasury officials said that if the United States ultimately pays its arrears to the IDA replenishment, early encashment income will then fully fund the U.S. MDRI commitment. However, to fully fund the U.S. MDRI commitment, (1) Treasury will need to release a withholding of $94 million by reporting to Congress that the World Bank has accomplished transparency reforms required under U.S. law, and (2) Congress will need to appropriate approximately $49 million to compensate for the rescissions. Moreover, GAO estimates that the early encashment approach will be insufficient to fully finance future U.S. MDRI commitments even if U.S. payments are made on time and in full because these commitments exceed projected early encashment income.

GAO estimates that the HIPC Initiative and MDRI debt relief from the four IFIs combined may provide countries for which data are available with nearly $44 billion in additional resources over the next 50 years, but the extent to which countries spend these resources on activities to reduce poverty is unknown. In addition to providing debt relief, the MDRI program for IDA and ADF provides for a reallocation of assistance, based in part on a consideration of the strength of country policies and institutions. The estimated amount of this MDRI assistance individual countries receive will vary. Although IFIs and the U.S. government encourage recipient countries to spend resources generated from debt relief on efforts to reduce poverty, the extent to which such spending occurs is unknown for two reasons. First, debt relief resources are difficult to track, because these resources cannot easily be separated from other types of financial flows such as international assistance and fiscal revenues. Second, country data on poverty-reducing expenditures are not comparable across countries and also may not be reliable.

The World Bank and IMF have improved their country debt sustainability analyses (DSA) since 2005, including by addressing weaknesses GAO previously reported. DSAs now consider the strength of a country's policies and institutions in determining sustainable debt loads and assess future debt sustainability under multiple scenarios that adjust economic assumptions. Furthermore, IDA and ADF now structure their assistance based on a country's risk of debt distress. While the new DSAs have identified numerous ambitious actions countries should take to avoid eroding their debt sustainability, implementing these actions could prove difficult.

ABBREVIATIONS

ADF	African Development Fund
CBO	Congressional Budget Office
CPIA	Country Policy and Institutional Assessment
DRF	Debt Reduction Facility
DSA	debt sustainability analysis
DSF	Debt Sustainability Framework
GAAP	generally accepted accounting principles
HIPC	Heavily Indebted Poor Country
IaDB	Inter-American Development Bank
IDA	International Development Association
IFI	International Financial Institution
IMF	International Monetary Fund
MDG	Millennium Development Goals
MDRI	Multilateral Debt Relief Initiative
MTDS	Medium-Term Debt Management Strategies
NPV	net present value
OECD	Organization for Economic Coordination and Development
PRGF	Poverty Reduction and Growth Facility
PRSP	Poverty Reduction Strategy Paper
PV	present value
UN	United Nations

January 26, 2009
Congressional Requesters

A buildup of foreign debt throughout the 1970s and 1980s—combined with low growth, falling commodity prices, and other economic difficulties— left many poor countries with significantly more debt than they could repay. In order to address this problem, the international community has provided increasing amounts of debt relief to 41 such heavily indebted poor countries over the last decade. These efforts include the Heavily Indebted Poor Country (HIPC) Initiative, which was launched in 1996 as an approach for international financial institutions (IFI), commercial creditors, and individual nations to lower the debt levels of the world's poorest and most indebted nations to "sustainable" levels. "Sustainable" means that a country can make its future debt payments on time and without rescheduling.

Multilateral debt relief efforts culminated in the Multilateral Debt Relief Initiative (MDRI), which was announced in 2005. MDRI involves fewer creditors than the HIPC Initiative, eliminating additional eligible debt that countries owe to four IFIs—the World Bank's International Development Association (IDA), the International Monetary Fund (IMF), the African Development Bank's African Development Fund (ADF), and the Inter-

American Development Bank (IaDB).[1] MDRI was created to assist countries in increasing their funding for poverty-reducing activities and accelerating progress toward achieving the United Nations (UN) Millennium Development Goals (MDG).[2] Countries must complete the HIPC Initiative before they can receive MDRI debt relief. Of the 41 countries that may benefit from both programs, 23 have received irrevocable HIPC Initiative and MDRI debt relief and another 11 have begun receiving debt relief under the HIPC Initiative. Another seven countries are potentially eligible for debt relief but have not yet met the requirements for such relief.

We estimate that IDA, IMF, ADF, and IaDB will provide about $58 billion in debt relief under the HIPC and MDRI Initiatives to 41 countries over the next several decades.[3] Donor governments (including the U.S. government) have agreed to help fund multilateral debt relief. Donor governments have provided funding to IFIs to support the HIPC Initiative through means such as a trust fund established at the World Bank. To fund MDRI, governments may (1) provide funding in addition to their regular contributions or replenishments to the institutions,[4] (2) provide their regular contributions early and generate credits through an approach known as early encashment, or (3) do both. The U.S. Department of the Treasury (Treasury) is currently using early encashment to fund the U.S. MDRI commitment. In July 2008, we reported that even if the U.S. government provides full funding for IDA, this early encashment approach results in a U.S. funding shortfall for MDRI by 2014.[5]

In response to your request, we (1) analyzed the U.S. financing approach for debt relief efforts; (2) reviewed the extent to which MDRI might affect resources available to countries for poverty-reducing activities;[6] and (3) assessed revisions to the analyses conducted by the World Bank and IMF to review and promote future debt sustainability. In addition, you asked us to review strategies for addressing legal actions brought by companies to collect outstanding claims from countries receiving HIPC and MDRI debt relief. These strategies are discussed in appendix II. We have previously reviewed debt-related issues, including the HIPC Initiative and MDRI.[7]

To address these objectives, we reviewed documents and analyzed data provided by Treasury, the World Bank, IMF, ADF, and IaDB, and spoke with officials at Treasury and these four institutions. We also examined poverty reduction strategy papers, country budget documents, and debt sustainability analyses. We prepared our own estimates regarding the sufficiency of the U.S. funding approach for MDRI as well as the amount of assistance that will be provided to beneficiary countries by the HIPC Initiative and MDRI. Our calculations reflect relevant data for debt relief countries as of November 21, 2008. All figures provided in this chapter are expressed in end-2008 present value dollars unless otherwise noted. To illustrate the impact of debt relief on individual countries, we selected five countries (Ethiopia, Ghana, Nicaragua, Rwanda, and Tanzania) as case studies based on several criteria, including geographic diversity and dispersion of country ranking in terms of the percentage of total HIPC and MDRI debt relief they received from the four institutions. In terms of percentage of debt relief received, we selected countries at or near the top, middle, and bottom of the ranking as examples of how the program works. Our choice of countries is meant to be illustrative, not representative. We assessed the reliability of the data analyzed and found the data to be sufficiently reliable for the purposes of this chapter.

We conducted this performance audit from December 2007 through January 2009 in accordance with generally accepted government auditing standards. Those standards require that we plan and perform the audit to obtain sufficient, appropriate evidence to provide a reasonable basis for our findings and conclusions based on our audit objectives. We believe that the evidence obtained provides a reasonable basis for our findings and conclusions based on our audit objectives. (See app. I for more detailed information regarding our scope and methodology.)

RESULTS IN BRIEF

Treasury's approach to financing MDRI, known as early encashment, does not fully fund current and future U.S commitments. The approach does not fully fund the current U.S. MDRI commitment because the United States is in arrears to the World Bank on its IDA replenishment. These arrears are due to requirements under U.S. law for withholdings and across-the-board rescissions. Under early encashment, the World Bank requires that the U.S. commitment to the IDA replenishment be paid in full before early encashment income can be used to fund MDRI. The World Bank deducts the U.S. arrears to IDA from any early encashment income before applying this income toward the U.S. MDRI commitment, resulting in a current MDRI shortfall of $149 million. Treasury officials said that if the United States ultimately pays its arrears to the IDA replenishment, early encashment income will then fully fund the U.S. MDRI commitment. However, to fully fund the U.S. MDRI commitment, (1) Treasury will need to release a withholding of $94 million from the IDA14 replenishment, by reporting to Congress that the World Bank has accomplished transparency reforms required under U.S. law, and (2) Congress will need to appropriate approximately $49 million in funds to compensate for the rescissions. Both actions will need to be completed by June 30, 2009. Moreover, we estimate that the early encashment approach will be insufficient to fully finance future U.S. MDRI commitments even if U.S. payments are made on time and in full because these commitments exceed projected early encashment income.

We estimate that HIPC Initiative and MDRI debt relief from the four IFIs combined may provide beneficiary countries for which data are available with a total of nearly $44 billion in additional resources over the next 50 years, but the extent to which countries spend these additional resources on activities to reduce poverty is unknown. According to our projections, HIPC assistance may provide over $21 billion in debt relief to recipient countries, while MDRI may generate over $22 billion in additional resources. In addition to providing debt relief, the MDRI program for IDA and ADF provides for a reallocation of assistance, based in part on a consideration of the strength of country policies and institutions. The estimated amount of this MDRI assistance individual countries receive will vary as countries realize increases or decreases in their assistance from IDA and ADF. Although IFIs and the U.S. government encourage recipient countries to spend resources generated from debt relief on efforts to reduce poverty, the extent to which such spending occurs is unknown. IMF and World Bank documents suggest an association between increased debt relief and increased poverty-reducing expenditures, but it is difficult to demonstrate that debt relief has led directly to increased poverty- reducing expenditures for two reasons. First, debt relief resources are difficult to track, because the resources generated by debt relief cannot easily be separated from other types of financial flows such as international assistance and fiscal revenues. Second, country data on poverty-reducing expenditures are not comparable across countries and also may not be reliable.

The World Bank and IMF have improved their country debt sustainability analyses (DSA) since 2005, including by addressing weaknesses that GAO previously identified, and these new DSAs have identified numerous ambitious actions countries should take in order to avoid future unsustainable debt levels. The new DSAs differ from other analyses by considering country performance in determining sustainable debt loads, and assessing debt sustainability under several scenarios that include varying assumptions of future economic growth. This approach addresses past GAO concerns that DSAs contained only one scenario, which may have been based on overly optimistic economic assumptions. Furthermore, IDA and ADF now structure their future assistance to countries based on a country's risk of future debt distress. Countries with a high risk of debt distress receive grant assistance, while countries with a low risk of debt distress receive concessional loans. This approach is aligned with our past reporting that the increased use of grant assistance would have a positive impact on poor country debt sustainability. The new DSAs have identified numerous actions countries should take in order to avoid future unsustainable debt levels. For example, for the 13 countries with a moderate or high risk of future debt distress, DSAs note that projected debt sustainability could be further eroded if countries do not take actions such as implementing sound macroeconomic policies or realizing sustained national income or export growth. Achieving such ambitious objectives could prove difficult for these poor countries over the course of the 20-year projection period.

To address limitations in the U.S. approach for financing MDRI, we recommend that the Secretary of the Treasury consider the use of different funding options that clarify the priority between paying U.S. arrears owed to IDA and paying MDRI obligations, such as requesting separate appropriations from Congress.

The Department of the Treasury, the World Bank, and IMF provided written comments on a draft of this chapter, which are reprinted in appendixes IX, X, and XI. Treasury stated that it is open to our recommendation that alternative U.S. funding approaches for MDRI be considered in the future. Treasury emphasized its objective to fully meet its current IDA and MDRI funding commitments while also noting that a lack of full funding would jeopardize this objective. Similarly, the World Bank stressed the importance of full funding for IDA and a sustainable U.S. funding approach to cover debt relief costs. IMF noted its disagreement with our position that the impact of debt relief on poverty- reducing spending is unknown. We maintain that our position is accurate since, while data compiled by IMF report that poverty-reducing spending has increased in countries receiving debt relief, it is not possible to link

such increases to debt relief. Treasury, the World Bank, IMF, and the African Development Bank provided technical comments on a draft of this chapter, which we have incorporated as appropriate. We requested comments from IaDB, but none were provided.

BACKGROUND

Bilateral creditors and IFIs created the HIPC Initiative in 1996 to address concerns that certain poor countries had accumulated unsustainable debt burdens, despite receiving debt relief from bilateral creditors. In response to concerns over the continuing vulnerability of poor countries, the World Bank and IMF enhanced the initiative in 1999 by reducing the qualifying thresholds and increasing the number of potentially eligible countries. Countries must meet numerous criteria in order to qualify for HIPC Initiative debt relief, such as establishing a track record of reform and sound policies. To fully benefit from HIPC debt relief, countries must progress through different phases of the initiative (see figure 1). At a country's "decision point," IDA and IMF use certain criteria to determine whether a country qualifies to receive HIPC Initiative debt relief. If a country is determined to qualify, it can begin to receive interim HIPC debt relief. Subsequently, at the "completion point," IDA and IMF determine whether the country meets additional criteria and can receive full and irrevocable HIPC debt relief. As of November 2008, of the 41 countries that may benefit from debt relief efforts, 23 had reached the completion point and 11 more had reached the decision point. An additional seven countries are considered "pre-decision point" countries and have not yet qualified for debt relief.[8] MDRI expands upon the HIPC Initiative and represents the most recent effort to provide debt relief to heavily indebted poor countries. To receive MDRI debt relief, countries must first complete the HIPC Initiative.

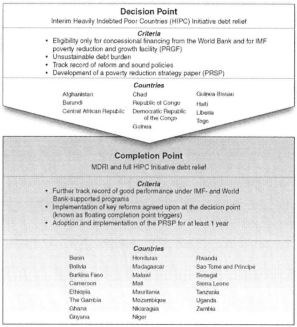

Source: IMF and World Bank documents.
Note: Countries develop a poverty reduction strategy paper (PRSP), which outlines the goals and objectives for reducing poverty, every 3 years through a participatory process involving domestic stakeholders as well as external development partners, including the World Bank and IMF.

Figure 1. Process for Receiving HIPC Initiative and MDRI Debt Relief

In addition, IMF has determined that it will provide MDRI debt relief to member countries with debt outstanding to IMF and a per capita income at or below $380 at end-2004 that do not otherwise qualify for debt relief.[9] While the HIPC Initiative provides for a reduction in the debt levels of eligible countries, the process associated with MDRI debt relief requires IDA and ADF to take additional actions that provide resources to poor countries beyond those countries benefiting from debt relief.[10]

We estimate that IDA, IMF, ADF, and IaDB will provide, in present value dollars, about $58 billion in debt relief (in end-2008 present value dollars) under the HIPC and MDRI Initiatives to 41 countries over the next several decades.[11] The amount of total debt relief provided under each initiative will be about equal, with over $28 billion provided under the HIPC Initiative and about $30 billion provided under MDRI. IDA is to provide the greatest level of debt relief at $34 billion (almost 60 percent of the total). IMF is to provide $10.6 billion, while ADF and IaDB are to provide $9.1 billion and $4.1 billion, respectively. Table 1 provides data on the amount of funding each institution will provide for each program.

For the 33 countries[12] currently receiving debt relief under both programs, IDA has secured about $8.6 billion for the HIPC Initiative and $4.4 billion for MDRI (for more detailed information, see app. III). This total of $13.1 billion represents 47 percent of the total required IDA financing of almost $27.8 billion for these countries under both debt relief initiatives. ADF will provide about $7.5 billion in HIPC Initiative and MDRI debt relief and has secured about $5.7 billion, about 76 percent of this amount. IMF and IaDB have fully financed their $8 billion and $3.8 billion of HIPC Initiative and MDRI debt relief for the countries currently receiving such relief, respectively, using internal resources and donor-provided funds. Because these two institutions have fully funded their HIPC Initiative and MDRI debt relief, almost 65 percent of total debt relief costs for all four IFIs has been secured.

Based on our projections, the United States has committed to provide a total of about $8.4 billion to the four IFIs to finance the total costs of their HIPC Initiative and MDRI debt relief (see table 2).

We estimate that the U.S. government is to provide $6.2 billion, or 74 percent, of its debt relief financing to IDA and $1.3 billion, or 16 percent, to ADF. The U.S. government has already provided $0.5 billion to IDA and $0.9 billion to ADF, leaving the majority of these costs ($5.7 billion for IDA and $0.4 billion for ADF) to be paid in the future. The U.S. government has provided $0.8 billion to IMF and $0.1 billion to IaDB. Of the $2.3 billion that the United States has already provided, $2.0 billion was for the HIPC Initiative and $0.3 billion was for MDRI. (App. IV provides information on bilateral debt relief that the United States has provided to countries under the HIPC Initiative.)

Table 1. Total HIPC Initiative and MDRI Debt Relief by International Financial Institution for 41 Countries (In billions of end-2008 present value dollars)

	IDA	IMF	ADF	IaDB	Total
HIPC	$15.0	$6.4	$5.3	$1.7	$28.4
MDRI	19.2	4.2	3.8	2.4	29.6
Total	**$34.2**	**$10.6**	**$9.1**	**$4.1**	**$58.0**

Source: GAO analysis of IMF and World Bank documents.

Table 2. Estimated U.S. Financing of Multilateral Debt Relief by International Financial Institution (In billions of end-2008 present value dollars)

	IDA		IMF		ADF		IaDB		Total	
	Estimate	Paid	Estimate	Paid	Estimate	Paid	Estimate	Paid	Estimate	Paid
HIPC	$2.3	0.3	0.7	0.7	0.9	0.9	0.1	0.1	4.0	2.0
MDRI	3.9	0.2	0.1	0.1	0.4	0.02	0	0	4.4	0.3
Total	**6.2**	**0.5**	**0.8**	**0.8**	**1.3**	**0.9**	**0.1**	**0.1**	**8.4**	**2.3**

Source: GAO analysis of Treasury, IADB, IMF, ADF, and IDA documents.

Note: Estimated U.S. financing for IMF includes transfers of the U.S. share of $0.47 billion from the PRGF-HIPC Trust fund for HIPC, $0.10 billion from the PRGF-ESF Trust Subsidy account for MDRI, and a commitment of $0.20 billion for HIPC debt relief to Liberia.

U.S. APPROACH TO FINANCING MDRI DOES NOT FULLY FUND CURRENT AND FUTURE U.S. COMMITMENTS

Treasury, IDA, and ADF have agreed to a financing approach for MDRI called early encashment, under which the U.S. government earns income for early replenishment payments to IDA and ADF. Since the U.S. government is currently in arrears on its replenishment payments to IDA14, early encashment does not fully fund the current U.S. MDRI commitment. We also estimate that U.S. early encashment income will be insufficient to fully finance future MDRI debt relief. Furthermore, the U.S. financing approach is more costly than other options.

Treasury Uses Early Encashment to Generate Income

The U.S. government currently uses an early encashment approach to fund U.S. MDRI obligations at both IDA and ADF.[13] Early encashment income is earned by IDA and ADF when the United States allows the IFI to draw funds on, or encash, its replenishment commitment early, rather than according to a standard encashment schedule that spans 9 years for IDA and 10 years for ADF. The standard encashment schedule represents the IFI's expected disbursement pattern of the funds committed during the 3- year replenishment period. Treasury has agreed to allow IDA and ADF to encash the U.S. replenishment commitment over an accelerated 4-year period. Since the early encashments exceed amounts required during the first 4 years under the regular 9-year or 10-year encashment schedule, IDA and ADF can invest these funds and earn income (see app. V). IDA and ADF guarantee fixed discount rates that determine the amount of income countries using the early encashment approach will receive for full and timely encashments according to the accelerated schedule, regardless of IDA's and ADF's actual earnings on early encashments over the period.

These amounts are then credited to the U.S. government and can be used toward paying the U.S. MDRI commitment. Treasury has separate agreements with IDA and ADF regarding the methodology used to estimate the amount of early encashment income that the United States will earn.

United States in Arrears on Its IDA14 Replenishment Commitment

The World Bank requires that the U.S. IDA14 replenishment be paid in full before early encashment income can be earned and used to fund MDRI; however, the United States is currently in arrears on its replenishment commitment. In recent years, Congress has withheld a portion of the U.S. replenishment contribution to encourage the World Bank to undertake specified reforms such as strengthened efforts to enhance transparency and combat corruption.[14] In fiscal year 2006, Congress required that 20 percent of the funds appropriated to IDA be withheld from disbursement until the Secretary of the Treasury reported to Congress that the World Bank had undertaken certain anticorruption reforms.[15] In fiscal year 2006, most of these funds were eventually disbursed pursuant to the requirements in the law; however, there was a shortfall in fiscal year 2006 of approximately $41 million due to both the anti-corruption withholding provision and an across-the-board rescission. In fiscal year 2007 there was an additional rescission of about $9.5 million. In fiscal year 2008, Congress rescinded $7.7 million and required that 10 percent, or $94 million, of IDA funds be withheld until Treasury reported that the World Bank had undertaken anticorruption reforms, and that another 10 percent be withheld until Treasury reported that the World Bank had enacted certain transparency reforms.[16] As of July 2008, Treasury had reported to Congress that the World Bank had enacted anti-corruption reforms called for in the fiscal year 2008 appropriations law and had disbursed the corresponding funds. However, Treasury still had not reported to Congress that the World Bank had accomplished all of the 2008 transparency reforms and continued to withhold funds. Treasury has complied with its legal obligation to withhold these funds that have created arrears.[17] When funds are rescinded or withheld from IDA, the shortfall amounts become arrears of the United States that remain until the appropriated funds are released from Treasury. We estimate that the U.S. government has arrears to the IDA14 replenishment of about $152 million, since the U.S. nominal contribution of $2,698 million is less than the U.S. commitment of $2,850 million.[18]

U.S. Early Encashment Income Insufficient to Fully Finance Current MDRI Debt Relief Due to Arrears

Because the United States is currently in arrears on its IDA14 replenishment commitment, the early encashment income the United States earns does not fully finance the current U.S. MDRI commitment. Under the early encashment process, the World Bank first uses early encashment income to fund the present value of the shortfall in the U.S. IDA replenishment before applying early encashment income to the U.S. MDRI commitment. As such, the present value of the U.S. replenishment to IDA14 will be fully funded before the MDRI obligation begins to be paid. As shown in figure 2, based on current U.S. payments, we estimate that the United States will generate sufficient early encashment income to fully fund the U.S. IDA14 replenishment commitment in present value dollars, with $83 million in encashment income applied toward the $232 million U.S. MDRI commitment. After applying its earned encashment income of $83 million, the United States will have a shortfall of $149 million in its MDRI commitment.[19]

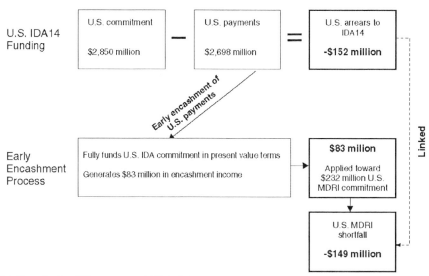

Source: GAO analysis of Treasury and IDA data.
Note: U.S. payments of $2,698 million include a payment of $47 million that will be encashed by June 30, 2009.

Figure 2. U.S. Replenishment, MDRI Commitment and Payments for IDA 14 (2006 through 2008, in millions of nominal dollars)

Treasury officials noted that if the United States ultimately pays its arrears to the IDA14 replenishment, early encashment income will then fund the U.S. MDRI commitment. However, to fully fund the U.S. MDRI commitment, (1) Treasury will need to release a withholding of $94 million from the IDA14 replenishment, by reporting to Congress that the World Bank has accomplished transparency reforms required under U.S. law, and (2) Congress will need to appropriate approximately $49 million in funds to compensate for the rescissions. Both actions will need to be completed by June 30, 2009. We estimate that the additional encashment income generated from releasing the $94 million will amount to $97 million and the shortfall in the U.S. MDRI commitment will decrease from $149 million to $52 million. A congressional appropriation of approximately $49 million by June 30, 2009 would generate enough early encashment income to finance the remaining $52 million U.S. MDRI commitment.[20]

Although it is unknown whether there will be any future shortfalls in U.S. replenishment payments, we assessed the impact of a shortfall on U.S. financing of MDRI similar to those that have occurred in recent years. The U.S. replenishment obligation for IDA for 2009 through 2011 is $3.7 billion, which includes $375 million for IDA's HIPC Initiative costs. In addition, the United States has agreed to pay $356 million for its MDRI commitment, which Treasury plans to finance using early encashment. We assumed a 5 percent across-the-board shortfall, slightly less than the current 5.3 percent shortfall during the 2006 through 2008 period. (See app. V for further information on this simulation.) Under this scenario, the U.S. government would make payments of $3.52 billion, leaving a shortfall of $185 million. U.S. early payments would generate investment income of $308 million. After first financing the replenishment shortfall, the remaining early encashment income of $146 million would be used to pay the U.S. MDRI commitment of $356 million, leaving a MDRI shortfall of $210 million.[21]

ADF and Treasury have agreed to a different approach to calculate early encashment income that does not prioritize paying replenishment shortfalls before funding MDRI. All encashment income is solely used to pay the U.S. MDRI commitment. Excess encashment income is used to pay future U.S. MDRI commitments when needed. Any arrears or shortfalls in U.S. replenishment payments reduce encashment income proportionately. None of the early encashment income is used to offset regular replenishment shortfalls.

U.S. Early Encashment Income Insufficient to Fully Finance Future MDRI Debt Relief

The approach of funding the U.S. share of MDRI through early encashment income will not generate sufficient funding to meet the future U.S. commitment under the projected growth rate for future IDA replenishments.[22] As we reported in our July 2008 correspondence, even if the United States pays its replenishments on time and in full, early encashment credits will be insufficient to finance U.S. MDRI obligations by 2014 for IDA and ADF.[23] Table 3 shows the relationship between the U.S. replenishments and the use of early encashment to finance U.S. obligations to MDRI under the World Bank's projected average 7 percent growth rate for IDA replenishments.

Table 3. Projected U.S. MDRI Shortfalls under Projected Growth Rates in U.S. IDA Replenishments for IDA13 through IDA19 (In millions of nominal dollars)

	IDA13 (2003-2005)	IDA14 (2006-2008)	IDA15 (2009-2011)	IDA16 (2012-2014)	IDA17 (2015-2017)	IDA18 (2018-2020)	IDA19 (2021-2023)
U.S. MDRI obligation	N/A	232	356	529	636	726	1,024
		Actual			Projection period		
U.S. replenishment	2,850	2,850	3,705	3,992	4,263	4,541	4,921
U.S. replenishment growth rate	18%	0%	30%	8%	7%	7%	8%
U.S. MDRI shortfall	N/A	-149	0	-145	-225	-289	-550

Source: GAO analysis of Treasury and IDA data.

Notes: The U.S. projected replenishment level is based on the World Bank's projected growth rate in total IDA resources and assumes full and timely payment. IDA14 funding, which was reduced because the U.S. government paid only $2,698 million due to withholdings and rescissions in U.S. law, is an exception. This circumstance has resulted in a shortfall in the U.S. MDRI obligation of $149 million. For IDA12, the U.S. replenishment amount was $2,410 million.

N/A – The U.S. government did not implement MDRI until July 2006.

The first row in table 3 shows the U.S. MDRI commitment from 2006 through 2023 in nominal dollars. Under this scenario, even if the U.S. government pays the replenishments on time and in full, there will be funding shortfalls for each replenishment period that will increase over time. We found that the U.S. government would need to increase its future replenishments to IDA by an average of 31 percent over the next 15 years, in order to fully fund its MDRI obligation using early encashment.

Early Encashment Is More Costly Than Other Options

Treasury's use of an early encashment approach to finance the U.S. share of MDRI debt relief has been more costly than paying U.S. MDRI costs directly because U.S. costs to borrow funds have been greater than the agreed-upon encashment interest rate for IDA and ADF. We estimate that during the replenishment period from 2009 through 2011, early encashment will cost the United States an additional $39 million, $41 million more for IDA and $2 million less for ADF. (See app. VI for more information on this cost differential.) In September 2008, the Congressional Budget Office (CBO) forecasted Treasury note borrowing interest rates. For the 4-year period from fiscal year 2009 through fiscal year 2012, CBO projected the average borrowing cost to the U.S. government to be 5 percent. This interest rate is greater than the 4 percent interest rate used by IDA and the 4.69 percent used by ADF to calculate early encashment credits.[24]

THE EXTENT TO WHICH COUNTRIES SPEND DEBT RELIEF RESOURCES TO REDUCE POVERTY IS UNKNOWN

We estimate that 41 countries[25] are to receive nearly $44 billion in additional MDRI and HIPC resources from the four IFIs, but the degree to which the countries target these resources at poverty-reducing activities is unknown. The $44 billion consists of freed-up resources resulting from HIPC Initiative[26] and MDRI debt relief, as well as a MDRI-related reduction and subsequent reallocation of IDA and ADF assistance.[27] The estimated amount by which IFI assistance will increase or decrease as a result of MDRI resource reallocation varies by country. The World Bank and IMF encourage countries to spend debt relief resources on activities to reduce poverty and make progress toward the UN Millennium Development Goals (MDG). Although the World Bank and IMF have suggested an association between reduced debt service payments and increased poverty-reducing expenditures, the extent to which countries spend debt relief resources on poverty-reducing activities is unknown. It is difficult to establish that debt relief has led directly to increased poverty-reducing expenditures for two reasons: (1) debt relief resources are difficult to track and (2) country spending data are not comparable and also may not be reliable.

Countries Projected to Receive Nearly $44 Billion in Additional HIPC Initiative and MDRI Resources

Overall, we project that the 41 countries receiving debt relief are to receive $43.8 billion in additional resources from the four IFIs between 2000 and 2054. As shown in figure 3, this estimate is based on three projected amounts:

- $21.4 billion in HIPC debt relief,
- $28.3 billion in MDRI debt relief[28] (IFIs will provide about 95 percent of MDRI debt relief by 2034), and
- $5.9 billion in reduced new IDA and ADF assistance resulting from MDRI's two-step process. Under this process, IDA and ADF reduce their new assistance to MDRI debt relief recipients by the amount of debt relief provided,[29] $18.9 billion, and reallocate $13.0 billion of this reduction to MDRI recipients.[30] IDA and ADF then reallocate the remaining approximately $5.9 billion to all low-income countries eligible to receive only concessional resources from IDA or ADF[31] that did not receive debt relief. IDA and ADF determine the amount of funding each country is to receive primarily on the basis of country performance.[32]

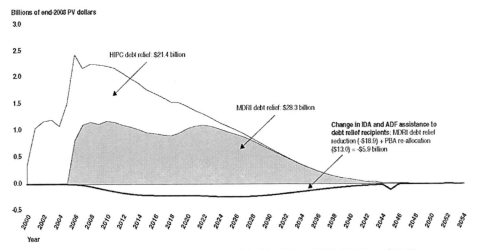

Source: GAO analysis of HIPC and MDRI data provided by IDA, ADF, IaDB, and IMF.

Note: The MDRI debt relief data covers the period 2006-2054 and includes all countries for IDA and ADF and only completion point countries for IMF and IaDB, as these latter IFIs did not provide us with data for the interim and pre-decision point countries. The associated MDRI disbursements cover the period 2006 to 2062.

The HIPC data in this figure cover the period 2000 to 2044 and include all 41 countries for IDA, the 25 completion point and decision point countries for ADF, and IaDB's 4 completion point countries. We obtained limited annual HIPC Initiative data from IMF for completion point and decision point countries covering the period from 2006 onward as IMF delivered the remaining HIPC debt relief as stock reduction rather than on a flow basis and did not provide us annual HIPC data for these countries.

Figure 3. Projected HIPC Initiative and MDRI Annual Debt Relief and IFI Assistance due to MDRI, 2000-2054 (Billions of end- 2008 present value dollars)

Table 4. Projected Change in New IDA and ADF Assistance due to MDRI for Five Countries (In millions of end-2008 present value dollars)

	Projected MDRI debt service relief	Projected change in new IDA and ADF assistance due to MDRI	Total net change in resources available due to MDRI
Ghana	$2,069.7	$(560.7)	$1,509.1
Ethiopia	1,447.9	776.0	2,224.0
Nicaragua	1,014.7	(149.7)	865.0
Rwanda	214.0	92.2	306.2
Tanzania	2,037.3	206.2	2,243.5

Source: GAO analysis of IDA, IaDB, ADF, and IMF MDRI data.

Notes: These calculations are linked to IDA14 performance. See app. I for more information.

Totals may not sum due to rounding.

Net Change in IDA and ADF Assistance for Each Country due to MDRI Varies

Based on our projections, individual countries will have different results from MDRI as they realize increases, decreases, or both in their annual IDA and ADF assistance due to the resource reallocation process. For example, while the overall net change in resources[33] available due to MDRI is positive for each of the five countries we analyzed (Ethiopia, Ghana, Tanzania, Nicaragua, and Rwanda), the countries are projected to receive different amounts of new IDA and ADF assistance. Table 4 illustrates the overall projected impact of MDRI, including the net change in IDA and ADF assistance, for our five case study countries.

We project that, even as MDRI debt relief frees up fiscal resources, Ghana and Nicaragua may experience a decrease in IFI assistance over the life of MDRI due to the MDRI netting out and reallocation process. In contrast, for Tanzania and Ethiopia, we project that this MDRI process may result in an increase in assistance from IDA and ADF. For Rwanda, MDRI may provide a mixture of increases and reductions in IDA and ADF's annual assistance over the MDRI period. (See app. VII for additional information on the impact of MDRI for our five case study countries, and app. VIII for additional information regarding the mechanics of the MDRI process.)

Countries Are Encouraged to Spend Debt Relief Resources on Poverty Reduction, but the Extent of Such Spending Is Unknown

While IFI and U.S. government documents state that countries should spend savings from debt relief on activities to reduce poverty and make progress toward the MDGs, the extent to which countries do so is unknown. In 2008, the World Bank and IMF suggested an association between reduced debt service payments and increased poverty-reducing expenditures, while acknowledging that it is difficult to show causation.[34] Specifically, these IFIs reported that since the late 1990s, the debt service payments of countries that received debt relief have declined by about 2 percent of GDP, while poverty-reducing expenditures have increased by about the same amount.[35] However, it is difficult to establish that debt relief has led directly to increased poverty-reducing expenditures for two reasons: (1) debt relief resources are difficult to track, and (2) country spending data are not comparable and also may not be reliable.

Debt Relief Resources Are Difficult to Track

The IFIs have suggested an association between debt relief and increased poverty-reducing expenditures. However, IMF and World Bank officials told us that they are unable to link debt relief resources directly to poverty-reducing expenditures because it is difficult to separate debt relief resources from other types of financial flows, such as international assistance and fiscal revenue. Based on the five case study countries, we found that these other resources often represent a much larger percentage of country budgets than savings from debt relief. For example, in the 2007 budgets of Ethiopia and Ghana, tax revenue and grant assistance represented at least 67 percent of government revenue combined, while HIPC Initiative and MDRI debt relief resources represented less than 8 percent (see figure 4).

Spending Data Are not Comparable and also May not Be Reliable

Although IMF and the World Bank publish aggregated poverty-reducing expenditures for all countries that received debt relief, individual countries can define and report such expenditures differently, resulting in data that are not comparable. We found that definitions of poverty- reducing expenditures vary. For most countries that receive debt relief, reported poverty-reducing expenditures include spending on primary education, basic health care, and rural development; however, countries can also choose to include additional categories.[36] For example, as shown in figure 5, some countries consider expenditures in areas such as energy development, transport, or judicial systems as poverty reducing, while other countries do not.

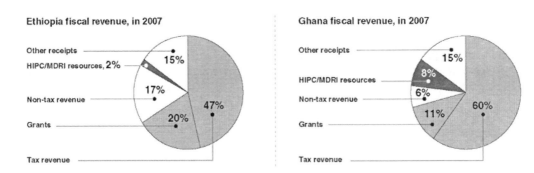

Source: GAO analysis of IMF and World Bank data, and country budget documents..
Note: HIPC/MDRI resources include bilateral and multilateral HIPC relief and multilateral MDRI relief. Other receipts include external and domestic financing. For Ethiopia, the total percentage exceeds 100 due to rounding.

Figure 4. Government Fiscal Revenue for Ethiopia and Ghana in 2007

	Ethiopia	Ghana	Nicaragua	Rwanda	Tanzania
Education	●	—	●	—	●
Primary education	—	○	—	○	—
Health	●	—	●	—	●
Public health	—	○	—	○	—
HIV/AIDs programs	—	—	—	—	○
Rural development	●	—	●	—	●
Poverty focused agriculture	—	○	—	—	—
Water/sanitation	—	—	●	—	●
Rural water	—	○	—	—	—
Roads/transport	●	—	●	—	●
Rural roads	—	○	—	—	—
Energy development	—	—	●	●	—
Rural electricity	—	○	—	—	—
Judicial systems	—	—	—	—	●

● Country reports on aggregate spending in this category, which it considers as poverty reducing

○ Country reports on specific spending in this category, which it considers as poverty reducing

— Country does not consider this category as poverty reducing

Source: GAO analysis of IMF and World Bank data, and country budget documents.

Note: Nicaragua's country budget defined additional categories as poverty reducing, such as the Ministry of Development Industry and Trade, the Nicaraguan Institute for Fishery and Aquaculture, and the Social Investment Fund of Emergency.

Figure 5. Reporting of Five Countries' Poverty-Reducing Categories in 2007

Country definitions of poverty-reducing expenditures can also change over time to include or exclude categories. For example, in 2005, Rwanda expanded its definition of poverty-reducing expenditures to include energy development, while Nicaragua no longer included institutional strengthening. Such differences in definitions between countries, as well as changing definitions for particular countries, complicate comparability across countries and over time.

In addition, we found that three of our five case study countries report aggregate spending in broad areas such as education, health and rural development rather than providing a detailed breakdown of poverty- reducing expenditures in these areas. For example, as shown above, while two countries (Ghana and Rwanda) reported specific spending in primary education and public health in their country budget documents, three countries (Ethiopia, Nicaragua, and Tanzania) reported only on aggregate spending in these two areas.[37] Aggregate spending data can include activities that do not directly affect the poor and may overestimate actual poverty-reducing expenditures. For example, a 2003 IMF and World Bank Poverty and Social Impact Analysis[38] for Nicaragua found that almost no public spending on university education affects the extremely poor, who generally do not participate at that level of the educational system.

Furthermore, country capacity to collect and report on poverty-reducing expenditures is questionable. According to several IFI assessments, countries receiving debt relief have numerous weaknesses in collecting and reporting information on poverty-reducing expenditures that raise doubts about the data's reliability. For example, a 2005 IMF assessment of country capacity to track poverty-reducing expenditures found that 19 out of 26 countries needed substantial upgrades to their data management systems and had weaknesses in tracking budgetary expenditures in areas such as budget formulation, execution and reporting.[39] IMF and the World Bank do not independently track poverty-reducing expenditures, and instead rely on country governments to provide such data even though the accuracy of these data and country capacity to provide such information are uncertain. [40] Additionally, the 2005 IMF assessment found that while 20 countries define poverty-reducing spending in their PRSPs, not all countries could identify these areas of expenditures in their budgets or report on such spending.[41] Limitations in country capacity to report on poverty-reducing spending raise further concerns about the reliability of the combined data published by IMF and the World Bank.

Moreover, while it is difficult to establish that debt relief has led directly to increased poverty-reducing expenditures, it is even more difficult to determine if debt relief has improved progress toward the MDGs. We found that for all five of our case study countries, progress data on the MDG targets were often either lacking or incomplete.[42] In 2008, IMF and the World Bank reported that it is difficult to quantify the impact of debt relief on the MDGs and that they have instead focused their analysis on linking debt relief and poverty-reducing expenditures.[43]

THE WORLD BANK AND IMF HAVE IMPROVED THEIR COUNTRY DEBT SUSTAINABILITY ANALYSES AND IDENTIFIED NUMEROUS ACTIONS COUNTRIES SHOULD TAKE TO AVOID FUTURE UNSUSTAINABLE DEBT LEVELS

The World Bank and IMF have improved their country debt sustainability analyses (DSA) since 2005, including by addressing weaknesses that GAO and others have previously identified. If countries do not realize the objectives outlined in the new DSAs, they once again may experience unsustainable debt levels. These objectives are ambitious and could prove difficult for these poor countries to achieve over the course of the 20-year projection period.

World Bank and IMF Established New Approach That Improves Projections of Country Debt Sustainability

The World Bank and IMF introduced the Debt Sustainability Framework (DSF) in 2005 to provide a new and improved approach to assessing debt sustainability in low-income countries. The DSF is intended to help guide financing for low-income countries' development needs, while also reducing the chances of another excessive build-up of debt in the future;

help detect potential problems early so that preventative action can be taken;

improve World Bank and IMF assessments and policy advice; and

provide guidance for country borrowing and creditor lending decisions.

Under the DSF, IMF and World Bank staff prepare DSAs, which project debt sustainability indicators over a 20-year period and are conducted roughly every 12 to 18 months for low-income countries.[44] These DSAs include elements that were lacking in the past and address weaknesses that had previously been identified by GAO, such as overly-optimistic economic assumptions. Furthermore, DSAs now result in a linkage between debt sustainability and the composition of future IFI assistance (grants and concessional loans), thus addressing a previous GAO assessment that IFIs should provide grants as a way of addressing future debt concerns.

DSAs Determine Risk Based on the Strength of Country Performance and Analysis of Numerous Possible Scenarios

In a departure from prior DSAs,[45] the new DSAs consider the strength of a country's policies and institutions in assessing risk and determining sustainable debt loads; countries with strong policies and institutions are considered capable of successfully carrying greater levels of debt. The DSF uses the World Bank's CPIA index to sort countries into three policy performance categories (strong, medium, or poor). Countries with strong policies and institutions have a higher CPIA rating.[46] An acceptable risk of debt distress for current strong performers, such as Tanzania, allows for higher levels of debt compared to countries with currently low CPIA ratings, such as Sierra Leone. Furthermore, performance categories are updated annually according to the latest CPIA ratings and, therefore, certain countries' annual performance categories have varied since the new process was introduced in 2005. For example, Burkina Faso's 2007 DSA noted that the country was a strong performer, but the country's CPIA rating was subsequently lowered and the 2008 DSA identified Burkina Faso as a medium performer. As a result, DSAs for Burkina Faso now require lower levels of debt in order to be categorized as debt sustainable. The new process provides flexibility to assess every country's risk differently based on individual performance, as well as an ability to adjust risk assessments within a specific country's DSA over time as CPIA ratings shift. Currently, of the 23 countries receiving HIPC Initiative and MDRI debt relief, a majority (14) have been identified as medium performers, 5 as poor performers, and 4 as strong performers.

DSAs conducted under the DSF now consider debt burden "threshold" indicators when assessing a country's debt sustainability position. Five thresholds have been established that provide key insights into a country's debt situation and that vary according to a country's CPIA-based performance category (see table 5). Other DSAs, on the other hand, assess primarily only one variable.[47] Strong performers have higher thresholds, indicating an ability to carry higher debt levels while maintaining debt sustainability.

Table 5. Debt Burden Indicator Thresholds Based on Country Performance Ratings

	Debt as a percentage of			Debt service as a percentage of	
	Exports	GDP	Revenue	Exports	Revenue
Strong	200	50	300	25	35
Medium	150	40	250	20	30
Weak	100	30	200	15	25

Source: Joint World Bank-International Monetary Fund, "Debt Sustainability Framework for Low-Income Countries."

In order to project a country's risk of future debt distress, these threshold indicators are compared against a country's performance under a "baseline" scenario based on assumptions of macroeconomic performance expected for the future in areas such as national income, inflation, exports, imports, and government revenues and expenditures. Various sensitivity scenarios are also used to test the robustness of the indicators to changes in key assumptions. These scenarios include the following: (1) numerous temporary standardized "stress" or "shock" scenarios that consider possibilities such as lower growth in national income or exports than experienced in the past; and (2) two additional scenarios: (a) a scenario that assumes a level of public loans on terms that are less concessional, and (b) a historical scenario that uses macroeconomic assumptions based on past performance (which has often, but not always, been less optimistic than the baseline scenario in the past). IMF and World Bank staff explained that baseline assumptions will diverge from the historical scenario if the institutions agree that the economic outlook of a country has changed. Such changes must be explained in the DSA. For example, in the case of Tanzania's 2007 DSA, a baseline GDP growth rate of 7.6 percent was used, rather than the historical 5.3 percent growth rate. According to the DSA, this change reflected "strong overall ratings of Tanzania's macroeconomic policies, as well as ongoing structural reforms in key areas."

A country's risk of future debt distress is then categorized as follows:

- *Low risk–* All scenario debt burden indicators are well below the thresholds throughout the 20-year projection period, and sensitivity testing does not result in significant breaches of thresholds;
- *Moderate risk–* Debt burden indicators are below the thresholds under the baseline scenario, but sensitivity testing causes them to exceed thresholds;
- *High risk–* Debt burden indicators exceed thresholds under the baseline scenario, and sensitivity testing further exacerbates the situation; or
- *In debt distress–* Debt burden indicators are currently in significant or sustained breach of thresholds, and the country is already experiencing repayment difficulties.[48]

As shown in table 6, for the 23 countries receiving HIPC Initiative and MDRI debt relief, 9 are classified at "moderate" risk of future debt distress, 4 at "high" risk, and 10 at "low" risk. IFI officials have considered refinements to the "moderate" risk classification that would provide greater distinctions within risk assessments, but have determined that there is currently no need to revise the category.

Table 6. Debt Risk Classification and CPIA Rating for Countries Receiving HIPC Initiative and MDRI Debt Relief

Performance rating	Risk of debt distress		
	Low	**Moderate**	**High**
Poor	Cameroon	Mauritania Sierra Leone	The Gambia Sao Tome & Principe
Medium	Bolivia Madagascar Mali Mozambique Senegal Zambia	Benin Ethiopia Guyana Malawi Nicaragua Niger	Burkina Faso Rwanda
Strong	Honduras Tanzania Uganda	Ghana	

Source: IMF-World Bank DSAs, 2007-2008.

Note: While Cameroon is classified as a poor performer under the CPIA rating system, it has a low risk of debt distress due to its low levels of external debt, according to IMF officials.

New DSA assessments of country debt sustainability under multiple scenarios address past concerns that DSAs only used one scenario, which may have contained overly-optimistic economic assumptions. For example, we reported in 1998, 2000, and 2004 that expected debt sustainability for debt relief countries was calculated based on one scenario that assumed high economic growth, including strong and sustained export growth.[49] We noted that such growth could be unrealistic given that many countries had very narrow export diversity (i.e., a limited number of exported goods), and these exports tended to be concentrated in the area of commodities that are highly vulnerable to events outside a country's control, such as drought or price fluctuations. IMF officials told us that current DSAs use assumptions that have been lowered to more realistic levels. They also stated that DSAs, which include descriptions of macroeconomic assumptions, are now transparent because they are publicly available and subject to scrutiny by outside parties.[50] In addition, IMF officials noted that because DSAs are conducted on an annual basis, DSAs can now begin to incorporate events such as increases in food or fuel prices in a timelier manner.

However, IMF officials also noted that the current approach for determining future macroeconomic performance assumptions is "not a perfect science," particularly when it makes projections over a 20-year period, and cannot be executed without potential forecast errors. In addition, a debt management capacity building group concluded that the sensitivity analyses contained in DSAs do not alter all relevant variables and exclude additional or secondary effects. It also reported that DSAs do not necessarily reflect all the risks that a country may think are likely in its own economic or borrowing prospects.[51]

IFIs Now Base Future Country Assistance on Risk of Future Debt Distress

IDA and ADF have adopted a revised system for providing future assistance based on DSA results. According to IDA officials, countries with a high risk of debt distress, or countries that are already in debt distress, receive 100 percent grant assistance, countries with a moderate risk of debt distress receive 50 percent grants and 50 percent concessional loans, and countries with a low risk of debt distress receive only concessional loans. ADF officials told us that ADF has adopted a similar system. According to World Bank officials, when a country's risk of future debt distress changes, the change is reflected in IDA allocations annually.[52] This approach directly aligns IDA and ADF assistance with a country's assessed ability to repay debt, and is relevant to our past reporting that the increased use of grant assistance would have a positive impact on future debt sustainability.[53] However, IDA and ADF reduce the volume of grant assistance provided under this system. Specifically, IDA and ADF reduce grant assistance by 20 percent for countries classified at a high or moderate risk of debt distress, thereby reducing resources available for poverty reduction. The 20 percent volume reduction is divided into an "incentives"-related portion and a "charges"-related portion.[54] The incentives-related portion is reallocated to IDA-only countries based on performance, and the charges-related portion is provided to creditworthy blend countries. According to IDA, this grant reduction was instated to maintain IDA's performance incentive.[55]

Other IFIs, such as IaDB and the Asian Development Bank, are also utilizing the new DSAs as part of their lending decision-making process, according to IMF and World Bank officials. In addition, OECD export credit agencies adopted a set of lending principles that adhere to IDA and IMF concessionality in January 2008.[56] Conversely, regarding borrowing decisions, IDA, ADF, and IMF officials stated that they work with country governments to improve their understanding and use of DSAs in future borrowing decisions. For example, IMF officials noted that DSAs are discussed as part of regular economic consultations with countries. Furthermore, according to an IMF and World Bank report, since 2005 eight training workshops have been organized in Africa, Asia, and Latin America and attended by officials from all 23 countries receiving HIPC Initiative and MDRI debt relief. However, IMF officials pointed out that countries. currently range widely in terms of their ability to use the DSA process to conduct their own analyses, and some country officials have said that they find the DSA process to be overly complicated.

DSAs Have Identified Numerous Ambitious Actions Countries Should Take in Order to Avoid Unsustainable Debt Levels

The new DSAs have cited many actions that countries receiving HIPC Initiative and MDRI debt relief should take in order to avoid unsustainable debt burdens in the future. Of the 23 countries receiving HIPC Initiative and MDRI debt relief, 13 (over 50 percent) have been found to have a moderate or high risk of future debt distress. These countries maintain this level of risk despite substantial HIPC Initiative and MDRI debt relief.[57] DSAs have stressed numerous policies or growth scenarios that countries should achieve in order to avoid further eroding their debt sustainability. For example, DSAs note that projected debt sustainability could be eroded if countries do not realize broad objectives that affect their overall economy, such as the following: continued concessional borrowing, implementation of sound macroeconomic policies, strengthened debt management capacity, sustained national income or export growth, and increased export diversity.

Such broad and ambitious objectives could prove difficult for countries to achieve over the course of the 20-year DSA period for various reasons. A country's debt position may be at risk even after it receives significant debt relief if, for example, its economy remains overly dependent on one export. For instance, Burkina Faso still held a moderate debt risk in 2007 despite World Bank and IMF reports that the HIPC Initiative and MDRI had substantially reduced its debt burden, because its economy is highly dependent on cotton exports (60 percent of total export value in 2006) which are vulnerable to large price fluctuations and weather shocks such as drought. In 2008, Burkina Faso's debt risk was elevated to high due to deteriorating country performance. Other unexpected factors beyond a country's control, such as oil and food import prices, may also affect economic position and debt sustainability. IMF and the World Bank have projected that countries may eventually return to pre-MDRI debt positions as they accumulate new debt over time.[58]

Continued concessional borrowing is cited frequently as an action countries must take to maintain debt sustainability.[59] IFIs have taken actions to address the issue of excessive nonconcessional borrowing. While IFIs aim to lower the risk of debt distress in low-income countries by providing new financial assistance on appropriately concessional terms, other creditors and borrowing governments may gain from nonconcessional lending that is made possible following large-scale debt relief or in conjunction with IFI grant assistance. According to the World Bank, rating agencies may upgrade commercial risk ratings for countries that have received MDRI debt relief, improving the countries' ability to secure nonconcessional loans. The risk of realizing an unsustainable nonconcessional debt burden is particularly high in resource-rich countries that can more easily obtain nonconcessional borrowing by using expected future export earnings as collateral to back such loans. In addition, IDA has noted that countries are experiencing significant risks associated with their weak debt management capacity. Debt management offices in low-income countries lack adequate capacity to monitor and accurately record debt data and new resource flows, let alone effectively manage them.[60]

IDA established a nonconcessional borrowing policy in 2006 to prevent the rapid reaccumulation of unsustainable debt.[61] This policy states that IDA has two instruments at its disposal to confront excessive nonconcessional borrowing— reducing its assistance volumes (primarily used in countries where debt sustainability is a major concern) and "hardening" its lending terms in countries with stronger debt sustainability and greater financial market access. According to IDA staff, hardened lending terms could include an increased interest rate, a shorter grace period, or a reduced repayment period. IDA has also reported that these options come with trade-offs as volume cuts reduce resources available to pursue poverty reduction, and hardened terms may exacerbate debt sustainability problems. As of June 2008, IDA reported that there had been two cases of hardened lending terms (Angola and Ghana) and, as allowed, one exception (Mali) granted under its nonconcessional borrowing policy.[62] IMF can impose limits on nonconcessional loans for countries that have a current arrangement with the institution.[63] For countries that do not have a loan arrangement with IMF, there is nothing IMF officials can do when countries borrow on a nonconcessional basis beyond consulting with borrowing country officials.

Conclusions

While HIPC Initiative and MDRI debt relief are projected to provide countries with additional resources, it is unknown how much of these additional resources countries will spend on poverty-reducing expenditures or pursuit of the MDGs. Furthermore, some countries may have difficulty maintaining debt sustainability, which requires demonstrating strong and sustained performance in numerous critical areas such as national income and export growth over the next several decades. The current U.S. approach for financing MDRI has several limitations. First, if the U.S. government does not fully pay its regular contributions to IDA on time, which is currently the case primarily due to withholdings, early encashment funding will be used to cover shortfalls in U.S. funding to IDA, rather than to solely fund debt relief. Second, according to our estimates, the U.S. financing approach will likely result in future shortfalls for funding MDRI for both IDA and ADF as early as 2014, even if the U.S. government provides full funding in a timely manner. Given these limitations, reassessing the options for funding U.S. MDRI commitments for IDA and ADF is critical.

Recommendation for Executive Action

To address limitations in the U.S. approach for financing MDRI, we recommend that the Secretary of the Treasury consider the use of different funding options that clarify the priority between paying U.S. arrears owed to IDA and paying MDRI obligations, such as requesting separate appropriations from Congress.

Agency Comments and Our Evaluation

The Department of the Treasury, the World Bank, and IMF provided written comments on a draft of this chapter, which are reprinted in appendixes IX, X, and XI. Treasury stated that it is open to our recommendation that alternative U.S. funding approaches for MDRI be considered in the future. Treasury emphasized its objective to fully meet its current IDA and MDRI funding commitments while also noting that a lack of full funding would jeopardize this objective. In addition, Treasury expressed a view that World Bank and IMF analyses produced under the Debt Sustainability Framework represent an improved ability to assess the debt sustainability outlook in low-income countries. Treasury explained that while debt relief can be a valuable tool, merely canceling debt is not sufficient to ensure long-term debt sustainability if underlying economic vulnerabilities remain.

The World Bank stressed the importance of full funding for IDA and a sustainable U.S. funding approach to cover debt relief costs. The World Bank also noted that our report could more explicitly state that it will not be possible for the United States to fund future MDRI costs through early encashment of the regular IDA contributions. The World Bank reported that the annual MDRI costs of IDA will more than triple over the next two decades, reaching an estimated $1.8 billion per year by 2025. Continuing the current practice would presuppose a commensurate increase in regular IDA contributions from the United States. The World

Bank further noted that funds from debt cancellation are small, relative to domestic revenues and external aid flows in countries benefiting from the debt relief, but represent a source of predictable financing for poverty-reducing expenditures.

IMF stated that poverty-reducing spending has increased in countries that have benefitted from debt relief - a point also made by Treasury. IMF further noted its disagreement with our position that the impact of debt relief on poverty-reducing spending is unknown. We maintain that our position is accurate since, while data compiled by IMF report that poverty- reducing spending has increased in countries receiving debt relief, it is not possible to link such increases to debt relief. Multiple factors, including challenges in tracking how debt relief resources are used and data reliability concerns, make it difficult to establish a linkage.

Treasury, the World Bank, IMF, and the African Development Bank provided technical comments on a draft of this chapter, which we have incorporated as appropriate. The World Bank's technical comments are included as part of its formal comment letter and suggested, as did IMF technical comments, that we better distinguish between recent debt sustainability analyses conducted under the Debt Sustainability Framework and other analyses conducted to establish the amount of debt relief needed to lower external public debt to agreed HIPC Initiative thresholds. We have altered our report to address this point. The African Development Bank provided comments on the U.S. costs for funding MDRI. We requested comments from IaDB, but none were provided.

APPENDIX I: OBJECTIVES, SCOPE, AND METHODOLOGY

Our objectives were to (1) analyze the U.S. financing approach for debt relief efforts, (2) review the extent to which the Multilateral Debt Relief Initiative (MDRI) might affect resources available to countries for poverty- reducing activities, and (3) assess revisions to the analyses conducted by the World Bank and IMF to review and promote future debt sustainability.

U.S. Financing for Debt Relief

To analyze U.S. financing for debt relief, we compiled data from Treasury and IFI staff and reviewed the U.S. contribution with these staff. To evaluate whether the U.S. approach to funding its IDA and ADF MDRI costs was adequate to fully pay U.S. commitments, we estimated total U.S. commitments in each IDA and ADF replenishment period and then used this amount in a simulation model of the U.S. payment schedule in order to estimate the amount of early payment credits that would be earned annually if Treasury continued to use the early encashment approach. To evaluate the early encashment approach the United States is using to finance its IDA and ADF MDRI costs during 2006-2011, we analyzed the statistical models that IDA and ADF are using to calculate U.S. encashment income. We performed simulations of shortfalls in U.S. replenishment payments and discussed our results with officials from Treasury and these IFIs. We developed a model to compare the costs to the United States of paying the MDRI obligation using the current early encashment approach rather than paying annual MDRI costs directly when due. Appendixes V and VI provide additional information regarding the costs associated with use of early encashment. We calculated and have presented all figures in this chapter in end-2008 present value dollars unless otherwise noted.[64] We assessed the reliability of the data analyzed and found the data to be sufficiently reliable for the purpose of this chapter.

MDRI and Resources Available for Poverty- Reducing Activities

To estimate the impact of MDRI debt relief on countries' resources, we calculated the aggregate net change in resources for MDRI recipient countries using an approach that considers the value of money over time. Our methodology reflects the three elements of MDRI's structure: MDRI debt relief, IDA and ADF reductions of annual assistance to the countries by the amount of debt relief provided in that year, and the reallocation of a portion of the cancelled debt service to countries based on their performance. IDA, ADF, and IaDB provided aggregate, annual debt relief and country-specific annual MDRI debt relief data for all current and expected future MDRI recipient countries, including our five case-study countries.[65] To calculate the aggregate reduction of annual assistance from IDA and ADF, we applied each IFI's encashment schedule to the disbursement of the annual MDRI debt relief that both IDA and ADF provided. While 1 year's debt relief is matched by a reduction in 1 year's IDA or ADF assistance, the reduction in assistance takes place over a 9- year disbursement cycle for IDA and a 10-year disbursement cycle for ADF.[66] This annual MDRI debt relief reduction, aggregated over all MDRI recipients, is the amount to be reallocated to IDA-only recipients—a larger subset of IDA recipients than those that receive MDRI debt relief—on the basis of performance. We refer to this as the performance-based reallocation, or PBA reallocation. We discussed our methodology with IMF and World Bank officials. The staff of both IFIs concurred that our approach was a valid way to analyze MDRI.

To determine the portion of the MDRI debt relief to be reallocated to recipients as additional HIPC countries reach their completion point, we created a weighted allocation index based on data provided by the World Bank. The World Bank told us that the group of 23 completion point countries is currently receiving 50 percent of the reallocated cancelled debt relief funds, and that this would rise to 60 percent as the interim (decision point) countries[67] reach their completion points, which is assumed to occur during 2009 and 2010. To determine the portion of the additional 10 percentage points that would go to each of the 10 interim countries, we created a weighted allocation index by dividing each country's projected percentage of IDA14 assistance flows by the portion of IDA14 assistance going to this group of 10 countries. To compute each country's share of the IDA PBA reallocation, we multiplied their weighted allocation index by the 10 additional percentage points to calculate the portion of the 10 percent that each would receive. Finally, to calculate the changing PBA allocation over the period as the individual countries reach their completion point, we added each country's respective share of the 10 percentage points on to the 50 percent base, arriving at 60 percent in 2010. We used the same methodology to determine the additional portion of the MDRI pool of debt relief that would go to 8 pre-decision point countries,[68] based on their projected completion point dates that the Bank provided. We assume that the pre-decision point countries will account for a proportional percentage of the 10 percentage points, reflecting their projected portion of IDA14 assistance flows. Based on this methodology, we estimate that, adding on the 8 pre-decision point countries, 41 HIPCs would receive about 67 percent of the reallocated MDRI debt relief and the remainder would go to all other low-income countries eligible to receive only concessional loans from IDA or ADF. ADF provided us with the amount of MDRI debt relief reallocated to all of its member countries, as well as the projected completion point dates for the HIPCs. To determine the portion of ADF's MDRI debt relief to be reallocated to recipients as additional HIPC countries reach their completion point, we added each country's percentage of total MDRI debt relief to the current reallocation percentage as countries successively reach their completion point. For ADF countries, by 2016, 33 HIPC countries would account for nearly 90 percent of ADF's reallocated MDRI debt relief. For all efforts to review the impact of MDRI on country resources, we assessed the reliability of the data analyzed and found the data to be sufficiently reliable for the purposes of this chapter.

We also included Enhanced HIPC Initiative debt relief in our analysis to present a more complete picture of the IFIs' contribution to debt relief. IDA, ADF, IaDB, and IMF provided annual data for Enhanced HIPC, by country. We included these data in our reported estimate of overall debt relief resources.

To calculate the impact of MDRI debt relief on individual countries, we selected five countries (Ethiopia, Ghana, Nicaragua, Rwanda, and Tanzania) as case studies based on several criteria, including dispersion of country ranking in terms of the percentage of total HIPC and MDRI debt relief they received from the four institutions, geographic diversity, and debt sustainability risk classification. In terms of percentage of debt relief received, we selected countries at or near the top, middle, and bottom of the ranking to use as examples of how the program works. Our choice of countries is meant to be illustrative, not representative. We used the same methodology to estimate the three components of MDRI debt relief for individual countries as we used in the aggregate.

To determine whether countries receiving debt relief are using the savings toward poverty reduction and achieving the MDGs, we reviewed documents provided by Treasury, the World Bank, IMF, ADF and IaDB, and spoke with officials at Treasury and these four institutions. We also examined publicly-available online data sources for poverty-reducing expenditures in areas such as education and health. To illustrate the impact of debt relief on individual nations, we examined the spending data for the five countries cited above. We reviewed the most recent Poverty Reduction Strategy Papers (PRSP) of the five countries in order to examine their poverty-reducing goals and objectives. In addition, we reviewed the most recent (2007) online country budgets and IMF Article IV consultation documents for our five case study countries to examine how countries were reporting their poverty-reducing expenditures.

Debt Sustainability Analyses

In order to assess revisions to IMF and World Bank debt sustainability analyses (DSA) since 2005, we first reviewed prior GAO reports issued between 1998 and 2004 that identified weaknesses in past DSAs. We then examined IMF and World Bank documentation explaining the Debt Sustainability Framework (DSF) and the related DSAs and other relevant issues, the following in particular:

- *Staff Guidance Note on the Application of the Joint Fund-Bank Debt Sustainability Framework for Low-Income Countries,*October 6, 2008;
- *Heavily Indebted Poor Countries (HIPC) Initiative and Multilateral Debt Relief Initiative (MDRI) – Status of Implementation,*September 12, 2008;
- *IDA's Nonconcessional Borrowing Policy: Review and Update,*June 2008;
- *Applying the Debt Sustainability Framework for Low-Income Countries Post Debt Relief,* November 6, 2006;
- *How to Do a Debt Sustainability Analysis for Low-Income Countries,* October 2006;
- *IDA Countries and Nonconcessional Debt: Dealing with the "Free Rider" Problem in IDA14 Grant-Recipient and Post-MDRI Countries,* June 19, 2006;
- *Review of Low-Income Country Debt Sustainability Framework and Implications of the MDRI,* March 27, 2006; and
- *Operational Framework for Debt Sustainability Assessments in Low- Income Countries – Further Considerations,* March 28, 2005.

We then collected and reviewed all DSAs performed for 23 completion point countries since the DSF was implemented in 2005 as part of IMF Article IV consultations, IMF Poverty Reduction Growth Facility (PRGF) arrangement requests or reviews, or other events. We identified the assumptions and scenarios used, and compiled the most recent risk determinations for each country. We did not independently assess the accuracy or comprehensiveness of the assumptions and data included in the DSAs. We discussed the DSA process with IMF and World Bank officials and found the DSA information sufficiently reliable for descriptive purposes.

We compared the current process against the weaknesses we had previously identified to determine whether the new process addressed these limitations. Furthermore, we identified additional alterations to the process and interviewed IMF, World Bank, IaDB, and AfDB officials to obtain their views on the new DSA process and results. Finally, we compiled the results of DSAs to determine the debt distress risk of countries currently receiving HIPC Initiative and MDRI debt relief, as well as DSA recommendations for actions such countries should take in order to avoid future downgrading of their debt risk classification and deterioration of their debt sustainability. Our work focused on analyses related to external debt and not domestic public debt.

We conducted this performance audit from December 2007 through January 2009 in accordance with generally accepted government auditing standards. Those standards require that we plan and perform the audit to obtain sufficient, appropriate evidence to provide a reasonable basis for our findings and conclusions based on our audit objectives. We believe the evidence obtained provides a reasonable basis for our findings and conclusions based on our audit objectives.

APPENDIX II: COMMERCIAL LAWSUITS TO COLLECT UNPAID DEBT FROM DEBT RELIEF COUNTRIES

Lawsuits by commercial creditors to collect on outstanding HIPC country debt can erode gains made through debt relief. International courts and U.S. federal courts have allowed commercial creditors to pursue legal action in order to recover funds owed to them, but these creditors are sometimes viewed as creating difficult circumstances for countries that have received debt relief from other creditors.[69] As of the end of 2007, based on survey data provided by country governments, 47 litigating creditors had filed suits against 11 countries receiving HIPC Initiative and MDRI debt relief (see table 7). Over $1 billion has been awarded by courts and is due to commercial creditors. About one-third of this total, or over $440 million, has been awarded against the Republic of Congo, followed by over $350 million against Liberia, and $100 million against the Democratic Republic of the Congo.

Treasury officials told us that while a court can award claims in favor of commercial creditors, actually enforcing the judgments and receiving payment is a separate, potentially more difficult exercise.

Table 7. Commercial Creditor Lawsuits against Countries Receiving HIPC Initiative and MDRI Assistance (As of the end of 2007)

(Dollars in millions)			
Country	**Number of litigating creditors**	**Creditor claims**	**Court awards**
Completion Point Countries			
Cameroon	4	$158	$51
Ethiopia	2	187	—[a]
Guyana	3	46	—
Honduras	1	1	—
Nicaragua	5	9	0[b]
Sierra Leone	5	29	25
Uganda	6	36	30
Zambia	2	55	16
Decision Point Countries			
Democratic Republic of the Congo	1	100	100
Republic of Congo	8	575	443
Liberia	10	130[c]	357
Total	**47**	**$1,326**	**$1,022**

Source: "Heavily Indebted Poor Countries (HIPC), Initiative and Multilateral Debt Relief Initiative (MDRI) – Status of Implementation," prepared by IDA and IMF staff, Aug. 2008; and IMF officials.

[a]Dashes indicate no information.
[b]Court awards against Nicaragua do not include amounts resolved through the Debt Reduction Facility.
[c]Creditor claims against Liberia appear to be less than court awards because data regarding creditor claims are incomplete.

The international community has taken numerous actions to address such cases:

- The World Bank's Debt Reduction Facility (DRF) allows governments to buy back—at a deep discount—country debts owed to external, commercial creditors. Through grants, the DRF supports heavily indebted IDA-only countries that undertake reforms to retain professional services necessary in preparing these commercial debt reduction operations and assists the countries in funding the cost of these operations. For example, court judgments against Nicaragua were settled through the DRF-supported buyback. All four litigating creditors participated in the buyback operation and accepted a significant cut in the value of their legal claims. The Nicaragua buyback extinguished about $1.3 billion in commercial debt. Another buyback operation has been concluded for Mozambique. Furthermore, according to Treasury officials, a DRF operation is currently being prepared for Liberia, and the United States intends to contribute $5 million to help fund the cost of this buyback.

- Paris Club creditors have committed as a group not to sell claims on HIPC countries to creditors who do not intend to provide debt relief.[70]

- In April 2008, AfDB approved a proposal to establish the African Legal Support Facility (ALSF), which would provide (1) technical legal advice to members of the facility in creditor litigation, and (2) technical legal assistance to members of the facility to strengthen their legal expertise and negotiating capacity in matters related to debt management and other issues.[71] The U.S. government was the only participating state to vote against establishment of the ALSF, and Treasury officials have noted that countries that have been the target of recent litigation have had very able legal representation to date, calling into question the need for ALSF assistance. In addition, Treasury staff expressed a position that some of the proposed activities for the ALSF are not an appropriate use of AfDB funds and noted concerns over the substantial administrative costs associated with ALSF. Furthermore, Treasury staff have emphasized that the DRF—an option already in operation that is achieving results in reducing country debt burdens to commercial creditors—is a preferred alternative.

APPENDIX III: FUNDING PROVIDED FOR THE HIPC INITIATIVE AND MDRI

IDA and ADF have not secured all financing that will be required to meet their HIPC Initiative and MDRI debt relief commitments for countries currently receiving such relief, though IaDB and IMF have secured all necessary funding. Overall, about 65 percent of the $47 billion in funding required to cover debt relief over the next several decades has been secured. Countries have currently received about $14 billion in debt relief. Overall, we project that the U.S. government is committed to provide about $8.4 billion in funding for the HIPC Initiative and MDRI.

IDA and ADF Have Not Secured All Necessary Financing

Of the $27.8 billion required to finance IDA's HIPC Initiative and MDRI debt relief for the 33 countries currently receiving such relief, IDA has secured about $8.6 billion for the

HIPC Initiative and $4.4 billion for MDRI (see figure 6).[72] This total of $13.1 billion represents 47 percent of the total required financing for both debt relief initiatives.[73]

IDA previously financed the HIPC Initiative primarily through transfers from the World Bank's International Bank for Reconstruction and Development.[74] Beginning in July 2006, this financing process changed and became part of the regular 3-year replenishment process. Donors have agreed to finance MDRI costs on a "dollar for dollar" basis (i.e., total MDRI costs will be covered) in conjunction with, and in addition to, replenishment contributions through 2044.[75]

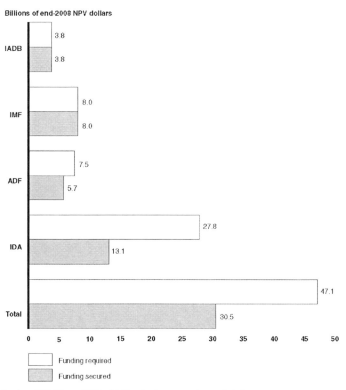

Source: GAO analysis of IMF and World Bank documents and data.

Note: Funding includes amounts for the 23 countries receiving HIPC Initiative and MDRI debt relief and 10 additional countries receiving only HIPC Initiative debt relief. Funding amounts do not include the eight countries that have not yet met the requirements to receive debt relief under either program.

Figure 6. IFI HIPC Initiative and MDRI Debt Relief Funding Required and Secured for Countries Currently Receiving Debt Relief Assistance

According to our projections, ADF is to provide about $7.5 billion in HIPC Initiative and MDRI debt relief and has secured about $5.7 billion, or more than 75 percent, of this amount. ADF has secured $4.6 billion for the HIPC Initiative and $1.1 billion for MDRI. ADF is financing the HIPC Initiative from internal African Development Bank resources and donor contributions, all of which are channeled through the HIPC Trust Fund administered by the World Bank. As with IDA, donors have agreed to finance ADF's MDRI costs on a "dollar for

160 United States Government Accountability Office

dollar" basis in conjunction with, and in addition to, replenishment contributions through 2054.

IMF and IaDB Have Secured HIPC Initiative and MDRI Funding

IMF and IaDB have fully financed their $8 billion and $3.8 billion of HIPC Initiative and MDRI debt relief for the countries currently receiving such relief, respectively, using internal resources and donor-provided funds.[76] Because these two institutions have fully funded their HIPC Initiative and MDRI debt relief for the countries currently receiving debt relief, almost 65 percent of total debt relief costs for all four IFIs have been secured. To fund HIPC Initiative and MDRI debt relief, IMF uses internal resources, including proceeds from its 1999 and 2000 off-market gold sales, and donor contributions. IMF has also secured some of the funds to cover its future debt relief costs for the countries not yet receiving debt relief.[77] IaDB has fully financed its HIPC Initiative debt relief from internal resources and donor funding through the HIPC Trust Fund. With the advent of its MDRI-like program in 2007, IaDB created a blended loan product made up of concessional and nonconcessional funds, according to Treasury officials. The process of creating this blended product freed up resources to be used for debt relief while allowing IaDB to continue to provide concessional lending. Furthermore, Treasury officials noted that IaDB took other measures to obtain additional resources, such as canceling undisbursed portions of nonperforming concessional loans, to gain access to additional funding. IaDB freed up sufficient internal resources to provide debt relief for its four member countries receiving HIPC Initiative and MDRI debt relief as well as reserves of about $0.4 billion for Haiti when it completes both programs.

Countries Have Realized $14 Billion in Debt Relief Assistance

Table 8. Total HIPC Initiative and MDRI Debt Relief Required and Delivered to 33 Countries Currently Receiving Debt Relief Assistance (In billions of end-2008 present value dollars)

	Total	IDA	ADF	IMF	IaDB
Funding required	47.1	27.8	7.5	8.0	3.8
Delivered debt relief	14.3	6.2	2.1	4.8	1.2
• HIPC debt relief	11.4	5.2	1.9	3.2	1.0
• MDRI debt relief	2.9	1.0	0.1	1.6	0.2
Delivered as % of required	30%	22%	28%	60%	32%

Source: GAO analysis of IMF, IDA, ADF, and IaDB documents and data.

Notes: Totals may not sum due to rounding.

Required funding includes 23 countries receiving HIPC Initiative and MDRI debt relief and 10 additional countries receiving only HIPC Initiative debt relief (MDRI funding is not included for these 10 countries). Funding does not include the eight countries that have not yet met the requirements to receive debt relief under either program.

Countries currently receiving debt relief have thus far realized less than a third of expected assistance. Countries realize the benefits of debt relief as annual debt service payments to IFIs that would have come due are no longer required to be paid. Debt relief provides the countries with additional available resources that they can spend on other activities, such as poverty-reduction programs. Table 8 shows the amount of debt relief assistance that each IFI has delivered compared to the required amount of assistance that has been approved.[78]

The IFIs have delivered a total of $14.3 billion in debt relief, which is 30 percent of the approved $47.1 billion for the 33 countries. IDA has delivered the largest amount, $6.2 billion, representing 22 percent of its approved $27.8 billion in debt relief assistance. IMF has delivered $4.8 billion, or 60 percent, of its approved $8 billion in debt relief. The HIPC Initiative has delivered nearly 80 percent, or $11.4 billion, of the debt relief delivered to date. Countries began receiving HIPC Initiative debt relief benefits in 1998, whereas MDRI debt relief began in 2006.

APPENDIX IV: U.S. BILATERAL HIPC INITIATIVE DEBT RELIEF

Table 9 shows the budget cost and the amount of bilateral debt relief the U.S. government has provided or is projected to provide to 30 countries under the HIPC Initiative.

Table 9. U.S. Bilateral Debt Relief Provided under the Enhanced HIPC Initiative

Country	HIPC Decision Point	Nominal bilateral debt (millions of dollars)	Budget cost[a]	Budget cost as percent of cancelled debt
Completion Point HIPCs				
Bolivia	Feb-00	$59.5	$28,926,235	49
Cameroon	Oct-00	47.7	15,585,552	33
Ethiopia	Nov-01	64.6	8,917,788	14
Ghana	Feb-02	11.3	3,660,831	32
Guyana	Nov-00	34.1	6,455,791	19
Honduras	Jun-00	54.1	20,430,401	38
Madagascar	Dec-00	8.5	6,500,000	76
Mali[b]	Sep-00	0	3,584	28
Mauritania	Feb-00	7.1	2,266,122	32
Mozambique	Apr-00	5.0	1,630,059	33
Nicaragua	Dec-00	42.2	11,359,365	27
Niger	Dec-00	4.1	1,330,360	32
Rwanda	Dec-00	1.6	117,121	7
Senegal	Jun-00	8.6	4,040,014	47
Sierra Leone	Mar-02	71.4	3,711,261	5
Tanzania	Apr-00	16.2	2,411,274	15
Uganda	Feb-00	0.2	101,141	51
Zambia	Dec-00	280.3	17,159,357	6
Sub-total		$716.5	$134,606,256	19

Table 9 (Continued)				
Interim HIPCs				
Afghanistan	Jul-07	$114.3	$7,148,394	6
Central African Republic	Sep-07	6.9	373,334	5
Congo, Democratic Republic of[c]	Jul-03	1,668.6	176,699,730	11
Congo, Republic of	Mar-06	56.9	5,067,204	9
Guinea	Dec-00	122.4	15,906,602	13
Haiti	Nov-06	14.4	2,798,751	19
Liberia	Mar-08	422.7	36,905,617	9
Sub-total		**$2,406.2**	**$244,899,632**	**10**
Pre-Decision Point		**(Estimated)**	**(Estimated)**	**(Estimated)**
Cote D'Ivoire, Eritrea, Somalia, Sudan, and Togo[d]	—	$1,600.0	$126 million	8
Total		**$4,722.7**	**$505,505,888**	**11**

Source: GAO analysis of U.S. Department of the Treasury data as of November 1, 2008.

Note: Eleven countries for which the U.S. government is or was not a creditor are omitted.

[a] Expected nominal bilateral debt relief as of HIPC Decision Point. For countries that have not reached HIPC Completion Point, full debt relief is dependent on successful completion of the HIPC Initiative requirements, and associated budget costs should be considered estimates.

[b] Amount of "0" indicates nominal debt was less than $50,000. Actual debt forgiven for Mali was $12,800.

[c] The expected nominal debt relief and estimated budget cost listed for the Democratic Republic of the Congo are contingent on the availability of sufficient appropriations and have not yet been fully committed.

[d] The aggregate amounts listed for these pre-decision point countries should be considered rough estimates only and may change over time. Inclusion on this list does not guarantee future debt relief. Potential bilateral HIPC debt relief for countries in this category is contingent on successfully meeting the HIPC Initiative requirements, as well as compliance with U.S. legal requirements and the availability of sufficient appropriations.

APPENDIX V: CALCULATION OF EARLY ENCASHMENT CREDITS

We calculated the outcome of the early encashment approach to funding the U.S. MDRI commitment under a scenario (1) where the U.S. government makes its payments in full and on time, and (2) where the U.S. contribution is 5 percent less than required. Our analysis demonstrates the significant impact on early encashment income and actual U.S. funding levels for MDRI when funding reductions, similar to those experienced in recent years, are realized.

The following is our explanation of the early encashment process. We use the same assumptions that are being used by Treasury and IDA, but describe the process in nominal dollars. The U.S. government plans to pay its share of IDA's debt relief costs for MDRI from the encashment income generated by paying its regular IDA replenishment commitment over a 4- year period, rather than over the standard 9-year period. Table 10 describes this process.

Table 10. Early Encashment Income When Replenishment Is Paid in Full

(Dollars in millions)				
Fiscal year	Standard encashment schedule	Early encashment schedule	Excess payment balance	Encashment investment income
	(a)	(b)	(c)	(d)
2009	$252	$1,112	$860	$34
2010	478	1,235	1,617	65
2011	678	1,235	2,174	87
2012	582	124	1,715	69
2013	519		1,197	48
2014	422		774	31
2015	322		452	18
2016	259		193	8
2017	193		0	0
Total (nominal)	$3,705	$3,705		$359
Total (present value)	$3,114	$3,414		
Percent face value		9.63		
Early encashment credits		$357		

Source: GAO analysis of Treasury and IDA documents.
Note: Totals may not sum due to rounding.

The U.S. replenishment obligation for IDA15, which covers the period 2009 through 2011, is $3.7 billion.[79] Column (a) describes the annual standard encashment or payment schedule over the 9-year period from 2009 through 2017. Column (b) is the annual U.S. payment over a 4-year period. Column (c) is the annual outstanding excess payment. In 2009, this amount consists of the difference between what the U.S. government pays, $1.1 billion, and the required amount of $252 million. In subsequent years, it consists of the annual excess in payment plus the outstanding excess payment balance. Beginning in the fifth year, no new payment is made. The excess payment balance is used to cover the required payment. In the ninth year, the excess payment balance is just sufficient to pay the last year's required payment. Column (d) is the annual encashment investment income. This amount is the estimated earned income calculated by multiplying the excess payment balance by the agreed-upon interest rate, which is 4 percent for the IDA15 replenishment. The line "Total (nominal)" shows that the total payments under the standard encashment schedule is equal to the total under the early encashment schedule. The total nominal dollar earned income is $359 million.

Treasury and IDA use a different method to compute early encashment income. Under their method, Treasury and IDA first calculate the present value sum of the payment schedules. The present value is a statistical method that takes into consideration the amount of annual payments, the time during which these payments are made, and the interest rate when computing the sum. Although the nominal sums of the two schedules are the same, the present value of the early encashment schedule, $3,414 million, is larger than that of the standard schedule, $3,114 million. Treasury and IDA compute the percent face value as the difference between these present values divided by the present value of the standard schedule.

The percent face value, 9.63 percent in this example, is multiplied by the nominal sum of early encashment payments, $3,705 million, to calculate the early encashment income of $357 million.[80] This is the agreed-upon methodology and $357 million will be used toward paying the U.S. IDA MDRI commitment of $356 million. The surplus $1 million can be used to pay future MDRI obligations.

In the previous example, the U.S. government pays its replenishment in full and all the early encashment income is used to pay its MDRI obligation. In the next example, we assume that the U.S. government does not pay its replenishment in full, either due to a rescission or a decision to withhold payment until certain reforms are made by the World Bank. Under the agreed-upon methodology, early encashment income is first used to pay off the replenishment shortfall. Any remaining encashment income is then used to pay the U.S. IDA MDRI commitment. Table 11 describes the calculation of early encashment income when there is a replenishment shortfall. We assume an across-the-board shortfall in U.S. annual payments of 5 percent, resulting in a shortfall of $185 million.[81] Thus, the total nominal early encashment payments are $3,520 million. Since the annual U.S. payments are less, the earned income in column (d) is less: $308 million or a 14-percent reduction. The calculated early encashment income to pay for the U.S. MDRI commitment is $146 million, a 59 percent reduction. Most of the earned encashment income is used to pay the replenishment shortfall. If the across-the-board shortfall were 8.8 percent or more of the replenishment, all of the earned encashment income would be used to pay the shortage and nothing would be used to pay the U.S. MDRI commitment.

Table 11. Early Encashment Income When There Is a 5 Percent Shortfall in Replenishment Payments.

(Dollars in millions)				
Fiscal year	**Standard encashment schedule**	**Early encashment schedule**	**Excess payment balance**	**Encashment investment income**
	(a)	(b)	(c)	(d)
2009	$252	$1,056	$804	$32
2010	478	1,173	1,499	60
2011	678	1,173	1,995	80
2012	582	117	1,530	61
2013	519		1,011	40
2014	422		589	24
2015	322		267	11
2016	259		7	0.3
2017	193		0	0
Total (nominal)	**$3,705**	**$3,520**		**$308**
Total (present value)	**$3,114**	**$3,243**		
Percent face value		4.15		
Early encashment credits		$146		

Source: GAO analysis.

Note: Totals may not sum due to rounding.

Treasury and ADF have agreed to use a different methodology to compute early encashment income. We applied this ADF approach to the IDA15 replenishment. If there is no funding shortfall, the results are identical between the two approaches. When there is a shortfall, the ADF approach implicitly reduces the standard encashment schedule payments by the average across-the-board percentage shortfall. Thus, the nominal total of the standard encashment schedule is the same as the total early encashment schedule payments. In the previous example with a 5 percent shortfall, the computed early encashment income would total $339 million and all of this amount would be used to pay the MDRI obligation. None of the earned encashment income would be used to pay the shortfall to IDA.

APPENDIX VI: EARLY ENCASHMENT COSTS MORE THAN ALTERNATIVE FINANCING

Under some conditions the early encashment approach to pay the U.S. MDRI commitment may be more costly than paying the annual MDRI obligations directly when they are due. If the cost for the U.S. government to borrow the funds exceeds the agreed upon interest rate used to compute early encashment income, then the early encashment approach is more costly than paying the U.S. replenishment and MDRI obligations annually as they come due. Conversely, if the borrowing cost to the U.S. government is less than the agreed-upon interest rate used to compute early encashment income, then the early encashment approach is less expensive.

According to the Congressional Budget Office, the average medium-term cost to borrow funds during fiscal year 2009 through fiscal year 2012 is projected to be 5.0 percent.[82] This amount is greater than the 4.0 percent agreed-upon interest rate used to compute early IDA encashment income. Under these conditions, the early encashment approach to finance the U.S. IDA MDRI commitment is more costly than paying the U.S. commitment directly.

Assuming that the full replenishment and IDA MDRI commitments are paid, we estimate that the cost to the U.S. government for early encashment payments, including financing costs for IDA15, will be $3,347.2 million in end-2008 present value dollars. This is about $38 million more than the cost of paying IDA15 replenishment and MDRI obligations annually as they come due, a total of $3,309.6 million. In nominal dollars, we estimate the additional cost is $42 million. Since early encashment income earned is $1 million more than MDRI obligations, the net additional cost is $41 million.

A similar cost analysis for ADF-11 in end-2008 present value terms shows that the early encashment cost, including financing costs, is $416.8 million, about $12.2 million more than the cost of paying ADF-11 replenishment and MDRI obligations annually as they come due, a total cost of $404.6 million. This reflects the higher government cost of borrowing, 5 percent, than the 4.69 percent used by ADF to calculate early encashment income. Again we have assumed that the United States pays its full replenishment and ADF MDRI commitment. In nominal dollars, we estimate the additional cost is $14 million. Since early encashment income earned is $16 million more than MDRI obligations, for ADF-11 early encashment results in a net benefit of $2 million as compared to paying replenishment and MDRI obligations annually as they come due.

Based on CBO's projections for the cost of U.S. borrowing, we estimate that during the replenishment period from 2009 through 2011, early encashment will cost the United States an additional $39 million, $41 million more for IDA and $2 million less for ADF.

APPENDIX VII: PROJECTED IMPACT OF MDRI ON FIVE CASE STUDY COUNTRIES

Based on our projections, while the overall net change in resources available due to MDRI is positive for each of the five countries we analyzed (Ethiopia, Ghana, Tanzania, Nicaragua, and Rwanda), individual countries may experience increases or decreases in their IFI assistance. The following graphs illustrate the projected overall impact of MDRI for these five countries. The shaded area indicates the negative (below the axis) or positive (above the axis) change in IDA and ADF assistance.

Ghana and Nicaragua are projected to experience a decrease in IFI assistance due to reduced IDA and ADF assistance over the life of MDRI, even as MDRI debt relief provides freed-up resources. (See shaded area in figures 7 and 8.)

In contrast, for Ethiopia and Tanzania, MDRI is projected to result in an increase in assistance from IDA and ADF. (See shaded area in figures 9 and 10.)

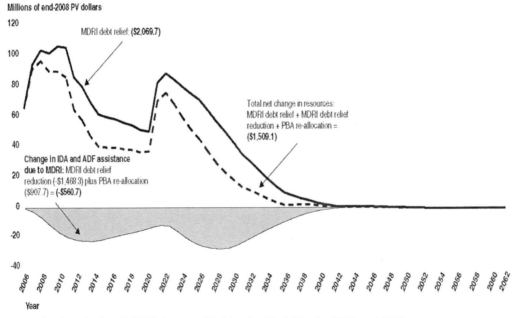

Source: GAO analysis of MDRI data provided by the World Bank, ADF, and IMF.

Figure 7. Projected Impact of MDRI on Ghana's Resource Availability, 2006-2062 (Millions of end-2008 present value dollars)

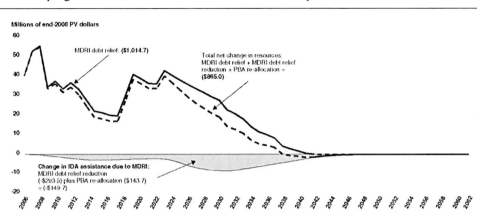

Source: GAO analysis of MDRI data provided by the World Bank, IaDB, and IMF.

Figure 8. Projected Impact of MDRI on Nicaragua's Resource Availability, 2006-2062 (Millions of end-2008 present value dollars)

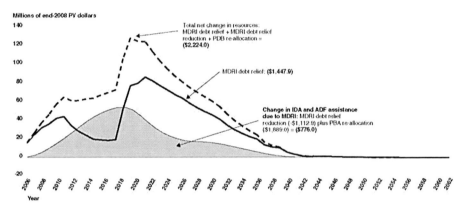

Source: GAO analysis of MDRI data provided by the World Bank, ADF, and IMF.

Figure 9. Projected Impact of MDRI on Ethiopia's Resource Availability, 2006-2062 (Millions of end-2008 present value dollars)

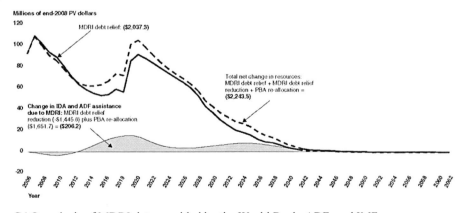

Source: GAO analysis of MDRI data provided by the World Bank, ADF, and IMF.

Figure 10. Projected Impact of MDRI on Tanzania's Resource Availability, 2006-2062 (Millions of end-2008 present value dollars)

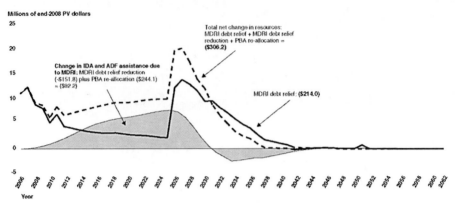

Source: GAO analysis of MDRI data provided by the World Bank, ADF, and IMF.

Figure 11. Projected Impact of MDRI on Rwanda's Resource Availability, 2006-2062 (Millions of end-2008 present value dollars)

As shown in figure 11, for Rwanda, MDRI is projected to provide a mixture of increases and reductions in IDA's and ADF's annual assistance over the MDRI period.

APPENDIX VIII: IMPLEMENTATION OF THE MULTILATERAL DEBT RELIEF INITIATIVE (MDRI) PROCESS

We found that countries receiving MDRI debt relief are projected to receive about $3 billion more than suggested in World Bank/International Development Association (IDA) documents describing MDRI. IDA documents state that, in a particular year, IDA is to reduce its commitments of financial assistance to countries receiving MDRI debt relief by the amount of debt relief provided, netting each other out. Donor governments have agreed to compensate IDA for the foregone debt service payments. IDA is to reallocate these funds to all countries eligible to borrow only from IDA, which includes countries that receive MDRI debt relief as well as those that do not. Thus, when IDA reallocates the donor funds, all IDA-only countries would be at the same starting point—with no net additional funds.

We compared the projected amount of debt relief to the projected amount of reduced assistance under two scenarios, each incorporating the time value of money. In the first scenario, we assumed that IDA reduces its assistance by the amount of debt relief provided in the same year, as described in World Bank documents. In the second scenario, we considered the disbursement pattern that IDA actually uses to distribute the reduction in allocations for MDRI recipients as well as the reallocation of those funds. Under the second scenario, because the disbursement pattern takes place over a 9-year period, the dollar value of MDRI debt relief is greater than the actual reduction in IDA disbursements.

In the first scenario, IDA is projected to provide $18.9 billion in debt relief and reduce its assistance commitments to MDRI recipients by the same amount. IDA is then projected to reallocate—on the basis of performance—a portion of this $18.9 billion of reduced assistance commitments to recipients of debt relief, $12.3 billion, and the remainder, $6.6 billion, to IDA-only countries that do not receive debt relief. (See figure 12.)

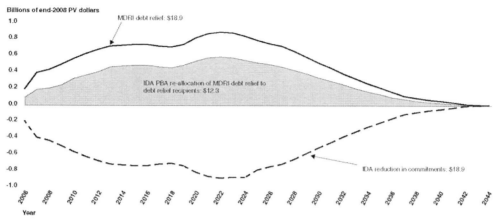

Source: GAO analysis of World Bank data.

Figure 12. Annual Projected IDA MDRI Assistance to Debt Relief Recipients, 2006-2044 (Billions of end-2008 present value dollars)

Under the second scenario, the overall annual amount of debt relief is greater than the overall annual reduction in assistance. When considering the disbursement pattern of IDA funds, the projected net present value of MDRI debt relief, $18.9 billion, is greater than the net present value of IDA's reduction in assistance, $15.8 billion, by $3.1 billion.[83] Countries that receive debt relief are projected to receive this $3.1 billion in addition to about $10.2 billion in reallocated assistance, for total MDRI benefits of $13.3 billion.[84] (See figure 13.)

The additional $3.1 billion places debt relief recipients in a more advantageous position at the outset of the reallocation process than their non-debt relief counterparts.

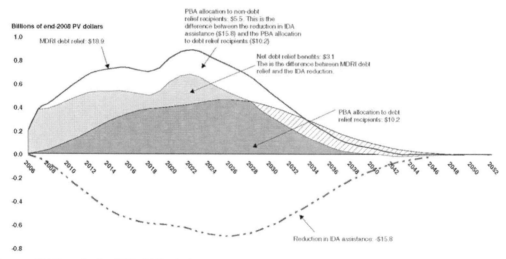

Source: GAO analysis of World Bank data.

Figure 13. Disbursement Pattern of Projected IDA MDRI Assistance to Debt Relief Recipients, 2006-2052 (Billions of end-2008 present value dollars)

While IDA documents indicate that donor funding provided to compensate for MDRI debt relief is to be reallocated to IDA-only countries, IDA is using donor finances to provide the $3.1 billion in net debt relief benefits to debt relief recipients, in addition to their performance-based reallocation of donor funds. Thus, the $18.9 billion in donor financing for MDRI is allocated as follows: $3.1 billion to net debt relief benefits, $10.2 billion in IDA reallocations to debt relief recipients, and $5.5 billion in reallocations to non-debt relief recipients.

APPENDIX IX: COMMENTS FROM THE DEPARTMENT OF THE TREASURY

Note: GAO comments supplementing those in the report text appear at the end of this appendix.

See comment 1.

DEPARTMENT OF THE TREASURY
WASHINGTON, D.C. 20220

JAN 0 9 2009

Thomas Melito
Director, International Affairs and Trade
Government Accountability Office
441 G Street N.W.
Washington, DC 20548

Dear Mr. Melito:

Thank you for the opportunity to comment on the draft report regarding international debt relief initiatives and debt sustainability. The United States has consistently provided strong international leadership on debt relief for the world's most heavily-indebted poor countries and on efforts to end the lend-and-forgive cycle and promote long-term debt sustainability. As such, we have great interest in your report and are providing comments on several aspects of your findings.

Financing the Multilateral Debt Relief Initiative

In examining U.S. financing for the Multilateral Debt Relief Initiative (MDRI), your report projects several scenarios. In the context of this analysis, we would like to be clear that it remains the Treasury Department's objective to fully meet the U.S. nominal commitment to the IDA14 replenishment, and thereby meet U.S. MDRI commitments from credits earned through early encashment. However, as the Treasury Department has repeatedly emphasized, including in its response to the previous GAO report on this subject, shortfalls in funding IDA14 would jeopardize the ability of the United States to meet its commitments to finance multilateral debt relief. If the United States meets its IDA14 commitments, the alternative scenarios you describe would not be relevant and the United States would simultaneously fully finance both IDA14 and its current MDRI commitments. In fact, our fiscal year 2009 budget request for payment of IDA arrears was specifically targeted at helping to fulfill this goal.

We remain open to your recommendation that alternative funding approaches be considered for MDRI in the future. There are a variety of potential methods by which MDRI could be funded and we are open to revisiting this issue as we move forward.

Effects of Debt Relief

The draft report states that the effects of debt relief on poverty reducing expenditures are unknown, due to the difficulty of tracking debt relief resources and data limitations. Without question, many low-income countries face serious capacity constraints, including in their ability to track and report on poverty and demographic outcomes. We recognize, further, that there is no internationally recognized definition of a poverty reducing expenditure, so, as described in the report, there can be significant variability in measurement across countries. Nonetheless, available evidence strongly suggests there has been increased spending for the poor in countries which have qualified for HIPC debt relief. For example, the IMF has found that before the HIPC Initiative, eligible countries were, on average, spending slightly more on debt service than on health and education combined. Based on available data, countries that have qualified for HIPC debt relief have now increased markedly their expenditures on health, education and other social services and, on average, poverty reducing spending was estimated at about eight times the amount of debt-service payments in 2007.

Moreover, the direct impact of redirecting resources from debt service to development expenditure is not the only avenue by which debt relief can have a positive effect. International debt relief initiatives can also help countries facing unsustainable debts to re-establish a sound economic footing and reengage with the international community. This process can thereby remove a significant barrier to economic growth and support their efforts to lift people out of poverty. For example, after years of conflict, Liberia has rejoined the international community, and debt relief under HIPC and MDRI has been an important part of this transition. The debt relief has been essential not only because of the massive debts that will be cancelled, but also because it is allowing Liberia to normalize its relations with its creditors, unlocking millions of dollars of new assistance every year from the international financial institutions.

Debt Sustainability

Debt sustainability in low-income countries is an issue to which the Treasury Department pays close attention, and we have been a strong supporter of efforts such as the World Bank and IMF Debt Sustainability Framework. We agree with your assessment that the World Bank and IMF analyses produced under the Debt Sustainability Framework represent an improved ability to assess the debt sustainability outlook in low-income countries. We will continue to work with these institutions and low-income countries to make further refinements as needed.

As the draft report highlights, despite significant debt relief, there are ongoing risks to debt sustainability in low-income countries. Although debt relief can be a valuable and sometimes necessary tool, merely canceling debt is not sufficient to ensure long-term debt sustainability if the underlying economic vulnerabilities remain. For this reason, continued effort is needed to assist countries in addressing weaknesses in their macroeconomic framework and financial management systems. The report correctly highlights the need to strengthen debt management capacity in low-income countries. Recognizing this need, the Treasury Department's Office of Technical Assistance and institutions such as the World Bank and IMF have been focusing significant attention on improving debt management in low-income countries. In fact, the Treasury Department has provided, at their request, direct technical assistance for debt management in eighteen of the countries that have received HIPC or MDRI debt relief.

Sincerely,

Karen Mathiasen
Acting Deputy Assistant Secretary
International Development Finance and Debt

The following is GAO's comment on the Department of the Treasury's letter dated January 9, 2009.

GAO Comment

1. GAO could not identify sufficient empirical evidence to suggest that increases in spending for the poor are directly related to savings from debt relief. It is difficult to establish that debt relief has led directly to increased poverty-reducing expenditures for two reasons: (1) debt relief resources are difficult to track, and (2) country spending data are not comparable and also may not be reliable. Because of these

limitations, it is difficult to establish if debt relief has caused these countries to increase or decrease their spending toward the poor.

APPENDIX X: COMMENTS FROM THE WORLD BANK

Note: GAO comments supplementing those in the report text appear at the end of this appendix.

The World Bank

Robert B. Zoellick
President

January 12, 2009

Mr. Gene L. Dodaro
Acting Comptroller General of the United States
Government Accountability Office
441 G St., NW
Washington, D.C. 20548

Dear Mr. Dodaro,

Thank you for the opportunity to comment on the U.S. Government Accountability Office's draft report entitled "The United States has not fully funded its share of debt relief, and the impact of debt relief on countries' poverty-reducing spending is unknown."

I welcome the report's recognition of the benefits of maintaining debt sustainability for low income countries to achieve their development objectives and, by extension, of the importance for donors to honor their pledges for additional funding covering the costs of IDA's debt cancellations over the long term.

The lack of additional funding would deprive not only the heavily indebted countries, but all IDA clients, of fresh loans and grants—in essence meaning that poor countries would themselves have to cover the cost of debt cancellations under debt relief initiatives, which the U.S. Government was instrumental in bringing to fruition. I believe that this report can serve as a useful reminder of the need for continued U.S. leadership in ensuring additionality of debt cancellations and new financing through replenishing IDA's resources to poor countries. I am also encouraged to see clear recognition of the need to shift to a more sustainable funding approach for the U.S. share of IDA's debt cancellation costs.

My staff has prepared comments of a more technical nature that address some of the points made in the report. They are attached to this letter, and I trust you will find them useful.

I would like to thank you and your staff for the fruitful cooperation in developing many of the findings contained in this report.

Sincerely,

Robert B. Zoellick

Attachment
cc: Mr. Eli Whitney Debevoise, Executive Director for the United States, The World Bank

1818 H Street, NW • Washington, DC 20433 • USA

World Bank Technical Comments on GAO's Draft Report
"The United States has not fully funded its share of debt relief, and the impact of debt relief on countries' poverty-reducing spending is unknown"
(GAO-09-162, January 2009)

1. The draft report rightly emphasizes that the additional resources which are freed up through debt cancellations granted by multilateral and bilateral creditors should be used to increase governments' poverty-reducing expenditures. It also points out that countries which receive debt relief may continue to face difficulties in maintaining debt sustainability.

2. Importantly, the report highlights that IDA's financial capacity to assist poor countries in the future would be impaired if donors fail to meet fully their commitments to IDA. Indeed, debt relief by a revolving credit fund such as IDA would be a mere accounting transaction and not provide benefits to recipients unless the lost credit reflows are replaced. That is why donors, including the United States, have committed to 'dollar-for-dollar' compensation under the Multilateral Debt Relief Initiative (MDRI) so that IDA's debt relief can lead to tangible development benefits.

3. The report rightly comments that the U.S. financing for MDRI will be increasingly insufficient if it is continued to be provided through accelerated encashment of regular IDA replenishment contributions. We believe that the report could more explicitly state that it will not be possible for the U.S. to fund future MDRI costs through early encashment of the regular IDA contributions. The annual MDRI costs of IDA will more than triple over the next two decades, reaching an estimated $1.8 billion per year by 2025. Continuing the current practice would presuppose a commensurate increase in regular IDA contributions from the U.S. As the report correctly states, the U.S. could instead employ separate budgetary appropriations for debt relief financing, which is the avenue that is employed by most other IDA donors.

4. In our view, GAO's draft report could also be strengthened by looking at debt relief costs beyond the 3-year timeframe of the current IDA replenishment. This is because IDA credits approved today will disburse over up to a decade - the maximum length of time that development projects need for completion. IDA can enter into these long term commitments based to a large degree on the value of future repayments under earlier credits. These credit reflows are however reduced through debt cancellation under the HIPC Initiative and MDRI. Thus IDA's ability to commit against them is correspondingly reduced. To mitigate this, and to ensure that the debt cancellations remain additional as intended, donor governments recognized the need to maintain IDA's financial capacity over the full disbursement period. The MDRI Agreement thus calls for firm donor financing commitments on a rolling basis over a decade. Many IDA donors have provided such commitments already, some even for the full (40-year) duration of MDRI. As currently drafted, the report may give the impression that all donor financing for the MDRI is limited to a rolling 3-year period, which is certainly not the case.

5. While the report rightly describes the challenges to improving the tracking and effectiveness of poverty reducing expenditures, the report could better acknowledge the progress being made in this area. In most low income countries, including heavily indebted poor countries (HIPCs), these expenditures are now aligned with countries' own poverty reduction strategies. It is important to remember that public expenditures in these countries are primarily financed through domestic revenues and fresh external aid flows. The funds released through multilateral debt cancellations are small relative to these other sources of financing for HIPCs. However, debt relief does represent a source of predictable financing as the repayment profile on the original

See comment 1.

174 United States Government Accountability Office

credits is well known in advance. Irrevocable, up-front cancellations of such credits leave governments with clarity on at least a portion of their income, which is typically rare in low income countries.

6. Consistent with the HIPC Initiative, poverty reducing expenditures are tracked and published in the HIPC Initiative Completion Point documents. The allocation of spending at the budget-wide level is analyzed to highlight the additionality of resources freed up through debt relief to finance country-defined development priorities. By design, once a country reaches its HIPC Initiative completion point, debt relief under the HIPC Initiative and MDRI is provided irrevocably. Thus, poverty reducing expenditures are not monitored for the purposes of these two debt relief initiatives beyond the completion point. However, in the context of periodic reviews of their national poverty reduction strategies, country authorities report poverty reducing expenditures to the IMF and World Bank. These are reported in the joint IMF-World Bank annual HIPC Initiative and MDRI Status of Implementation reports. In addition, since 2005, the Public Expenditure and Financial Accountability (PEFA) framework has also been used to evaluate the quality of public expenditure in low and middle income countries. As of end-2008, PEFA assessments have been conducted in 16 HIPCs, of which 11 post-completion point countries.

7. The report rightly notes that debt sustainability analyses (DSAs) are now more rigorous in defining the risk of debt distress for all LICs, thanks to assessments based on standardized and country specific shocks. However, the report should clearly distinguish between DSAs conducted under the HIPC Initiative and DSAs under the Low Income Country Debt Sustainability Framework (LIC DSF). HIPC DSAs are designed to establish the amount of debt relief needed to lower external public debt to the agreed HIPC Initiative thresholds. In contrast, DSAs under the LIC DSF are forward-looking to support LICs in their efforts to achieve their development goals without creating future debt problems. Efforts to improve their public debt management capacities are also being made through appropriate technical assistance.

The following is GAO's comment on the World Bank's letter dated January 12, 2009.

GAO Comment

1. We have revised our report language to clarify this distinction between DSAs.

APPENDIX XI: COMMENTS FROM THE INTERNATIONAL MONETARY FUND

Note: GAO comments supplementing those in the report text appear at the end of this appendix.

See comment 1.

INTERNATIONAL MONETARY FUND

WASHINGTON, D.C. 20431

Facsimile Number
1-202-623-4661

January 8, 2008

Mr. Thomas Melito
Director, International Affairs and Trade
Government Accountability Office
Washington, D.C.

Dear Mr. Melito:

Thank you for seeking our comments on the draft GAO report titled "The United States Has Not Fully Funded Its Share of Debt Relief, and the Impact of Debt Relief on Countries' Poverty-Reducing Spending Is Unknown." This report covers topics of great importance to the international community. We welcome the close collaboration between GAO and IMF staff during its preparation over the past few months.

We broadly agree with the report's main findings relevant for the IMF. We were particularly gratified with the finding that the IMF and the World Bank have improved their debt sustainability analyses since 2005. The report describes well the methodology of the debt sustainability framework (DSF) as well as its benefits. As mentioned in the report, the DSF is being used by an increasing number of lenders and borrowers.

We also concur that debt relief initiatives—both the Heavily Indebted Poor Countries (HIPC) Initiative and the Multilateral Debt Relief Initiative (MDRI)—have freed up substantial resources for recipient countries, a point abundantly made in the report although not reflected in the title. This is an important conclusion that is well worth stressing, as we have done in our 2008 Report with the World Bank on the Status of Implementation of the HIPC Initiative and MDRI and other publications.

However, we do not share the report's headline message on the impact of debt relief initiatives on poverty-reduction spending. As rightly argued in the report, it is generally not possible to track how debt service savings are used, as money is fungible and debt service savings are just one of the many ways to finance higher poverty-reducing spending. Thus, a feasible approach is to measure how much fiscal space has been created by debt relief and whether this has been associated with higher poverty-reducing spending. The former is done in the report; the latter is a difficult task, particularly when attempting comparisons across countries, because of differences in data and definitions. Analysis for specific countries is not affected by these latter problems, however, and does show that poverty-reducing spending has increased significantly in most of the countries that have benefited from debt relief. It is

> true that these data may be subject to other, idiosyncratic, weaknesses in some countries, so precision is not always possible. But we do not think that these weaknesses are so pervasive as to invalidate the conclusion that poverty-reducing spending has generally increased. Moreover, we would note that many of the report's observations regarding data shortcomings are based on five countries, a sample that GAO staff acknowledges is "illustrative, not representative."
>
> In short, we believe this is a good report, and that it would merit a title that accords more closely with the evidence on which it is based. We hope that, even at this late stage, this is a suggestion you might consider.
>
> Sincerely yours,
>
> Reza Moghadam
> Director
> Strategy, Policy, and Review Department

The following is GAO's comment on the International Monetary Fund's letter dated January 8, 2009.

GAO Comment

1. Based on our evidence, we found that the impact of debt relief on poverty-reducing expenditures is unknown. Our report shows that additional resources have been created by debt relief, but it is difficult to establish that debt relief has led directly to increased poverty- reducing expenditures for two reasons: (1) it is not possible to track how debt relief resources are used, and (2) country spending data are not comparable and also may not be reliable. In addition, based on our review of five MDRI case study countries, we found that debt relief resources are often much less than other types of resources such as tax revenue and grants. Therefore, while we agree that associations between debt relief and poverty-reducing expenditures may exist, the impact is unknown.

End Notes

[1] IaDB was not included in MDRI but decided in 2007 to provide equivalent debt relief under a similar initiative. IaDB's Fund for Special Operations is the entity responsible for providing debt relief. For the purpose of this chapter, references to MDRI also include the IaDB initiative. IMF, ADF, and IaDB plan to cancel all eligible debt countries owed them as of the end of 2004. IDA plans to cancel all eligible outstanding debt as of the end of 2003.

[2] The UN MDGs, which have a target completion date of 2015, are to (1) eradicate extreme poverty and hunger; (2) achieve universal primary education; (3) promote gender equality and empower women; (4) reduce child

Developing Countries: The United States Has Not Fully Funded Its Share of Debt... 177

mortality; (5) improve maternal health; (6) combat HIV/AIDS, malaria, and other diseases; (7) ensure environmental sustainability; and (8) develop a global partnership for development.

[3] This estimate is in end-2008 present value dollars. The present value of debt is a measure that takes into account the concessional, or below-market, terms that underlie most of these countries' loans. Present value debt is defined as the sum of all debt-service obligations (interest and principal) on existing debt, discounted at the market interest rate. The nominal value of the debt relief, estimated at more than $122 billion (more than $68 billion for the HIPC Initiative, not including predecision point countries for whom data are unavailable, and $54 billion for MDRI), is greater than the present value. These nominal dollar amounts do not take into consideration the time value of money.

[4] Replenishment refers to periodic contributions by member countries that are agreed upon by the institution's board of governors to fund concessional lending operations over a specified period of time, normally every 3 years. IDA14 covers the period 2006 through 2008, and IDA15 covers the period 2009 through 2011.

[5] GAO, *Developing Countries: U.S. Financing for Multilateral Debt Relief InitiativeCurrently Experiencing a Shortfall,* GAO-08-888R (Washington, D.C.: July 24, 2008).

[6] Countries describe their poverty-reducing spending as targeted toward activities, categories, sectors, clusters, programs, and ministries that we refer to in this chapter as activities, areas, or categories.

[7] See related GAO products at the end of this chapter.

[8] Pre-decision point countries are Comoros, Cote d'Ivoire, Eritrea, Kyrgyz Republic, Nepal, Somalia, and Sudan.

[9] Using this criterion, IMF has identified two non-HIPC Initiative countries, Cambodia and Tajikistan, as eligible for MDRI debt relief. As of the end of September 2007, IMF had provided $82 million and $100 million in MDRI debt relief to these two countries, respectively.

[10] Countries eligible for these additional actions are low-income countries that receive only concessional loans from IDA and ADF. While some of these countries receive debt relief under the HIPC Initiative and MDRI, others do not.

[11] While other creditors, including other IFIs and individual countries, also provide debt relief under the HIPC Initiative, our report focuses solely on debt relief provided by IDA, IMF, ADF, and IaDB. Total HIPC Initiative debt relief from all creditors is estimated at $74.5 billion.

[12] We did not include Togo in our calculations of debt relief costs because it reached the decision point on November 25, 2008, which is outside the scope of this review.

[13] Early encashment is an existing World Bank financing approach that Treasury chose to use in a new way. Previously, donors were allowed, if they so chose, to pay their nominal replenishment commitment at a discount and earn early encashment income to meet the full value of their obligations. Donors could also pay their commitment in full and the early encashment income would add to IDA's liquid assets. Treasury instead chose to use the early encashment income to finance the U.S. MDRI commitment. For more information on the use of early encashment to finance U.S. MDRI obligations, see *Developing Countries: U.S. Financing for Multilateral Debt Relief Initiative Currently Experiencing a Shortfall,* GAO-08-888R (Washington, D.C.: July 24, 2008).

[14] Pub. L. No. 109-102, §599D (Nov. 14, 2005); Pub. L. No. 110-161, §668(c) (Dec. 26, 2007).

[15] Pub. L. No. 109-102, §599D (Nov. 14, 2005), as amended by §20407 of Pub. L. No. 110-5, Div. B (Feb. 15, 2007).

[16] Pub. L. No. 110-161, §668(c) (Dec. 26, 2007).

[17] Some shortfalls in IDA funding are due to across-the-board funding rescissions reducing overall U.S. government funding levels, rather than withholdings specifically targeted at the World Bank to encourage reforms.

[18] The outstanding U.S. arrears to IDA are in nominal terms, which is the basis for U.S. commitments to IDA. Treasury officials emphasized that the nominal U.S. commitment to IDA is the required amount that must be paid. Early encashment has more than fully funded IDA on a present value basis.

[19] In 2008, the World Bank reported that the United States had a MDRI credit of $232 million. This assumes that the United States will meet most of its obligations to the U.S. IDA14 replenishment under the early encashment schedule by June 30, 2009. *Debt Relief Provided by IDA under MDRI and HIPC Initiative: Update on Costs and Donor Financing, as of June 30, 2008,* International Development Association (Washington, D.C.: Oct. 1, 2008).

[20] The amount of encashment income earned will depend on when IDA receives the $94 million and $49 million. If IDA receives this funding between July 1, 2009, and June 30, 2010, then encashment income credited to MDRI will be $228 million, leaving a shortfall of $4 million.

[21] The sum of MDRI encashment income ($146 million) and replenishment shortfall ($185 million) does not equal the amount of investment income ($308 million). Different methods are used to estimate these nominal dollar amounts. Investment income is the sum of simple and not compound interest income. MDRI encashment income is estimated by using a present value methodology and then converting the figure to nominal dollars. In July 2007, IDA moved to a new accounting framework using U.S. generally accepted accounting principles (GAAP). Under U.S. GAAP, the IDA balance sheet will show that the U.S. government paid $3.52 billion and will not count the $185 million of earned investment income under this scenario. However, the IDA

replenishment process will still allow countries to use encashment income to meet their replenishment obligations.

[22] In contrast, the U.S. government has agreed to an approach that will result in full funding for the HIPC Initiative for IDA. As part of its regular replenishment, the United States will pay its share of IDA's HIPC debt relief on a pay-as-you-go basis. The HIPC cost share of donors' replenishments is paid over a 3-year period.

[23] As we reported in July 2008, encashment income generated during ADF-12 is insufficient to cover U.S. MDRI costs for that period. However, in January 2009 ADF officials told us that accumulated surpluses from previous replenishment periods could offset the shortfall. Nonetheless, the shortfalls would increase during subsequent replenishment periods, rising to almost $19 million by 2025.

[24] For CBO forecast data see http://www.cbo.gov/budget/data/econproj.xls.

[25] Debt relief resources for this analysis are based on varying numbers of countries depending on which IFI and debt relief program, HIPC or MDRI, we are analyzing. For IDA, our analysis of the annual MDRI program is based on 41 countries.

[26] While other creditors, including other IFIs and individual countries, also provide debt relief under the HIPC Initiative, our report focuses solely on debt relief provided by IDA, IMF, ADF, and IaDB.

[27] In addition to providing debt relief, each year IDA and ADF are to reduce the amount of planned assistance to each eligible country by an amount equivalent to the debt relief to be provided that year. IDA and ADF are then to reallocate the aggregate amount of this funding to all eligible low-income countries (i.e., countries eligible to receive concessional loans from IDA or ADF, only some of whom receive debt relief) based on the institution's assessment of each country's performance.

[28] For the purposes of this discussion, the combined total of HIPC Initiative and MDRI debt relief, $21.4 billion and $28.3 billion, respectively, is $49.7 billion. This amount differs from the $58 billion in total debt relief cited earlier—$28.4 billion for HIPC and $29.6 billion for MDRI—primarily due to differences in HIPC Initiative data. The $21.4 billion HIPC amount does not include annual HIPC debt service relief data for all countries, as ADF, IaDB, and IMF did not provide annual data for all completion point, decision point, and pre-decision point countries. After 2006, IMF delivered the remaining HIPC assistance on a stock basis for countries that reached HIPC Completion Point, and therefore did not provide annual HIPC debt service relief data for the completion point countries after 2006. IDA told us that discrepancies between its aggregate reported HIPC data ($15.0 billion) and our calculation based on the annual HIPC debt service relief ($12.7 billion) was due, in part, to the arrears clearance mechanism. The MDRI amounts differ by $1.3 billion primarily because the data for IMF covers only the 23 completion point countries.

[29] According to IDA's MDRI process, IDA reduces its annual commitments to a country by the amount of that year's MDRI debt relief. However, the associated annual reduction in disbursed assistance is only a portion of the reduction of the annual commitments. This is because the associated reduction in disbursements occurs over a 9-year period for IDA and a 10-year period for ADF. When analyzed taking into account the time value of money and these disbursement patterns, the aggregate net present value of MDRI debt relief, $28.3 billion, is greater than the aggregate net present value of the reduction in disbursed assistance, $18.9 billion, for countries receiving MDRI debt relief.

[30] The annual MDRI debt relief reduction, aggregated over all MDRI recipients, is the amount to be reallocated to IDA-only recipients—a larger subset of IDA recipients than those that receive MDRI debt relief—on the basis of performance. We refer to this as the performance-based reallocation, or PBA reallocation.

[31] There are 23 IDA-only countries that will not receive MDRI debt service relief, but will receive the MDRI debt relief reallocation: Angola, Bangladesh, Bhutan, Cambodia, Cape Verde, Djibouti, Kenya, Kiribati, Kyrgyz Republic, Lao People's Democratic Republic, Lesotho, Maldives, Moldova, Mongolia, Nigeria, Samoa, Solomon Islands, Tajikistan, TimorLeste, Tonga, Vanuatu, Vietnam, and Yemen. Three inactive IDA-only countries are excluded, namely Burma, Somalia, and Sudan.

[32] IDA bases the distribution of its resources on Country Performance Ratings, which reflect primarily an assessment of a country's policy and institutional framework, or CPIA, as established by the World Bank. The CPIA consists of 16 criteria representing the different policy and institutional dimensions of an effective poverty reduction and growth strategy. These 16 criteria are grouped into four clusters as follows: (1) *economic management:* macroeconomic management, fiscal policy, debt policy; (2) *structural policies:* trade, financial sector, business regulatory environment; (3) *policies for social inclusion/equity:* gender equality, equity of public resource use, building human resources, social protection and labor, policies and institutions for environmental sustainability; and (4) *public sector management and institutions:* property rights and rule-based governance, quality of budgetary and financial management, efficiency of revenue mobilization, quality of public administration, and transparency, accountability, and corruption in the public sector. Population and per capita income are also determinants of IDA allocations.

[33] Net change in resources is the sum of MDRI debt relief, the IDA and ADF reduction in assistance due to MDRI debt relief, and the performance-based reallocation.

[34] *Heavily Indebted Poor Countries (HIPC) Initiative and Multilateral Debt Relief Initiative (MDRI) —Status of Implementation,* IMF and World Bank (Washington, D.C.: Aug. 27, 2008).

Developing Countries: The United States Has Not Fully Funded Its Share of Debt... 179

[35] IMF and World Bank officials told us that it is difficult to estimate the amount of annual debt relief provided to countries due to lack of bilateral and private creditor data. As a result, the association discussed in IMF and World Bank documents is between debt service payments and poverty-reducing expenditures. The World Bank and IMF do not show any causation between debt service payments and poverty-reducing expenditures, but present a graphical representation of an association between rising levels of poverty- reducing expenditures and declining debt service payments. The underlying implication is that declining debt service payments are resulting from increased amounts of debt relief from the HIPC Initiative and MDRI.

[36] We reviewed the most recent online country budget documents available on the five countries' Ministry of Finance Web sites to determine how countries were reporting their poverty-reducing expenditures.

[37] According to IMF officials, countries report to the IMF country teams on their poverty- reducing expenditures as outlined in their PRSPs. Each country determines the level of aggregation in its reporting, which can range from an aggregated total to a detailed breakdown of spending.

[38] In 2001, the World Bank and IMF committed to a systematic assessment of poverty and the social impacts of policy reforms in low-income countries. The Policy and Social Impact Analysis applies tools and techniques of social and economic analysis to analyze impacts of economy wide policy reforms before those reforms are carried out (ex ante analysis), and more systematic use of that analysis to inform policy advice and policy design.

[39] International Monetary Fund and World Bank, *Update on the Assessments and Implementation of Action Plans to Strengthen Capacity of HIPCs to Track Poverty- Reducing Public Spending*(Washington, D.C.: Apr. 12, 2005). Most recent assessments of HIPC performance in tracking budgetary processes are conducted under the Public Expenditure and Financial Accountability (PEFA) framework. PEFA is a partnership between the World Bank, IMF, the European Commission and several bilateral aid agencies. We found for the five case study countries that only three had PEFA assessments online, of which the most recent information provided was collected in 2006. For more information on PEFA, see http://www.pefa.org/.

[40] According to IMF officials, when IMF country teams visit countries, they collect and attempt to standardize the countries' poverty-reducing expenditure data and send them to other IMF officials, who aggregate the data into one line item to be reported as poverty- reducing expenditures. The World Bank and IMF jointly publish annual poverty-reducing expenditure data in an annual debt relief status of implementation report. The reports show actual data from 2001 through 2007 and estimates from 2008 through 2012.

[41] Additionally, according to a 2006 ADF country assessment report, countries such as Ethiopia and Ghana experienced a number of weaknesses and challenges in their public expenditure management systems that caused delays in pro-poor spending and prevented timely internal reporting of budget execution. For additional information on this assessment, see the African Development Fund's *Implementation Modalities of the Multilateral Debt Relief Initiative* (Apr. 10, 2006).

[42] We found for our five case study countries that some targets, such as access to drinking water, net enrolment ratio in primary education, and infant mortality rates, had more complete information.

[43] World Bank officials also told us that insufficient time has passed since the inception of MDRI to assess the impact of poverty-reducing expenditures on attaining the MDGs, given that it takes time to realize the effects of investing in areas such as education and health care. However, some recent studies have attempted to examine the impact of the various aspects of the debt relief process, including the formulation of the PRSP on MDG outcomes. For additional information on these studies, see http://www1.worldbank.org/economicpolicy/debtconf08/DebtConferenceMaterials.asp

[44] For IMF, DSAs are required in the context of Article IV consultation or a Poverty Reduction Growth Facility (PRGF) arrangement request or review. Article IV consultations are usually conducted annually with member countries, and IMF economists travel to the countries to gather and report on information collected from government, central bank, and other officials. PRGF arrangements link IMF low-interest lending closely to poverty- reducing efforts of countries, specifically to country PRSPs. IMF officials also noted that DSAs could be done on a stand-alone basis if, for example, the World Bank needed a joint DSA for its operations but there was no scheduled Article IV consultation or program review at that time. For the World Bank, the DSA is required for Country Assistance Strategies and IDA allocation purposes. For the purposes of this chapter, we are addressing DSA components relating to external debt sustainability and not the public debt issues also included in the analyses.

[45] Prior to establishment of the DSF, IMF and the World Bank conducted analyses at a country's decision point and completion point to determine the level of debt relief that was required to bring a country's debt level to within HIPC Initiative targets. These debt relief analyses are still conducted and are not the focus of this chapter.

[46] Strong performing countries have a CPIA rating of 3.75 or higher, while medium performers have a rating between 3.25 and 3.75 and poor performers have a rating of 3.25 or lower. In order to reduce uncertainty regarding appropriate creditor assistance that could be associated with potential annual fluctuations in a country's CPIA rating, a 3-year moving CPIA average is used to determine a country's performance. IMF officials explained that the empirical evidence establishing that countries with better policies and institutions can carry substantially higher debt burdens without increasing the risk of debt distress was reported by Aart

Kraay and Vikram Nehru in "When Is External Debt Sustainable," World *Bank Economic Review*, Vol. 20, No. 3, August 28, 2006.

[47] Prior to the establishment of the DSF, almost all countries' debt sustainability was assessed in the same manner and was defined as maintaining a debt stock-to-exports ratio of 150 percent or lower.

[48] IMF and World Bank officials told us that while the debt burden indicator analysis is the basis for determining a country's future risk of debt distress, officials also use their judgment in making a final decision. For example, if a threshold is breached in a marginal or temporary way, a risk determination would take this circumstance into account.

[49] See GAO, *Developing Countries: Status of the Heavily Indebted Poor Countries Debt Relief Initiative*, GAO/NSIAD-98-229 (Washington, D.C.: Sept. 30, 1998); *Developing Countries: Debt Relief Initiative for Poor Countries Faces Challenges*, GAO/NSIAD-00-161 (Washington, D.C.: June 29, 2000); and *Developing Countries: Achieving Poor Countries' Economic Growth and Debt Relief Targets Faces Significant Financing Challenges*, GAO-04-405 (Washington, D.C.: Apr. 14, 2004).

[50] DSAs are available on the World Bank Web site at www.worldbank.org/debt and the IMF Web site at www.imf.org/dsa.

[51] *Strategies for Financing Development*, newsletter of the HIPC CBP and the FPC CBP, Issue 35, 2nd quarter 2008.

[52] For example, when Mauritania's risk rating changed from "low" to "moderate" in fiscal year 2008, IDA's assistance to the country changed from 100 percent loans in fiscal year 2007 to 50 percent grants and 50 percent loans in fiscal year 2008. According to World Bank staff, this risk reclassification is due, in part, to the emergence of substantial arrears to external creditors that were previously considered "passive debt," or debt for which creditors had not requested payment for many years. After Mauritania passed the completion point, the holders of these claims indicated that their claims had not been waived.

[53] In 2002 we reported that a shift of multilateral loans to grants would lessen poor countries' debt burdens, increasing their ability to repay future debt. See *Developing Countries: Switching Some Multilateral Loans to Grants Lessens Poor Country Debt Burdens*, GAO-02-593 (Washington, D.C.: Apr. 19, 2002).

[54] During IDA14, the divide between the incentives-related portion and the charges-related portion was 11 percent and 9 percent, respectively. According to the World Bank, in fiscal year 2009, the divide was changed to 13 percent and 7 percent, respectively, reflecting no IDA commitment charge in fiscal year 2009.

[55] IDA documentation notes that "Given the negative correlation between risk of debt distress and performance, grants based on debt sustainability can result in higher resource transfers to low-performing countries, thereby weakening the performance incentive. This weakening is moderated by applying the 20 percent discount to grant volumes." See *The Role of IDA in Ensuring Debt Sustainability: A Progress Report*, International Development Association Resource Mobilization Department, September 2007.

[56] IFI outreach to commercial creditors has been less active, with IMF and World Bank reports noting that progress is needed to improve DSA visibility with this group of creditors.

[57] For example, IMF and the World Bank reported that at the end of 2007, countries receiving both HIPC Initiative and MDRI debt relief had an average debt-to-exports ratio of 63 percent, while countries not yet benefiting from both programs had an average debt-toexports ratio of 200 percent.

[58] This projection includes stable assumptions regarding borrowing and growth of national income and exports. See *Review of Low-Income Country Debt Sustainability Framework and Implications of the MDRI*, International Development Association and International Monetary Fund (Mar. 27, 2006).

[59] A concessional loan is a loan extended by a creditor at below market terms. IDA's nonconcessional borrowing policy defines a loan with at least a 35 percent grant element as concessional. The grant element is the difference between the nominal value of a loan and the present value of a loan.

[60] The World Bank and IMF are providing assistance to help low-income countries improve their debt management capabilities. For example, countries can use the Debt Management Performance Assessment as a diagnostic tool for identifying strengths and weaknesses in debt management operations. The World Bank and IMF also provide technical assistance in designing Medium-Term Debt Management Strategies (MTDS). An MTDS helps to operationalize a country's debt management objectives by outlining cost-risk tradeoffs in meeting a government's financing needs and payment obligations.

[61] See *IDA Countries and Non-Concessional Debt: Dealing with the 'Free Rider' Problem in IDA14 Grant-Recipient and Post-MDRI Countries*, Resource Mobilization Department (FRM) (June 19, 2006).

[62] In 2007, IDA granted Mali an exception to its nonconcessional financing policy to finance a power plant that would help ease a short-term crisis in the energy sector by increasing the country's electricity generation capacity. Mali entered into a nonconcessional financing agreement for over $70 million for this project. The country's strong policies and institutions indicated an ability to manage modest levels of nonconcessional borrowing for a critical economic need. In addition, the power plant is expected to generate sufficiently high economic and financial rates of return to justify the loan. IDA has since granted to Rwanda and Mauritania two additional preliminary exceptions to its nonconcessional borrowing policy.

[63] For example, IMF can impose ceilings on nonconcessional borrowing when countries have a PRGF arrangement loan or a Policy Support Instrument to help design IMF- approved economic programs that signal strong

country policies to other parties. According to IMF officials, IMF can provide for exceptions to its nonconcessional borrowing limits.

[64] We used a discount rate of 4.9 percent to compute present values. The IMF/IDA September 2008 "Status of Implementation" report used this rate in their present value cost updating exercise.

[65] Both IMF and IaDB are providing MDRI debt relief as debt stock reduction rather than on a flow basis. IMF provided data for 17 of the 23 MDRI recipients. We calculated IMF's annual debt service reduction based on outstanding MDRI-eligible debt for the remaining six countries (Cameroon, The Gambia, Malawi, Mauritania, São Tomé and Príncipe, and Sierra Leone) using data from IMF's external Web site.

[66] A World Bank official noted that the 9-year encashment schedule may vary on a countryby-country basis.

[67] The 10 interim countries used in this analysis are Afghanistan, Burundi, Central African Republic, Chad, Democratic Republic of the Congo, Republic of the Congo, Guinea, Guinea-Bissau, Haiti, and Liberia. Togo is not included in the list of interim countries because it reached the decision point on November 25, 2008, which is outside the scope of this analysis.

[68] The eight pre-decision point countries used in this analysis are Comoros, Cote d'Ivoire, Eritrea, Kyrgyz Republic, Nepal, Somalia, Sudan, and Togo.

[69] Under the Foreign Sovereign Immunities Act, foreign states are not immune from the jurisdiction of U.S. courts in any case in which immunity has been waived, or in which the action is based upon a commercial activity carried on in the United States by the foreign state; or upon an act performed in the United States in connection with a commercial activity of the foreign state elsewhere; or upon an act outside the territory of the United States in connection with a commercial activity of the foreign state elsewhere and that act causes a direct effect in the United States (28 U.S.C. §1605(a)(1), §1605(a)(2)).

[70] *Press Release of the Paris Club on the Threats Posed by Some Litigating Creditors to Heavily Indebted Poor Countries*, Paris Club (May 22, 2007).

[71] The African Legal Support Facility, which is not yet operational, will come into existence when the agreement creating the facility is signed by at least 10 participating states or international organizations, and instruments of ratification, acceptance, or approval are deposited by at least 7 of those participating states or international organizations.

[72] Secured funding includes donor commitments that are part of the IDA15 replenishment to cover IDA's costs for the HIPC Initiative ($1.7 billion) and arrears clearance for HIPC countries ($1.1 billion).

[73] In addition, IDA, ADF, IaDB, and IMF will need an estimated $11 billion in additional financing to cover countries that are not yet eligible to receive debt relief: 8 countries under the HIPC Initiative and 18 countries under MDRI.

[74] These IBRD transfers were from income earned primarily from interest payments by middle-income borrower countries.

[75] While donors provide funding for the HIPC Initiative as part of their regular replenishment funding, donors provide additional funding for MDRI in conjunction with their replenishment funding.

[76] While IFIs can provide debt relief either by canceling debt service payments as they come due (referred to as "flow" debt relief) or by canceling a portion of a country's outstanding debt (known as "stock" debt relief), the approach makes no difference to the countries receiving debt relief as they only realize the benefits of additional available resources as debt payments that would have come due are no longer required to be paid. The present value costs of either approach are the same for the IFI.

[77] IMF has an estimated $0.54 billion to cover un-anticipated HIPC Initiative costs (referred to as topping-up assistance) as well as future debt relief costs for Somalia and Sudan, countries with protracted arrears of about $1.8 billion as of the end of November 2008. Additional financing may be required when these countries are ready to clear their arrears and embark on the HIPC Initiative.

[78] In order to provide comparable debt relief delivered figures for the four IFIs, we estimated the amount of debt service relief through 2008 implied by the debt stock cancellation by IMF and IaDB.

[79] IDA15 covers the period July 1, 2008, through June 30, 2011, the IDA fiscal year 2009 through fiscal year 2011.

[80] The early encashment credits are not exactly the same as the interest income earned. Two different computation techniques are used. The present value approach is the agreed-upon methodology used to calculate early encashment credits.

[81] The preliminary shortfall for IDA 14 is $152 million, about 5.3 percent of the replenishment commitment. This was not an across-the-board reduction.

[82] Congressional Budget Office, Table C-2, CBO's Year-by-Year Forecast and Projections for Fiscal Years 2008 to 2018, *The Budget and Economic Outlook: An Update* (September 2008), at http://www.cbo.gov may not add due to rounding.

[84] The $3.1 billion consists of a $4.9 billion gain between 2006 and 2027 and a $1.7 billion loss between 2028 and 2052.

INDEX

A

academics, 57, 99, 126
access, 11, 17, 22, 50, 54, 55, 61, 75, 76, 78, 80, 82, 83, 84, 86, 90, 103, 109, 119, 120, 151, 160, 179
accountability, 45, 49, 52, 59, 60, 63, 66, 74, 82, 83, 84, 116, 178
accounting, 54, 59, 131, 177
accuracy, 146, 156
aerospace, 79
Afghanistan, 51, 125, 162, 181
Africa, ix, 10, 30, 31, 32, 33, 34, 57, 67, 72, 96, 98, 107, 112, 115, 117, 126, 150
agencies, 15, 17, 19, 32, 53, 62, 66, 73, 89, 111, 112, 120, 150, 179
agriculture, 3, 72, 73
AIDS, 33, 76, 100
Albania, 11, 96
Algeria, 13, 96
Angola, 96, 151, 178
appropriations, viii, 20, 21, 22, 28, 45, 61, 63, 110, 114, 116, 119, 130, 134, 138, 152, 162
Argentina, 13, 14, 15, 28, 67, 100, 101, 103
Armenia, 96
Asia, 10, 57, 77, 94, 98, 150
Asian countries, 30, 71, 93
assessment, 49, 52, 61, 67, 81, 84, 116, 146, 147, 178, 179
assets, 78, 87, 88, 110
assumptions, 130, 134, 147, 148, 149, 156, 162, 180
Attorney General, 75
auditing, 58, 59, 119, 132, 156
audits, 70, 73, 108, 119
Australia, 13, 15, 18, 28, 91, 94, 101, 103
authorities, 48, 72, 82
authority, 15, 16, 23, 30, 37, 48, 69, 83, 84, 90, 97, 104

B

background, ix, 108
balance of payments, 27, 90
balance sheet, 177
Balkans, 77
Bangladesh, 60, 178
bank financing, 79
banking, 78, 79, 95, 120
banking sector, 78, 120
banks, vii, 1, 6, 8, 9, 10, 12, 14, 27, 36, 37, 43, 45, 46, 48, 49, 51, 53, 54, 57, 58, 59, 61, 62, 64, 65, 66, 67, 79, 84, 85, 95
Barbados, 11
Belgium, 26
Bhutan, 178
bilateral aid, vii, 2, 17, 18, 109, 179
Bolivia, 92, 96, 97, 100, 125, 128, 149, 161
bondholders, 12
bonds, 14, 27, 30
borrowers, 12, 32, 43, 47, 110, 112, 115
borrowing, 12, 14, 24, 49, 50, 53, 65, 68, 82, 92, 97, 112, 141, 147, 149, 150, 151, 165, 166, 180
Bosnia, 11, 96
Botswana, 10, 67, 68, 96, 104
Brazil, 11, 13, 14, 15, 28, 91, 96, 97, 101, 103
breaches, 148
breakdown, 145, 179
Britain, 71, 78
budget deficit, 67, 71
budget surplus, 110
Bulgaria, 96
Burkina Faso, 96, 147, 149, 151
Burma, 23, 178
business education, 85

C

Cambodia, 60, 96, 125, 177, 178

Index

Cameroon, 125, 149, 157, 161, 181
Canada, 13, 14, 15, 28, 30, 37, 91, 93, 101, 103
capacity building, 149
capital account, 92
capital flows, 56, 63, 127
capital markets, 11, 12, 34, 36, 50, 55, 86, 91, 109
capitalism, 47, 94
Caribbean, 22, 27, 88, 92, 96
Caribbean countries, 88
case study, 69, 70, 143, 144, 145, 146, 155, 176, 179
cash flow, 69
causation, 143, 179
CEE, 6, 10
Central African Republic, 162, 181
Central Asia, 57, 77, 96
central bank, 67, 179
Central Europe, 10, 86
Chad, 96, 125, 181
challenges, 22, 57, 61, 63, 70, 74, 85, 118, 124, 153, 179
Chief Justice, 75
Chile, 13, 60, 69, 70, 100
China, 10, 11, 13, 14, 16, 28, 60, 80, 83, 91, 96, 101, 103, 117
CIS, 79, 100
City, 28
civil servants, 15
civil society, 49, 52, 53, 58, 72, 73, 75, 81, 99
classification, 148, 155, 156
clients, 77, 79, 86, 87, 95
climate, 22, 53, 56, 59, 115
climate change, 22, 53, 56, 59
clusters, 177, 178
Cold War, 92
Colombia, 13, 96
commodity, 31, 67, 77, 131
Commonwealth of Independent States, 79, 100
communist countries, 6
community, 23, 25, 47, 50, 56, 60, 63, 74, 83, 84, 85, 131, 157
comparative advantage, 73
compensation, 75, 108
compensation package, 75
competition, 57, 77, 78
competition policy, 78
complaints, 54, 75, 84
compliance, 83, 84, 162
components, 20, 155, 179
concessional terms, 6, 27, 116, 151
confidence, 31, 46, 62, 71, 126
conflict, ix, 50, 51, 52, 53, 67, 74, 81, 108, 117, 118
congestion, 69

Congress, iv, v, vii, viii, 1, 2, 3, 19, 21, 23, 24, 28, 29, 30, 32, 34, 35, 37, 42, 45, 47, 48, 49, 50, 51, 52, 57, 59, 62, 63, 64, 69, 84, 88, 89, 90, 99, 104, 107, 109, 110, 116, 118, 119, 120, 121, 123, 124, 126, 127, 128, 130, 133, 134, 138, 139, 152
Congressional Budget Office, 131, 141, 165, 181
congressional hearings, viii, 2, 23
consent, 23, 83, 120
Consolidated Appropriations Act, 23, 28, 30, 116
Constitution, 96, 111
construction, 33, 55, 76
consultants, 59, 60, 84
consulting, 87, 151
control, vii, 1, 15, 18, 24, 32, 37, 62, 78, 87, 90, 109, 149, 151
Cook Islands, 10
coordination, 58, 85, 108, 118
corporate governance, 63, 78, 79
corruption, 23, 24, 25, 33, 46, 47, 48, 49, 53, 54, 57, 58, 59, 60, 61, 63, 64, 67, 70, 72, 73, 74, 76, 82, 83, 99, 115, 116, 138, 178
cost, 18, 43, 51, 55, 58, 65, 75, 80, 98, 108, 109, 125, 127, 141, 158, 161, 162, 165, 166, 178, 180, 181
Costa Rica, 11, 88, 96, 97
costs, 11, 17, 22, 48, 58, 59, 64, 85, 112, 134, 136, 139, 141, 152, 153, 158, 159, 160, 162, 165, 177, 178, 181
Côte d'Ivoire, 29, 33
country of origin, 25
covering, 30, 65, 142
credibility, 50, 80, 108
credit, 53, 56, 67, 79, 88, 89, 150, 177
credit market, 89
credit rating, 88
credit squeeze, 79
creditor nation, 124, 125
creditors, 36, 105, 125, 131, 134, 151, 156, 157, 158, 177, 178, 180
creditworthiness, 30, 112
crisis management, 50
criticism, 27, 71, 114, 124
critics, 78, 114
Croatia, 96
CRP, 82, 83, 84, 101
CRR, 77, 101
Cuba, 4
culture, 49, 118
Cyprus, 91, 117
Czech Republic, 86, 101

D

debt service, 22, 60, 124, 127, 141, 143, 154, 160, 168, 178, 179, 181

Index

debtor nation, 127
debtors, 127
debts, ix, 64, 65, 71, 80, 123, 124, 126, 127, 157
decentralization, 34
decision making, 119
decision-making process, 150
decisions, 15, 16, 32, 37, 49, 63, 64, 66, 74, 80, 82, 89, 113, 120, 147, 150
definition, 67, 127, 145
democracy, 6, 47, 56, 72, 76, 77, 95
denial, 69, 83
developed countries, 18
developing countries, vii, 1, 2, 3, 4, 5, 6, 11, 17, 18, 19, 22, 24, 25, 27, 36, 37, 47, 49, 52, 56, 62, 63, 64, 65, 104, 109, 114, 115, 120
developing nations, 90
development assistance, 19, 109, 118
development banks, vii, viii, 1, 2, 6, 15, 16, 24, 27, 33, 35, 45, 46, 48, 49, 51, 52, 53, 54, 55, 57, 58, 59, 60, 61, 62, 63, 64, 65, 66, 67, 89, 94, 95, 99, 117, 120, 121, 123, 125
directives, 15, 48, 51
directors, 66, 89, 119
disaster relief, 48
disbursement, 3, 24, 73, 116, 137, 138, 154, 168, 169, 178
discipline, 48, 51
disclosure, 49, 52, 54, 55, 59, 60, 61, 66, 86, 116
diseases, 57, 177
dispersion, 132, 155
distress, 130, 134, 147, 148, 149, 150, 151, 156, 179, 180
diversity, 90, 132, 149, 150, 155
division, vii, 1, 111, 117
division of labor, vii, 1, 117
doctors, 109
domestic investment, 85
domestic resources, 128
Dominican Republic, 96, 97
donations, 88, 91, 113, 117
donors, vii, 1, 12, 17, 18, 24, 30, 31, 32, 33, 34, 36, 37, 47, 60, 62, 63, 64, 65, 73, 74, 81, 85, 86, 91, 108, 109, 110, 111, 112, 113, 117, 118, 124, 125, 159, 177, 178, 181
draft, 134, 152, 153
drinking water, 179
drought, 149, 151
drugs, 23, 109
duplication, 27
dynamics, 86

E

earnings, 68, 137, 151

East Asia, 96, 112
Eastern Europe, 6, 96, 112
economic assistance, 18, 32
economic crisis, 47, 49, 50, 56, 90
economic development, viii, 17, 19, 27, 52, 65, 74, 85, 91, 92, 107, 109, 120
economic downturn, 80
economic growth, 17, 46, 65, 81, 118, 124, 126, 127, 134, 149
economic performance, 30
economic policy, 60, 65, 67, 72, 110, 114, 125
economic resources, 76
economics, 79
economy, viii, 2, 12, 18, 26, 27, 51, 61, 71, 72, 77, 80, 90, 109, 150, 151, 179
Ecuador, 96
educational system, 145
Egypt, 10, 13, 14, 36, 62, 91, 96, 117
El Salvador, 88, 96, 97
electricity, 3, 78, 180
eligible countries, 112, 113, 125, 126, 135
emerging markets, 63, 98
employees, 58, 82, 83, 91, 93, 118
employment, 46, 62
endangered species, 84
energy, 33, 51, 54, 56, 57, 73, 77, 78, 79, 144, 145, 180
energy efficiency, 78
environment, 22, 48, 75, 91, 178
environmental impact, 49, 51, 54, 70, 83, 89
environmental issues, 11, 89
environmental sustainability, 177, 178
equipment, 80
equity, 4, 5, 36, 78, 79, 81, 92, 94, 95, 120, 121, 178
Eritrea, 125, 162, 177, 181
Estonia, 91, 101, 117
ethics, 57, 59
ethnic groups, 81
EU, 77, 80, 86, 101
Europe, 14, 57, 91, 98, 113
European Commission, 111, 179
European Community, 13
European Investment Bank, 13
European Union, 28, 33, 37, 90, 101
excess demand, 33
exchange rate, 47, 56, 93
execution, 116, 146, 179
exercise, 23, 24, 86, 89, 157, 181
expenditures, 53, 57, 74, 81, 130, 133, 141, 143, 144, 145, 146, 148, 152, 153, 155, 171, 176, 179
expertise, 33, 47, 158
experts, 47, 84, 88, 108, 118, 119
export ratio, 124

186   Index

exports, 31, 80, 124, 148, 149, 151, 180
extreme poverty, 176

F

farmers, 76
FDI, 27, 85, 101
FDI inflow, 85
federal courts, 156
Federal Reserve Board, 89
feedback, 70
Ferdinand Marcos, 76
filters, 52, 67
finance, viii, ix, 22, 31, 56, 64, 73, 78, 85, 88, 107,
    109, 123, 126, 130, 133, 136, 137, 138, 139, 140,
    141, 153, 158, 159, 165, 177, 180
financial crisis, vii, viii, 2, 6, 12, 19, 47, 48, 50, 51,
    56, 63, 67, 86, 95, 104
financial institutions, 52, 56, 57, 66, 67
financial market, 151
financial resources, 31, 124
financial sector, 178
financial stability, 27, 46, 48, 51
financial support, 27, 90
financial system, 72
firms, 3, 4, 5, 23, 24, 25, 36, 71, 77, 79
fiscal policy, 82, 178
fluctuations, 56, 149, 151, 179
focusing, 11, 109, 118
food, 17, 22, 54, 56, 149, 151
foreign aid, vii, ix, 1, 17, 18, 27, 74, 108, 111, 114,
    117, 121, 127, 128
foreign assistance, ix, 108, 115, 117, 123, 124, 127
foreign direct investment, 27, 85
foreign exchange, 77
foreign policy, viii, 45, 47, 51, 64, 109, 126
forgiveness, 124, 125, 127
formula, 26, 115
France, 13, 15, 28, 78, 93, 101, 103, 113
fraud, 55, 57, 58, 59, 67, 70, 73
funding, vii, viii, 2, 22, 23, 32, 33, 36, 46, 48, 50, 54,
    58, 61, 62, 64, 66, 69, 73, 75, 88, 90, 108, 109,
    110, 111, 115, 119, 120, 129, 132, 134, 136, 140,
    141, 142, 152, 153, 158, 160, 162, 165, 170, 177,
    178, 181

G

Gabon, 96
GDP, 26, 67, 72, 85, 101, 144, 148
gender, 73, 176, 178
gender equality, 176, 178
General Accounting Office, 32
generation, 180

Georgia, 10, 96
Germany, 13, 15, 18, 28, 93, 101, 103, 113
global leaders, 61
goals, 47, 53, 54, 59, 61, 62, 72, 78, 84, 85, 89, 115,
    116, 118, 120, 126, 135, 155
gold, 53, 56, 60, 68, 124, 160
goods and services, 24, 61
governance, 11, 23, 32, 46, 48, 52, 57, 61, 63, 73, 77,
    83, 84, 95, 115, 117, 118, 121, 178
government budget, 73
government revenues, 148
government spending, 71
grant programs, viii, 45
grants, vii, viii, ix, 1, 2, 3, 4, 5, 11, 14, 27, 29, 33, 52,
    53, 54, 56, 60, 62, 64, 68, 72, 91, 92, 93, 94, 95,
    107, 109, 110, 112, 114, 115, 121, 147, 149, 157,
    176, 180
Great Depression, 56
greenhouse gas emissions, 22, 54
growth, 17, 22, 47, 56, 64, 90, 114, 115, 126, 127,
    128, 131, 134, 140, 148, 149, 150, 152, 178, 180
growth rate, 140, 148
Guatemala, 96, 97
guidance, 74, 147
guidelines, 50, 53, 73, 87, 116
Guinea, 10, 96, 125, 162, 181
Guyana, 92, 125, 128, 149, 157, 161

H

Haiti, 53, 56, 60, 68, 92, 96, 97, 125, 128, 160, 162,
    181
harmonization, 25, 117, 121
headquarters, 33, 48, 50, 72, 73, 91, 93, 94
health, vii, 1, 3, 17, 23, 50, 53, 65, 70, 84, 109, 115,
    121, 144, 145, 155, 177, 179
health care, 65, 144, 179
Hezbollah, 74
Highlands, 74, 75, 76, 101
highways, 3, 73
HIPC, ix, 20, 21, 22, 28, 30, 123, 124, 125, 126, 127,
    128, 129, 130, 131, 132, 133, 134, 135, 136, 137,
    139, 141, 142, 144, 147, 148, 149, 150, 151, 152,
    153, 154, 155, 156, 157, 158, 159, 160, 161, 162,
    177, 178, 179, 180, 181
HIV, 33, 58, 76, 101, 109, 177
HIV/AIDS, 33, 58, 76, 109, 177
Honduras, 92, 96, 97, 125, 128, 149, 157, 161
hopes, 85
host, 54, 60, 70, 77, 83
hostilities, 50, 53, 74
House, 20, 69, 90, 101
human development, 84
human dignity, 17

human resource development, 73
human resources, 55, 178
human rights, 23, 28, 64
Hungary, 101

I

ICC, 22
Iceland, 56
immunity, 58, 181
impacts, 75, 179
implementation, ix, 24, 49, 53, 54, 64, 65, 68, 69, 70, 72, 81, 85, 86, 123, 150, 179
import prices, 151
imports, 148
in transition, 87
incentives, 73, 85, 118, 150, 180
inclusion, 121, 178
income, vii, viii, ix, 1, 2, 3, 4, 5, 11, 12, 14, 22, 27, 29, 30, 36, 55, 68, 73, 77, 90, 91, 93, 107, 109, 110, 112, 115, 120, 124, 127, 130, 133, 137, 138, 139, 140, 142, 146, 147, 148, 151, 152, 153, 155, 162, 163, 164, 165, 177, 178, 179, 180, 181
income distribution, 73, 115
independence, 58, 68, 84, 118
Independence, 84, 119
India, 10, 11, 13, 14, 28, 60, 70, 101, 103, 112
indicators, 32, 49, 53, 65, 70, 81, 115, 116, 147, 148
indices, 78
indigenous, 75
indigenous peoples, 75
Indonesia, 13, 28, 60, 71, 72, 96, 101, 103, 104, 105, 112
industrialized countries, 56
inertia, 48, 74, 83
institutional reforms, viii, 2, 32, 63
institutions, vii, viii, 2, 3, 12, 16, 18, 19, 24, 27, 45, 46, 48, 49, 50, 51, 64, 66, 70, 72, 76, 89, 118, 120, 124, 125, 130, 132, 133, 136, 147, 148, 155, 160, 178, 179, 180
instruments, 56, 63, 87, 90, 95, 151, 181
insurance, 27, 61
Inter-American Development Bank, viii, ix, 2, 4, 10, 21, 35, 45, 47, 51, 53, 56, 57, 62, 63, 64, 65, 67, 68, 69, 87, 89, 92, 97, 99, 101, 102, 103, 104, 105, 120, 123, 128, 129, 131
interest rates, vii, 1, 3, 4, 11, 12, 68, 92, 141
internal controls, 46, 53
international affairs, 88
International Bank for Reconstruction and Development, viii, 3, 62, 68, 91, 101, 107, 109, 159

International Development Association (IDA), v, viii, ix, 3, 21, 43, 72, 91, 105, 107, 108, 109, 129, 131, 168
international financial institutions, ix, 17, 46, 47, 50, 51, 52, 56, 57, 61, 62, 63, 65, 66, 67, 68, 89, 129, 131
International Financial Institutions, v, 28, 45, 56, 90, 100, 110
international investment, 36
International Monetary Fund, viii, ix, 3, 27, 45, 47, 52, 71, 87, 88, 89, 90, 92, 101, 102, 103, 104, 105, 107, 121, 123, 128, 129, 131, 148, 174, 176, 179, 180
international terrorism, 23, 109
investment, 3, 56, 61, 78, 79, 80, 85, 87, 88, 95, 115, 120, 126, 127, 139, 163, 164, 177
investors, 27, 87, 120, 126, 127
Iran, 109, 120
Iraq, 51
issues, viii, ix, 2, 3, 19, 23, 33, 37, 48, 50, 61, 62, 66, 74, 79, 81, 82, 84, 87, 116, 117, 118, 123, 132, 155, 158, 179
Italy, 13, 15, 28, 78, 101, 103

J

Jamaica, 88
Japan, 13, 14, 15, 18, 28, 31, 36, 37, 62, 90, 94, 101, 103, 113
job creation, 56
jobs, 47, 85, 119
jurisdiction, 90, 181

K

Kazakhstan, 10, 96
Kenya, 72, 73, 178
knowledge economy, 79
Korea, 13, 72, 91, 96, 101, 103, 104

L

labor, 72, 178
language, 105, 174
Latin America, 4, 10, 22, 36, 57, 87, 88, 89, 92, 96, 98, 127, 128, 150
Latvia, 91, 101, 117
leadership, vii, viii, 1, 18, 45, 46, 47, 48, 51, 63, 64
learning, 25
Lebanon, 60, 74, 96, 101, 105
legislation, vii, 2, 3, 19, 20, 21, 23, 42, 47, 48, 59, 69, 89, 90, 97, 120
lender of last resort, 73
liberalization, 78
Liberia, 96, 125, 137, 157, 158, 162, 181

Index

line, 67, 69, 78, 86, 88, 119, 163, 179
linkage, 147, 153
liquefied natural gas, 85
liquid assets, 177
liquidity, 79, 88
Lithuania, 91, 101, 117
litigation, 158
living conditions, 93
local community, 84
local government, 120
low risk, 134, 149, 150
lower prices, 85

M

Macedonia, 96
macroeconomic management, 178
macroeconomic policies, 134, 148, 150
majority, 27, 31, 32, 37, 90, 119, 136, 147
Malaysia, 13, 72
management, 15, 31, 32, 36, 48, 49, 52, 53, 54, 56,
  60, 63, 64, 67, 71, 73, 74, 75, 81, 82, 83, 87, 116,
  119, 121, 128, 146, 149, 150, 151, 158, 178, 179,
  180
mandates, viii, 2, 23, 51, 57, 67, 87
market, vii, viii, 1, 3, 4, 6, 11, 12, 26, 27, 28, 29, 34,
  36, 37, 43, 47, 54, 55, 56, 62, 71, 77, 85, 87, 88,
  91, 94, 107, 109, 110, 160, 177, 180
market economics, 77, 95
markets, viii, 2, 3, 11, 36, 63, 77, 86, 109
Mauritania, 125, 149, 161, 180, 181
measurement, 32, 114, 115, 118
measures, 53, 58, 59, 61, 66, 67, 116, 126, 160
membership, 4, 11, 30, 31, 90
methodology, 130, 133, 137, 154, 155, 164, 165,
  177, 181
Mexico, 11, 13, 14, 15, 27, 28, 36, 96, 101, 103
Miami, 128
Middle East, 57, 96, 98
migrant workers, 88
military, 19, 28, 47, 50, 53, 71, 80, 81
military spending, 50, 81
missions, 46, 47, 50, 56, 62, 95
mobile phone, 79
model, 68, 84, 85, 153
models, 127, 153
Moldova, 11, 96, 178
monetary policy, 71
money, vii, 1, 11, 12, 14, 17, 18, 19, 21, 36, 37, 47,
  49, 53, 54, 58, 60, 61, 64, 74, 75, 76, 77, 79, 80,
  83, 87, 95, 108, 118, 124, 125, 126, 154, 168,
  177, 178
money supply, 126
Mongolia, 10, 94, 96, 178

Montenegro, 96
Morocco, 10
mortgage-backed securities, 87, 88
Moscow, 55, 78, 79
movement, 57, 71
Mozambique, 125, 149, 158, 161
MTS, 79, 101
multilateral aid, vii, 2, 17, 18, 28, 108, 111, 112, 127

N

NAFTA, 36
nation, 126
national income, 134, 148, 150, 152, 180
national policy, 128
national security, viii, 18, 45, 61, 82
nationality, 24, 25, 28
natural habitats, 84
negotiating, 110, 158
Nepal, 83, 125, 177, 181
Netherlands, 13, 15, 26
network, 69
New York Stock Exchange, 79
NGOs, 86, 116
Nicaragua, 92, 96, 97, 125, 128, 132, 143, 145, 149,
  155, 157, 158, 161, 166, 167
Nigeria, viii, 13, 29, 30, 31, 36, 62, 93, 178
North Africa, 31, 96
North America, 27, 35, 36, 101, 120
North American Free Trade Agreement, 36
North Korea, 4
Norway, 15, 90
nutrition, 22, 23, 121
nutrition programs, 23

O

Obama Administration, 16
objectives, 91, 109, 114, 116, 118, 119, 132, 133,
  134, 135, 146, 150, 153, 155, 156, 180
obligation, 47, 138, 139, 140, 141, 153, 163, 164,
  165
obstacles, 47, 115
OECD, 18, 19, 28, 111, 120, 131, 150
Office of Management and Budget, 32, 128
Official Development Assistance, 19, 111, 120
oil, 31, 37, 52, 55, 77, 78, 79, 85, 151
oil revenues, 85
opacity, 66, 73
opportunities, 23, 33, 73, 74, 81, 85, 115
optimism, 30
order, vii, ix, 2, 3, 12, 14, 24, 27, 33, 49, 52, 115,
  123, 127, 131, 134, 135, 141, 147, 148, 150, 153,
  155, 156, 157, 179, 181

Organization for Economic Cooperation and
  Development, 18
overhead costs, 24, 25
oversight, viii, 2, 3, 19, 23, 45, 46, 48, 49, 53, 73, 87,
  89, 90, 120

P

Pacific, 94, 96
Pakistan, 83, 112
palm oil, 23
Paraguay, 60, 96, 97, 100
Paris Club, 124, 128, 158, 181
Parliament, 74
partnership, 72, 177, 179
passive, 119, 180
per capita income, 43, 112, 120, 125, 135, 178
performance, 49, 61, 69, 84, 114, 115, 118, 121, 125,
  132, 134, 142, 143, 147, 148, 149, 150, 151, 152,
  154, 156, 168, 170, 178, 179, 180
performance indicator, 118
performers, 147, 179
Peru, 60, 96, 100
Philippines, 60, 72, 76, 94
planned economies, 6
planning, 12, 85
pluralism, 77, 95
Poland, 86, 101
policy makers, 124
policy making, 110
policy reform, vii, 1, 3, 18, 36, 61, 179
political crisis, 33
political instability, 29, 72
politics, 108, 117, 120
poor, vii, ix, 1, 14, 30, 36, 46, 54, 56, 57, 61, 64, 65,
  76, 86, 105, 114, 118, 119, 120, 123, 124, 126,
  127, 129, 131, 134, 136, 145, 146, 147, 149, 171,
  179, 180
poor performance, 76, 126
population, 23, 69, 85, 115
portfolio, 10, 55, 56, 63, 73, 76, 78, 87
portfolios, 8, 9, 80
poverty alleviation, 4, 55, 91, 95, 109, 115, 118
poverty reduction, 49, 54, 56, 60, 65, 73, 85, 124,
  126, 127, 132, 135, 150, 151, 155, 178
power, viii, 2, 3, 12, 16, 23, 26, 27, 31, 37, 46, 56,
  61, 78, 109, 180
power plants, 3, 78
present value, 131, 132, 136, 137, 138, 142, 143,
  154, 160, 163, 164, 165, 166, 167, 168, 169, 177,
  178, 180, 181
president, 33, 35, 36, 103, 120, 121, 126
pressure, 49, 58, 71, 77, 88, 108, 119
prices, 31, 56, 67, 77, 131, 149

private firms, 4, 24, 87
private investment, 36, 127
private sector, 3, 4, 5, 6, 34, 36, 47, 54, 66, 69, 85,
  86, 91, 95, 120, 127
private sector investment, 47
problem-solving, 84
procurement, viii, 2, 23, 24, 25, 54, 57, 58, 61, 73,
  108, 116
profits, 54, 60, 68, 95, 126
program, ix, 21, 32, 34, 36, 37, 49, 53, 55, 65, 70,
  71, 72, 77, 78, 80, 81, 117, 123, 124, 126, 127,
  130, 132, 133, 136, 155, 159, 160, 178, 179
programming, 65, 73
project, 24, 43, 45, 48, 49, 52, 53, 54, 55, 57, 58, 59,
  64, 65, 66, 67, 69, 70, 72, 73, 74, 75, 76, 81, 82,
  83, 84, 86, 94, 95, 108, 109, 110, 118, 142, 143,
  147, 148, 158, 180
proliferation, 34, 57, 117
property rights, 178
protocol, 54
public administration, 178
public debt, 153, 156, 179
public expenditures, 24
public finance, 73
public health, 145
public opinion, 86
public policy, 80
public sector, 66, 178
public support, 48, 66

Q

quality of life, 94, 115

R

range, 60, 71, 77, 83, 120, 150, 179
rating agencies, 151
ratings, 65, 86, 116, 121, 147, 148, 151
raw materials, 79
real estate, 79
real terms, 108, 110
reason, viii, 45, 77, 83, 116, 126
recognition, 58, 120
recommendations, iv, 34, 45, 46, 48, 49, 50, 52, 53,
  57, 58, 60, 65, 72, 88, 99, 116, 156
reconciliation, 20, 81
reconstruction, ix, 51, 81, 108, 117
reforms, 18, 19, 24, 31, 32, 34, 46, 47, 50, 51, 52, 53,
  56, 57, 59, 62, 63, 64, 65, 70, 72, 74, 77, 85, 88,
  95, 99, 108, 116, 119, 124, 125, 128, 130, 133,
  138, 139, 158, 164, 177, 179
region, 4, 5, 11, 12, 36, 55, 72, 73, 78, 80, 94
regional cooperation, 4

relationship, 70, 71, 120, 140
reliability, 132, 146, 153, 154, 155
renewable energy, 22
Republic of the Congo, 96, 157, 162, 181
reputation, 73
resentment, 71, 80
reserves, 11, 12, 33, 77, 80, 81, 87, 105, 160
resolution, 81, 94, 120
resource management, 84
revenue, 49, 50, 52, 54, 60, 61, 144, 176, 178
rewards, 119
rights, iv, 48, 51, 52
risk, 27, 36, 56, 73, 83, 86, 87, 95, 117, 120, 130,
    134, 147, 148, 149, 150, 151, 155, 156, 179, 180
risk assessment, 147, 148
risk factors, 73
rural development, 144, 145
rural poverty, 21
Russia, 11, 13, 14, 28, 55, 77, 78, 79, 80, 87, 91, 96,
    101, 103
Rwanda, 60, 96, 125, 132, 143, 145, 149, 155, 161,
    166, 168, 180

S

sales, 53, 77, 160
Samoa, 178
sanctions, 15, 58
Saudi Arabia, 13, 28, 101, 103
savings, 48, 65, 143, 144, 155, 171
scarce resources, 54
scores, 32
SDRs, 90
Secretary of Commerce, 23
Secretary of the Treasury, 15, 58, 59, 60, 89, 116,
    119, 121, 127, 129, 134, 138, 152
security, 22, 54, 56, 57, 74, 82
security assistance, 54, 74
Senate, 16, 17, 20, 23, 28, 34, 45, 46, 48, 57, 59, 60,
    63, 72, 75, 89, 90, 99, 102, 103, 104, 105, 118,
    121
Senate approval, 89
Senate Foreign Relations Committee, 17, 34, 45, 46,
    48, 57, 59, 60, 63, 72, 75, 89, 90, 99, 102, 103,
    104, 105
sensitivity, 51, 81, 148, 149
Serbia, 96
shareholders, viii, 32, 45, 94, 95
shares, 11, 12, 22, 26, 30, 36, 37, 48, 51, 62, 64, 88,
    94, 113, 119
Sierra Leone, 96, 125, 147, 149, 157, 161, 181
simulation, 139, 153
Slovakia, 101
social development, vii, 1, 2, 18, 27, 64, 93

social services, 89, 126
soft loan, 49
Solomon I, 178
Somalia, 125, 162, 177, 178, 181
South Africa, 10, 13, 14, 28, 31, 60, 75, 76, 96, 99,
    101, 103
South Asia, 96, 117
South Korea, 28
Soviet Union, 6, 78, 94, 117
Spain, 13, 15
Spring, 20, 26, 27
Sri Lanka, 52, 60, 67, 80, 81, 83, 100, 105
St. Petersburg, 78
stability, 47, 56, 67, 72, 81, 90
staffing, 61, 73, 75, 84
stakeholders, 72, 83, 84, 135
standard of living, 115
standards, viii, 2, 24, 25, 36, 50, 53, 54, 120, 132,
    156
State Department, 62, 74, 89, 109
stock, 12, 36, 60, 91, 92, 94, 126, 142, 178, 180, 181
strategies, 63, 85, 132
strategy, 32, 34, 54, 56, 57, 67, 77, 78, 80, 85, 87,
    88, 114, 118, 132, 135, 178
strength, 78, 115, 130, 133, 147
stress, 148
structural reforms, 71, 74, 148
sub-Saharan Africa, 108
subscribers, 37, 62
Sudan, 96, 125, 162, 177, 178, 181
supply, 67, 83, 109, 115, 121
surplus, 11, 164
surveillance, 72, 90
sustainability, ix, 127, 129, 130, 131, 132, 134, 146,
    147, 149, 150, 151, 152, 153, 155, 156, 179, 180
sustainable development, 46
sustainable economic growth, 29
sustainable energy, 78
sustainable growth, 56
Sweden, 15
Switzerland, 15, 26, 91

T

Tajikistan, 96, 125, 177, 178
Tanzania, 60, 96, 112, 125, 132, 143, 145, 147, 148,
    149, 155, 161, 166, 167
targets, 114, 125, 146, 179
technical assistance, 11, 29, 34, 49, 53, 61, 68, 73,
    90, 91, 92, 93, 94, 109, 180
Thailand, 72, 82, 104
thinking, 48
Third World, 104
threshold, 147, 148, 180

Index

191

thresholds, 127, 135, 147, 148, 153
Togo, 96, 125, 177, 181
Tonga, 178
total costs, 136
tourism, 79
tracking, 146, 153, 179
trade, 47, 114, 115, 151, 178
trade-off, 151
tradition, 66, 80, 120, 121
training, 57, 79, 85, 150
transition, 6, 26, 77, 79, 86, 95
transparency, 17, 45, 49, 50, 53, 54, 55, 58, 59, 60,
61, 63, 66, 67, 74, 78, 86, 87, 114, 116, 119, 130,
133, 138, 139, 178
transport, 69, 73, 83, 144
transportation, 33, 69, 76, 78, 115
trust, viii, 20, 21, 22, 29, 81, 118, 132
Turkey, 28, 95, 96, 101, 103

U

U.N. Security Council, 15
U.S. Department of the Treasury, 32, 120, 132, 162
U.S. policy, 23, 48, 89
U.S. Treasury, 88, 99, 115, 128
Ukraine, 96
UN, 85, 102, 131, 132, 141, 176
uncertainty, 83, 179
unemployment, 88
unions, 72
unit of account, 105
United Kingdom, 13, 14, 15, 18, 28, 91, 93, 94, 95,
101, 103, 113, 117
United Nations, ix, 15, 33, 52, 102, 111, 123, 126,
128, 131, 132

Uruguay, 100

V

Vanuatu, 96, 178
Vatican, 4
Venezuela, 13, 14, 96, 97
veto, 16, 31, 48, 51, 109
Vietnam, 112, 178
voting, viii, 2, 3, 12, 16, 19, 26, 27, 28, 31, 32, 36,
37, 48, 51, 56, 62, 66, 90, 91, 92, 93, 94, 95, 113,
121

W

war, 52, 74, 80, 81, 91, 120
wealth, 33, 56, 77
weapons, 57, 80
web, 51, 64, 75, 104, 105, 120
Western Europe, 14
windows, vii, 1, 2, 3, 4, 6, 8, 9, 10, 12, 13, 14, 19,
21, 27, 28, 49, 54, 64, 68, 90
witnesses, 58, 99, 100
World Trade Organization, 3
World War I, 47, 90
WTO, 3

Y

Yemen, 60, 84, 85, 96, 102, 105, 178
Yugoslavia, 94

Z

Zimbabwe, 96